SPECIAL CHILDREN—SPECIAL RISKS
The Maltreatment of Children
with Disabilities

MODERN APPLICATIONS OF SOCIAL WORK

Edited by JAMES K. WHITTAKER

SPECIAL CHILDREN—SPECIAL RISKS
The Maltreatment of Children with Disabilities

James Garbarino
Patrick E. Brookhouser
Karen J. Authier
and Associates

ALDINE DE GRUYTER
New York

ABOUT THE EDITORS

James Garbarino is President, Erikson Institute for Advanced Study in
Child Development, Chicago. He has authored more than sixty
articles on social development, child welfare, and education, and
eight books, including *Protecting Children from Abuse and Neglect,
Understanding Abusive Families, Successful Schools and Competent Students, Children and Families in the Social Environment,
Social Support Networks: Informal Helping in the Social Environment, Troubled Youth, Troubled Families* and *The Psychologically
Battered Child.* In 1985 he received the first C. Henry Kempe award
for the "outstanding professional contribution to the field of child
abuse and neglect."

Patrick E. Brookhouser is Director of the Boys Town National Institute
for Communication Disorders in Children, Omaha, Nebraska.

Karen J. Authier is Administrative Director of the Center for Abused
Handicapped Children and Director of the Family Support Systems
at the Boys Town National Institute for Communication Disorders
in Children, Omaha, Nebraska.

ALDINE DE GRUYTER
A Division of Walter de Gruyter, Inc.
200 Saw Mill River Road
Hawthorne, New York 10532

Library of Congress Cataloging-in-Publication Data

Garbarino, James.
    Special children, special risks.

    (Modern applications of social work)
    Bibliography: p.
    Includes indexes.
    1. Handicapped children—United States—Abuse of—
Congresses.   I. Brookhouser, Patrick E.   II. Authier,
Karen J.   III. Title.   IV. Series.
HV888.5.G37   1987   362.4'088054   86-24170
ISBN 0-202-36045-8 (lib. bdg.)
ISBN 0-202-36046-6 (pbk.)

Printed in the United States of America
10 9 8 7 6 5 4 3 2 1

CONTENTS

PREFACE

Abused children. Handicapped children. Abused handicapped children. Putting these two topics together is an important piece of the puzzle that is protective services. What are the special risks faced by abused handicapped children? How does one investigate a child maltreatment case in which the victim is blind? mute? deaf? mentally retarded? confined to an institution? Are such children at special risk for being abused and neglected? Are they in greater jeopardy in "the system" once a report of maltreatment is made to a protective services or law enforcement agency? Are handicapped children at special risk for maltreatment?

This book brings together a diverse group of experts—to pool their knowledge and share their concerns. As a former Fellow at the Boys Town Center for the Study of Youth Development, Jim Garbarino was asked to develop and edit this volume. In this effort he was joined by Patrick Brookhouser, Director of the Boys Town National Institute and Karen Authier, Administrative Director of the Center for Abused Handicapped Children. Both are expert professionals experienced in dealing with the intricacies of both handicapping conditions and child maltreatment, Brookhouser from medicine, Authier from social work. The other authors represent developmental psychology, psychiatry, clinical psychology, education, child welfare, law, public policy, and journalism.

Boys Town's Executive Director, Rev. Val Peter, gave freely and generously of his support for this project. Secretarial staff at the Boys Town National Institute helped in the preparation of the manuscript. We believe this book will prove useful to those who seek to deal with abused handicapped children.

James Garbarino
Patrick E. Brookhouser
Karen J. Authier

LIST OF CONTRIBUTORS

Karen J. Authier
Center for Abused Handicapped
Children and Family Support
Systems
Boys Town National Institute for
Communication Disorders in
Children
Omaha, Nebraska

Faith A. Bolick
Human Development Research and
Training Institute
Western Carolina Center
Morganton, North Carolina

Patrick E. Brookhouser
Boys Town National Institute for
Communication Disorders in
Children
Omaha, Nebraska

Carolyn S. Cooper
Human Development Research and
Training Institute
Western Carolina Center
Morganton, North Carolina

Carl J. Dunst
Human Development Research and
Training Institute
Western Carolina Center
Morganton, North Carolina

Wendy C. Gamble
University of Denver
Denver, Colorado

James Garbarino
Erikson Institute for Advanced
Study in Child Development
Chicago, Illinois

Thomas C. Gregory
Father Flanagan's Boys' Home
Boys Town, Nebraska

Helen V. Howerton
National Center on Child Abuse
and Neglect
U.S. Department of Health and
Human Services
Washington, D.C.

Robert B. McCall
Father Flanagan's Boys' Home
Boys Town, Nebraska

Susan M. McHale
The Pennsylvania State University
University Park, Pennsylvania

Gary B. Melton
Department of Psychology
University of Nebraska at Lincoln
Lincoln, Nebraska

William Modzeleski
Office for Victims of Crime
Washington, D.C.

John M. Scanlan
St. Paul-Ramsey Mental Health and
Hearing Impaired Program
St. Paul, Minnesota

Patricia M. Sullivan
Center for Abused Handicapped
Children
Boys Town National Institute for
Communication Disorders in
Children
Omaha, Nebraska

James K. Whittaker
School of Social Work
University of Washington
Seattle, Washington

part ▮

AN INTRODUCTION
TO THE ISSUES

chapter 1

THE ABUSE AND NEGLECT OF SPECIAL CHILDREN: AN INTRODUCTION TO THE ISSUES

James Garbarino

WHAT KIND OF SOCIETY PERMITS CHILD MALTREATMENT?

The serious mistreatment of children by their parents and guardians arouses public indignation, motivates professional service providers, and frustrates researchers—perhaps more than any other single public issue (Garbarino, 1980). Despite the high level of public attention given to the topic of child abuse, however, major factual and ideological issues remain unresolved. For example, although there are volumes of research, theory, and speculation on the topic, there is still no totally satisfactory definition of abuse. Broadly speaking, of course, child abuse is *willful* behavior by parents or guardians that harms a child in their care. However, the unresolved issue is what constitutes harms. While few would doubt that savage and severe beatings, burnings or assault with a deadly weapon constitute abuse, it is difficult to draw a firm line between corporal punishment and abuse in cultures, such as our own, that sanctions the use of physical assault as a legitimate means of discipline with the family. For this reason, we must rely jointly upon community standards and scientific expertise for knowing what behaviors by a parent are threatening to a child (Garbarino & Gilliam, 1980). Community standards tell us what is normal in a culture—for example, scarification in some tribal African communities and spanking in North America. Scientific expertise gives us a basis with which to evaluate values and norms, for example, the finding that "rejection" is psychologically damaging no matter what its standing culturally.

In the broad prospective, we see the principal social causes of child abuse and neglect as being of three types. First, there is cultural support for domestic violence and inadequate child care. Our values permit a range of behaviors by parents and guardians that set the child up for maltreatment. Second, there are the joint concepts of family autonomy and parental ownership of children. Together these deeply entrenched ideas conspire to reduce a sense of community responsibility for children, to permit and even encourage social isolation, and break the weak link in our chain of concern. They permit us to define the problem in a particular family as "belonging" to someone else, rather than being a matter of collective responsibility *and* obligation. Third, there are the stresses of day-to-day social and economic life that feed the fires of personal inadequacy and permit family vulnerability to become risk, which ultimately translates into abuse and neglect. These three factors together provide a social machine quite adequate to the task of producing large quantities of abuse and neglect. It is this "social machine" that is most dangerous to infants and children, in general, and handicapped children, in particular.

All of the many causes and contributing factors involved in child maltreatment combine to produce psychosocially impoverished families and physically damaged children. This process is inevitable if we allow it to flourish in the social isolation that is characteristic of our individualistic culture. Our growing knowledge base makes this quite clear.

WHAT HAVE WE LEARNED ABOUT CHILD MALTREATMENT?

Empirical and clinical studies of child maltreatment now number in excess of 1000, and each study contains numerous "findings." However, based on research (Garbarino, 1983, 1984), the following has been suggested by the available evidence: Much of the confusion and uncertainty in studying, legislating against, treating, and preventing child maltreatment derives from the variety and lack of precision in the definitions used in research, policy, law, and practice. Thus, for example, estimates of the incidence of child maltreatment range from the tens of thousands if only life-threatening assault and total failure to offer care are used as criteria, to the millions if we define maltreatment as any form of damaging treatment (emotional, sexual, educational, or physical). Nonetheless, analyses based upon a comparison of officially reported cases (as compiled by the American Human Association) and a broader survey of cases known to any community professional dealing with families (the federally funded National Incidence Study) are reassuring in telling us that we *are* beginning to get reliable information about incidence and prevalence. What is more, real progress has been made in differentiating among physical, sexual, and psychological maltreatment. Also, preliminary studies of adolescent victims of maltreatment (more than 25% of the total number of reported cases) suggest the causes, correlates, and consequences probably are somewhat different from cases involving children, and that sex differences in victimization exist across the period from infancy to adolescence.

Even given the problem of definition, however, we do know something about the factors that contribute to child maltreatment.

- It is clear that both psychological and social factors play a role in producing child maltreatment, although debate continues about which is more important. Low income and other aspects of social stress are associated with higher rates of child maltreatment, which is evident during economic recessions and their accompanying increases in unemployment. This relationship between economic deprivation and maltreatment appears stronger with respect to infants and young children than with adolescents.
- Some cultures, societies, and communities have more child maltreatment than others. Economic pressure, values concerning the role of the child in the family, attitudes about the use of physical punishment, and the degree of social support for parents seem to account for these differences. Ethnic and cultural differences appear to exist in both overall incidence and in differences in the relative frequency of different forms of maltreatment—e.g., abuse versus neglect.
- Poor general coping skills and parenting skills (including those directly involved in discipline) play a significant role in child maltreatment. Social isolation is associated with a greater likelihood of child maltreatment, both because abuse-prone individuals isolate themselves and because they lack the means to participate in their communities. Personal characteristics of parents (e.g., untimely childbearing, physical illness and poor ability to empathize) and children (e.g., aversive crying and unresponsiveness) can substantially increase the likelihood of child maltreatment, *particularly* when social stress and social isolation characterize the family. These find expression in relative lack of success in dealing nonviolently with problematic behavior by children.
- A history of maltreatment in the parent's background increases the likelihood of child maltreatment, as does the contemporary presence of interspousal violence.
- Families involved in child maltreatment tend to exhibit a pattern of day-to-day interaction characterized by low level of social exchange, low responsiveness to positive behavior, and high responsiveness to negative behavior. This style may extend beyond the family to the work place for the parents and school for the children.
- Although many abusive parents exhibit barely adequate personality characteristics, overt mental illness plays a small overall role in child maltreatment.

Based on analyses of community responses to child maltreatment, we know that it is very difficult if not impossible to identify reliably, *before the fact,* families that will mistreat their children. However, predicting the degree of risk is possible, based upon the known correlates of maltreatment.

Most community responses to specific cases of maltreatment have been ineffective (Garbarino, 1985):

- To reduce risks to the youngster, protective services should hold as their foremost goal an adequate permanent family placement for the child. This means preventing removal, if possible, by offering supportive and therapeutic services to the family sufficient to protect the child *and* improve the family functioning. If removal is necessary, however, a realistic decision should be made quickly regarding permanent placement of the child. If the goal is returning the child to the family, then the family should remain in contact with the child in foster care, and rehabilitative services should be offered. If the child is to be permanently separated from the family, the child should be placed in a new *permanent* home as soon as possible.

- Conventional casework approaches typically result in a 50% success rate (at best). Some intensive and resource-laden programs report very low recidivism rates with selected clientele, however.

- Interdisciplinary teams for case management and development of community services are best. Paraprofessional and volunteer staff in conjunction with mutual help groups can provide effective social support and concrete aid in meeting day-to-day problems. Comprehensive implementation of high-quality programs dependent upon heavy involvement of professional staff exceeds current and projected levels of fiscal resources devoted to protective services. Using paraprofessionals, volunteers, and mutual help groups is highly cost effective under most circumstances. Teaching parents skills for successfully handling the problem behavior of children in a nonviolent manner is often useful. Most current treatment addresses parents, although exclusive treatment of parents does not appear to reverse damage of children. Children generally receive no treatment at all, and may even be harmed by outside intervention that places them in foster care or institutional care that is often traumatic in its own right. Even if the initial placement is benign, the risk of repeated placements is high and a matter of great concern. The issues involved in serving adolescent victims differ somewhat from those involved in serving the needs of children. Resolving custody issues and dealing with negative behavior appear to be greater problems with adolescents.

- Prevention remains underdeveloped. However, several strategies exist that have generated very encouraging results. Home-health visitors, family-centered childbirth, and social skills training aimed at improving parent effectiveness are among these. We are rapidly approaching a point at which it will be feasible to set specific goals for preventing child maltreatment and have realistic expectations for meeting those goals.

We know that child maltreatment and the family environments associated with it pose a clear and present developmental danger to the children involved.

- Specific acts of maltreatment produce acute and chronic medical problems that impair growth and development.
- Even if specific acts of abuse are not present, growing up in a family at high risk for maltreatment is associated with developmental damage.
- Children who experience maltreatment may be at substantially increased risk for later delinquency, psychiatric disorders, school failure, self-destructive behavior, domestic violence, and sexual dysfunction, depending upon the nature, age of onset, duration, and family climate of the maltreatment. However, existing research does not include sufficient large-scale, longitudinal, and well-controlled studies to permit a definitive conclusion about the precise effects of maltreatment. Of particular concern are two issues: the role of sexual abuse in generating later sexually dysfunctional behavior; and, the dynamic links between child maltreatment and juvenile delinquency.

This outline of our knowledge base sets the stage for our efforts to focus attention on the crucial questions of whether, how, and why handicapping conditions and maltreatment are connected in the lives of children. We first address the issue of abuse/neglect as the cause of developmental harm.

CHILD MALTREATMENT AS THE CAUSE OF DEVELOPMENTAL HARM

A complete and unambiguous analysis of the outcomes of child maltreatment is certainly beyond the knowledge available to us at this point in the history of scientific inquiry into child abuse and neglect. Most of the existing research is retrospective, limiting our ability to detect causal relations. In the case of the link between child abuse and juvenile delinquency, for example, a review by Garbarino and Plantz (1986) indicated that virtually all the available studies were retrospective. None-

theless, concern about the consequences of child maltreatment is justifiable on multiple grounds—clinical and empirical.

On the one hand, most of us are convinced that child maltreatment
has multiple and often severe consequences. On the other hand, we
must acknowledge that the prevalence of specific forms of harm, the
mediators of damage, and the processes of influence are not as yet
completely clear (to say the least). When discussing socioemotional
consequences of physical abuse, Egeland and Sroufe (1981) assert:

> In the area of socioemotional development, even the obvious is often dif-
> ficult to demonstrate. . . . Uncovering the developmental consequences
> of child abuse is a prime example. . . . Yet, no one can doubt that there
> are consequences of being physically abused (p. 77).

What are some of those consequences? Even a cursory review of
the literature reveals numerous possibilities. These include death, permanent disability, developmental delay, speech and learning problems,
impaired attachment relations, self- and other-directed aggression,
psychosis (particularly multiple personalities), juvenile delinquency,
depression, deficient social skills, and sexual dysfunction. Indeed, it
is difficult to identify *any* problem that has not been linked to child
maltreatment on the basis of clinical observation, survey research, or
informed speculation.

In a comprehensive review of the consequences of abuse and neglect, Martin (1980) identified three major forms of harm: *medical
problems* (ranging from nutritional deficiencies to hearing loss to brain
damage); *developmental problems* (from mental retardation to language deficiencies to impaired motor skills); *psychological problems*
(encompassing the extremes on most dimensions of personality—for
example, being either very shy and inhibited *or* very aggressive and
provocative—as well as general unhappiness, poor attachment, and
inadequate peer relations). Martin sheds some light on the "dynamics
of the effect of abusive environment on development." He includes
the idea that a pattern of transactions develops (cf. Sameroff & Chandler, 1975) in which the damaged child elicits responses that reinforce
the damage, for example, brain damage adversely affects personality,
a pattern of entrapped parent–child conflict releases a pattern of abuse,
mastery languishes, increasingly iatrongenic interventions occur as
foster placement occurs and then fails. All of this is plausible, and the
reality of damage appears undeniable. It is the form, severity, prevalence, and duration of harm that remain at issue. We must bear this
in mind as we consider the question of whether handicapped children
are at special risk for being abused and neglected, because handicapping conditions may well be the *result* of maltreatment early in life and

then become the *cause* of maltreatment in later interactions with parents, peers, teachers, and other caregivers.

ARE HANDICAPPED CHILDREN AT SPECIAL RISK FOR ABUSE AND NEGLECT?

We use the word "special" here with particular intent. While it may seem obvious that our main task is to demonstrate that handicapped children and youth are disproportionately represented among victims of maltreatment, this is neither the only nor the best way to express the issue. For one thing, we are interested in knowing that the maltreatment handicapped children experience follows from their handicap rather than vice versa. This is often difficult (if not impossible) to establish. Cause and effect are intertwined. But even this is not the only empirical challenge we face.

Our real interest lies in specifying the ways in which the factors that produce or prevent maltreatment in the lives of nonhandicapped children operate for handicapped children. This focus upon children in social context underlies our work here. Some handicapped children may be at greater risk than would nonhandicapped children in the same situation, while others well might be at reduced risk. For example, if being handicapped elicits greater nurturance, surveillance, and resources being brought to bear upon a child's family, then the child in such a situation might be at *less* risk than a nonhandicapped child in the same family. By the same token, difficulties in comprehension and communication and heightened dependence upon caregivers might make a handicapped child less able to seek protection from maltreatment when it does occur. Thus the degree of risk for handicapped children may derive from the very meaning and community implications of being "special," for that label may invoke extra resources in some settings and rejection in others. No *simple* compilation of statistics reporting the incidence of maltreatment for handicapped versus nonhandicapped children is sufficient. Embry (1980) highlighted this when he observed that the increased stress experienced by the family that has a handicapped preschool child lacking in the behaviors that normal children use to attract caretaking and attention and having a developmental history that decreases mother–child bonding increases the risk for severe family dysfunction, which may exhibit itself in the most extreme form, child abuse (Farber & Ryckman, 1965; Helfer & Kempe, 1976; Martin, 1976). Thus a family that would have established a successful, supportive relationship with a normal child or children can develop serious problems when a child with special needs enters the family system. Finally, dysfunctional family interactions appear only to exacerbate a child's developmental delay. Given this nexus of developmental difficulties facing the handicapped child, not only does the task of intervention become far more sophisticated but the risks of nonintervention become much more severe (Embry, 1980, pp. 30–31). We are not simply interested in knowing "what are the differences?" but in knowing "what difference do the differences make?"

Many studies report that handicapped children (particularly mentally retarded children) account for more than their proportionate share of the total number of abused and neglected children and youth (Martin, 1980), while others do not (Starr, Dietrich, Fischhoff, Ceresnie, & Zweier, 1984). Some report high levels of handicap among maltreated children. In one study, 43% of the abused children had handicaps, and 65% of the handicapped children were abused (Lightcap, Kurland, & Burgess, 1982). Sandgrund, Gaines, and Green (1975) reported that serious mental retardation was eight times more common in abused and neglected children than in similar but not maltreated children. However, other studies report no significant difference between maltreated and comparison groups (Starr et al., 1984) and offer the hypothesis that child maltreatment is implicated primarily as a cause of handicap (Egeland & Sroufe, 1980).

We begin our comparisons of risk with generally accepted estimates that about 12% of all children and youth are handicapped—with about 60% of these handicaps occurring after birth. The incidence of handicap appears to be higher for low-income families, however, a fact that makes it difficult to know exactly who to use as comparison groups in research on this topic. What is more, some handicapping conditions (such as mental retardation) have a significant genetic component that functions through intergenerational transmission (i.e., they may be inherited from parents). This compounds our difficulties because it makes it even more troublesome to disentangle cause and effect.

The fact that handicapped children are likely to elicit special resources for families from their communities in some settings means that the "true expectable rate" (in a nonsupportive community) is higher than the observed actual rate. Thus, we might expect that the strength of any causal relationship between handicap and child maltreatment varies from time to time and place to place as a function of the overall resource implications of being and having a "special" child.

We know that abuse and neglect early in life (even prenatally) can produce physical damage. Experts estimate that only about 40% of all handicaps are attributable to prenatal and genetic conditions. Deafness, mental retardation, blindness, and other handicapping conditions can all be the *result* of maltreatment. This damage may then predispose the child to further victimization by impairing the child's ability to meet parental expectations, by requiring special care that exceeds the parent's resources, by leading the parent to reject the child, or by causing the parent to institutionalize the child (a factor that, itself, can be a cause of maltreatment).

Similarly, we must recognize that handicapping conditions may be linked to other factors that are themselves the real cause of maltreatment. Researchers and clinicians have long sought to identify factors that increase the likelihood of a child being maltreated. Their efforts have identified five broad categories of risk. Two refer primarily to the individuals involved in the family. The first concerns the parents. Individual adults may not possess the personal resources they need to function adequately as parents, particularly if they are subjected to greater than normal demands. One such personal characteristic identified in research on abuse is lack of empathy (i.e., the ability to perceive and appreciate the feelings and motives of others). In the case of neglect, depression and apathy figure prominently as personal risk factors. A second category of individual risk factors concerns characteristics of the child. Characteristics of children or youth that make them especially challenging or difficult to care for are associated with increased risk of maltreatment. These include fussiness, a chronic illness that requires special care, and delinquent or aggressive behavior.

A third documented risk factor involves aspects of the relationship between a particular adult and a particular child or youth that produce a deteriorating pattern of interaction—either escalating conflict or progressive withdrawal. The fourth risk factor lies in elements of the immediate situation that stimulate abuse or neglect (e.g., by increasing the level of stress beyond tolerable limits or by isolating the adult–child relationship from the support of spouse, friends, relatives, or professional helpers). A fifth is any feature of the culture or the society that encourages maltreatment or permits it to occur (e.g., values and institutions that approve of harsh physical punishment as a form of normal discipline or that define children as the disposable property of parents). Each of these five factors plays a role in the maltreatment of children and youth; not all are necessarily present in any single case.

Handicapped children and youth may be at special risk for maltreatment because of any or all of these five factors. They appear to be particularly vulnerable to maltreatment when faced with parents who, themselves, are lacking important personal resources. Raising a handicapped child is a challenge that makes great demands upon parents. Thus, for example, parents who lack the ability to empathize are a special danger for the handicapped child or youth, who usually requires a parent with *heightened* rather than diminished ability to understand feelings and respond sympathetically.

When we turn to the second risk factor (i.e., characteristics of children that increase the likelihood of maltreatment), we again find that handicapped children and youth may be at special risk under some conditions. The very existence of a handicap that reduces the ability to communicate, to respond, and to otherwise meet parental and community expectations can make some children more vulnerable. They become both more likely to experience maltreatment and less able to respond in adaptive ways that range from accommodating to the parent's needs, to offsetting the effects of neglect by caring for self, to seeking assistance from adults and peers outside the family. In this we see a parallel to the distinctions being drawn between abuse as it affects infants versus adolescents. The former is a "perfect victim" (i.e., easily victimized, having few self-protective resources, and having access to a broad base of public sympathy), the latter is an imperfect victim in these same three senses.

Both personal risk factors can play a role in heightening the risk that a particular parent–child relationship will become enmeshed in a negative cycle that leads to escalating conflict (and thus to abuse) or progressive withdrawal (and thus to neglect). Similarly, the presence of a handicapped child or youth within a family may raise the level of stress beyond the family's ability to cope and may lead to a process of social withdrawal and estrangement that produces the kind of social isolation in which maltreatment flourishes. Indeed, research repeatedly has identified a pattern in which families with handicapped children evidence a worsening pattern of social isolation (Embry, 1980). This is both in the sense of less contact and narrower social contact (i.e., more and more exclusively focused upon kin), a factor which when coupled with stress, has been identified as a correlate of elevated family violence (Straus, 1980).

Here we see most clearly an important theme that emerges as a hypothesis in research and clinical reports. It appears that the presence of a handicapped child in a family tends to push families toward extremes—either unusually strong and positive family interaction or particularly negative family functioning. Like all such special circumstances, the presence of a handicapped child can act as a growth-inducing challenge or as a stressful event that precipitates deteriorating functioning. This is true of economic events (e.g., unemployment) as well as more social or psychological circumstances (such as the birth of a handicapped child).

Certainly one key to how well a family responds is their overall level of functioning. A second is the level of available and accessible social support (nurturance and guidance). This highlights the importance of social support systems for families with handicapped children and youth. Not surprisingly, the research and clinical evidence indicates that handicapped children and youth experience maltreatment primarily when their families are isolated from such formal and informal social support systems—or when they isolate themselves (Embry, 1980).

The availability and accessibility of social support for families with handicapped children and youth is not simply a personal or even a family matter. It reflects the community's willingness and ability to provide such support, assuming responsibility for *all* children. Culture plays a role in this, as does the organization and policy of culturally defined classes of children who are designated "damaged" or otherwise less desirable than normal children (Korbin, 1981). These "damaged" children can include illegitimate or racially mixed offspring, and, in addition, handicapped children. The existence of such a culturally derived stigma appears to heighten the risk for maltreatment among handicapped children and youth. It leads to a lowering of standards for care and a kind of license to abuse them. We see this most clearly by examining the problem of institutional abuse and neglect.

A recent federally funded study of institutional abuse conducted under the auspices of Ohio State University (Rindfleisch, 1984) concluded that "there are factors inherent in institutions not necessarily found in family homes that may result in abuse or neglect (e.g., emotionally detached caretakers, use of psychotropic drugs, large numbers of resident children). This and other findings about the incidence of institutional maltreatment have a special relevance for handicapped children and youth because they are disproportionately likely to be institutionalized at some point in their lives.

Handicapped children and youth are at special risk for institutional maltreatment in the three forms that have been identified by investigators: institutional child abuse (including corporal punishment, misuse of psychotropic drugs, isolation exceeding 2 hours, and restraint by mechanical device); institutional child neglect (including failure to provide specific services, negligence in the administration of psychotropic drugs, and failure to notify the placing agency when a child's continued residence is detrimental to him/her); and wrongful abrogation of rights (including tampering with mail, racial or other improper segregation, restricting visitation and other contact, and interference with a resident's ability to consult with outside agents).

If these children experience such maltreatment, they face special difficulties in seeking and receiving protection and assistance because of their difficulties in communicating and because they and their families may be highly dependent upon the institution for essential services (e.g., in the case of deaf or blind students enrolled in the only school geographically or financially available to them). In such conditions of heightened dependence, handicapped children and youth will require special protective services.

All in all, it seems clear that handicapped children and youth do experience special risks for maltreatment. Many handicaps observed in children are probably the *result* of earlier maltreatment. Many handicapped children experience heightened risk of abuse and neglect (or *additional* abuse and neglect). Many maltreated children exhibit handicaps. However, under some conditions, handicapped children may actually be at *lower* than usual risk (e.g., when born to or adopted by highly motivated and competent parents who have special resources for caring for handicapped children). A strong, positive community response geared to the special needs of the family with a handicapped child can alter the context in which the handicap—maltreatment dynamic operates.

Beyond drawing conclusions about the level and conditions of risk for handicapped children, we must recognize and deal with the special issues involved in preventing maltreatment or, if failing that, in identifying cases of actual maltreatment and in designing interventions. The task before us is to protect handicapped children and youth by preventing the conditions under which they are at special risk and by correcting problems when they do occur. This is our goal in this volume.

part **II**

IDENTIFYING
SPECIAL RISKS FOR
HANDICAPPED
CHILDREN

chapter 2

SUPPORTING FAMILIES OF HANDICAPPED CHILDREN

Carl J. Dunst
Carolyn S. Cooper
Faith A. Bolick

INTRODUCTION

The major purpose of this chapter is to examine the manner in which supporting and strengthening families contributes to preventing the maltreatment of handicapped children. It is well documented that both personal well-being and family integrity are often threatened by the birth and rearing of a handicapped child (Crnic, Friedrich, & Greenberg, 1983a; Dunst, 1985a; Dunst & Trivette, 1984), which place the family at-risk for a host of psychological and emotional problems, including abuse and neglect (Garbarino, 1986; Starr, Dietrich, Fischoff, Ceresnie, & Zweier, 1984). Recent evidence, however, strongly suggests that many of the negative consequences associated with the rearing of a handicapped child can be prevented or lessened if the family is provided support that strengthens well-being and family integrity (Garbarino & Stocking, 1980; Hobbs, Dokecki, Hoover-Dempsey, Moroney, Shayne, & Weeks, 1984; Parke, 1982; Trivette & Dunst, 1986). The major thesis of our chapter is that developing and maintaining effective support systems for families of handicapped children (Garbarino & Stocking, 1980; Hobbs et al., 1984) can have positive influences on parent and family functioning and decrease the probability of child maltreatment.

We make a fundamental distinction between prevention-oriented and treatment-oriented programs that has major implications for conceptualizing and implementing intervention trials with handicapped children and their families. Prevention programs tend to be *proactive* in their orientation. That is, interventions focus on the promotion and enhancement of positive functioning that reduces the possibility of a negative outcome. The effect is an overall reduction in the incidence and prevalence of one or more disorders or dysfunctional behaviors. In contrast, treatment programs tend to be *reactive*. Thus, interventions focus on the treatment of a problem after its manifestation, with the hope that the intervention will deter subsequent occurrences of the undesirable outcome.

According to Cowen (1983), prevention programs have several before-the-fact qualities that distinguish them from treatment programs. He noted that prevention programs have the following characteristics:

> (a) they must be mass- or group-oriented, not targeted to individuals; (b) directed to essentially "well" people, not to the already affected, though targets can appropriately include those who, by virtue of life circumstances or recent experiences are known (epidemiologically) to be at risk for adverse psychological outcomes; (c) "intentional," that is, rest on a knowledge base which suggests that a program's operations hold promise for strengthening psychological health or reducing psychological maladjustment (p. 15).

Stated differently, prevention programs are those that substantially reduce the probability of a negative consequence by strengthening psychological and physical functioning through provision of supportive experiences known or believed to have positive influences upon persons at-risk for maladjustment. Cowen's (1983) exacting requirements provide a framework for altering the ways in which we view child maltreatment as a social problem and the manner in which we go about preventing abuse and neglect.

COMPONENTS ANALYSIS OF CHILD MALTREATMENT

Most models of child maltreatment, regardless of their particular theoretical or conceptual orientation, view abuse and neglect as the result of one or more risk factors that individually, in aggregation, or transactionally[1] cause or correlate with maltreatment. This relationship may be depicted as:

$$M = f(R)$$

where M (maltreatment) is caused by, results from, or varies as a function (f) of one or more R (risk factors).

The $M = f(R)$ model, despite its heuristic value, often treats risk factors and intervening variables as belonging to the same "causal"

[1]The term transactional (Sameroff & Chandler, 1975; Vietze et al., 1980) refers to the reciprocal interactions among person and setting variables that affect developmental outcomes, with special emphasis on the continuous and mutual influences among variables.

class, when in fact they are more likely to be causally linked themselves. For example, poverty, crowding, unemployment, and stress are factors often implicated as correlates or causes of maltreatment; yet stress is likely to be a consequence of the other factors and *temporally* manifests itself as a negative outcome of the other risk factors.

As part of our efforts toward the prevention of the maltreatment of handicapped children, we have found it useful to conceptualize abuse and neglect as taking the form:

$$M = f(R_{t_1}, I_{t_2})$$

where M is maltreatment, I is a set of intervening variables (stress, marital discord, isolation, etc.), R is a set of risk factors (difficult child temperament, unemployment, unrealistic child expectations, etc.), t_1 and t_2 indicate that R temporally occurs before I and that I is caused or mediated by R. In this paradigm, R moderates the magnitude or degree of I which, in turn, increases the probability that these variables will intervene in producing maltreatment (M).[2] The model predicts a relationship between the risk factors category and child maltreatment only in those instances where R causes I to reach a level that is beyond a person's capacity to cope. Consequently, monitoring the level of behaviors in the I category should provide an index of the probability of maltreatment to the extent that the base rate levels of I are known or can be established. Given this hypothesized sequence of occurrences, prevention efforts are directed toward affecting the levels of I, keeping them at or below the base rate levels, which should, in turn, reduce the probability of maltreatment (M).

Similar component analyses of abuse and neglect have been proposed by others. For example, Straus (1980) proposed a model of maltreatment in which stress causes abuse only if certain mediating variables are present (e.g., situational factors that do not allow a person to remove him/herself from the immediate context as a means of avoiding a maltreatment episode). Likewise, Meier (1985) offers a perspective of abuse in which risk factors aggravate precipitating factors which, in turn, lead to child abuse episodes. Belsky's (1980) model of maltreatment views abuse and neglect as caused by multiple factors related to the characteristics of the child, family, community, and culture, which

[2]The mathematically and functionally correct formula is

$$M = b_0 + b_1 R + b_2 I + b_3 (R \times I)$$

where b_0 is a constant, b_1 is an estimate of the main effect of the risk factors (R) on maltreatment (M), b_2 is an estimate of the main effect of the intervening variables (I) on maltreatment (M), and $b_3 (R \times I)$ is a multiplicative interaction between the risk factors (R) and the intervening variables (I).

interact and increase the likelihood of episodes of maltreatment. These as well as other components analysis models provide the type of conceptual frameworks necessary to (1) move away from treatment toward prevention models and (2) explicitly state both the causative and mediating role that different risk factors play in child maltreatment.

While similar in many ways to other perspectives of maltreatment, our model differs in a number of important respects. First, our model is prevention rather than treatment oriented. Second, we use a causal analysis paradigm that attempts to order the occurrences of different events and their consequences temporally so that causal as well as mediational relationships can be discerned. Third, a fundamental if not the most important dimension of the model is how provision of support alleviates or lessens the consequences of risk factors and thus decreases the likelihood that the intervening variables will precipitate episodes of maltreatment.

TOWARD A PROACTIVE PERSPECTIVE OF PREVENTION

If stress, marital discord, isolation, etc., are the negative consequences of different risk factors, then personal well-being, family integrity, and other positive intra- and interpersonal behavior characteristics ought to be the positive consequences resulting from supporting and strengthening families. There is now a substantial body of evidence that indicates that provision of support can influence personal and familial well-being and health (Bott, 1971; Cohen & Syme, 1985; Dean & Lin, 1977; Gore, 1985; McCubbin, Joy, Cauble, Comeau, Patterson, & Needle, 1980; Mitchell & Trickett, 1980). In our own work on the mediational influences of support in families of handicapped children (discussed in detail below), we have repeatedly found that different forms of support have positive effects on parent, family, and child functioning (e.g., Dunst, 1985a; Dunst & Leet, 1985; Dunst & Trivette, 1984, 1986; Dunst, Trivette, & Cross, 1986a, 1986b, in press; Trivette & Dunst, 1986, in preparation). The results of our studies have shown that social support has positive influences on personal well-being, family integrity, parental attitudes toward their child, and parental styles of interaction. To the extent that positive functioning can be promoted through provisions of support, well-being and family integrity ought to be enhanced and child maltreatment will be prevented.

THE SOCIAL CONTEXT OF MALTREATMENT

Evidence increasingly points to the role that social context plays in child maltreatment (Belsky, 1980; Garbarino, 1981; Garbarino & Stocking, 1980; Meier, 1985; Parke, 1982; Pelton, 1981). In contrast to models of maltreatment that focus primarily on the individual characteristics of the abuser and abused, social systems models emphasize the interdependencies of events in different contexts and the manner in which these events affect the behavior of the members of different social units. A social systems perspective of child maltreatment views episodes of abuse and neglect as the consequence of the interactions and transactions of different factors that transform individual risk into maltreatment (Belsky, 1980; Garbarino & Stocking, 1980).

A fundamental tenet of a social systems perspective of behavior is that social units and their members do not act in isolation but rather interact so that events occurring in different units or subunits reverberate and influence the behavior of members in other units (Bronfenbrenner, 1979). In addition there is emphasis and concern for the "progressive accommodation(s) between a growing organism and its immediate environment, and the way in which this relation is *mediated by forces emanating from more remote regions in the larger physical and social milieu"* (Bronfenbrenner, 1979, p. 13, emphasis added).

An ecological perspective of child maltreatment views abuse or neglect as resulting, in part, from events beyond the family unit that both directly and indirectly influence the family members (Garbarino, 1981). This is not to suggest that the personal characteristics of parents and their children do not contribute to abuse, but rather that these personal characteristics often attain risk status as a result of other factors external to the family. Belsky (1980), Kempe and Kempe (1978), and Meier (1985) offer perspectives of child maltreatment consonant with this viewpoint. These investigators suggest that abuse and neglect are a result of the interaction of parent, child, and environmental factors that combine to "cause" maltreatment. Garbarino (1976, 1977, 1981), Garbarino and Crouter (1978), Garbarino and Ebata (1983), Garbarino, Sebes, and Schellenbach (1986), and Garbarino and Sherman (1980) have amassed an array of evidence to support the contention that forces outside the family intrude into the home and affect the manner in which risk factors are transformed into abuse. For example, one of their findings is that social and economic conditions beyond the family unit impact upon the family in a way that exacerbates already volatile situations, increasing the probability of abusive behavior.

Social Network Theory and Social Support

The proposition that different ecological settings are interconnected and events in one setting affect occurrences in other settings is a fundamental principle of social network theory. Network analysis attempts to describe the properties of social units, the nature of linkages among units, and how *provision of support* from members of different units contributes to the *promotion* of individual, family, and community well-being and health (Hall & Wellman, 1985).

Social networks have long been viewed as powerful mediators of social support (Mitchell & Trickett, 1980). Broadly defined, social support includes emotional, physical, informational, instrumental, and material assistance provided to others to maintain well-being, promote adaptations to different life events, and foster development in an adaptive manner. There is general consensus among network theorists that social networks function to nurture and sustain linkages among persons that are supportive of one another on both a day-to-day basis and in times of need and crises (e.g., Brim, 1974; Caplan, 1974; Cobb, 1976; Cohen & Syme, 1985; Walker, MacBride, & Vachon, 1977; Weiss, 1974). For example, parenthood has been found to be a crisis situation for some (Hobbs, 1965; LeMasters, 1957). However, simply reintegrating extended family members into the nuclear family has been found successful in buffering some new parents from stressful reactions associated with the birth of their firstborn child (Litwak, 1960). Recent work has shown that the effects of provision of support go beyond moderating intrapersonal and intrafamily physical and psychological well-being. Evidence indicates that social support influences attitudes toward parenting (Crnic, Greenberg, Ragozin, Robinson, & Basham, 1983b), parental styles of interaction with their children (Colletta, 1981; Crnic *et al.*, 1983b; Crockenberg, 1981; Embry, 1980; Giovannoni & Billingsley, 1970; Hetherington, Cox, & Cox, 1976, 1978; Philliber & Graham, 1981; Weinraub & Wolf, 1983), parental expectations and aspirations for their children (Lazar & Darlington, 1982), and child behavior and development (Crockenberg, 1981; Crnic *et al.*, 1983b; Crnic, Greenberg, & Slough, 1986). These direct and indirect influences of social support are examples of first-, second-, and higher order effects resulting from the provision of support (Bronfenbrenner, 1979).

A Social Systems Perspective of Prevention

Both ecological psychology (Bronfenbrenner, 1979) and social network theory (Mitchell & Trickett, 1980) provide frameworks for conceptualizing and conducting prevention trials aimed at alleviating or lessening the adverse effects of different risk factors associated with child maltreatment. To the extent that provisions of support can proactively affect parent, family, and child functioning, the probability of risk factors having negative consequences should be lessened and child maltreatment prevented. Paradigmatically, this set of hypothesized relationships is shown in Figure 2.1. In instances where social support is inadequate in moderating the negative consequences of one or more risk factors, they are likely to produce effects that increase the prob-

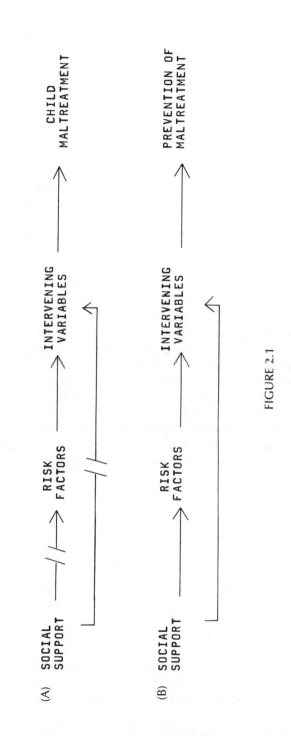

FIGURE 2.1

ability of maltreatment (Figure 2.1A). In contrast, where provision of support moderates the consequences of risk factors as well as promotes positive functioning, the probability of maltreatment should be lessened (Figure 2.1B).

OVERVIEW OF THE LITERATURE

We now turn to an examination of the literature to discern the extent to which the relationships central to our model are supported by empirical evidence. We focus primarily on the manner in which the negative consequences associated with the birth and rearing of a handicapped child can be affected by forces both within and outside the family, with special emphasis on the manner in which social support promotes parent, family, and child functioning.

There have been numerous attempts to identify the "causes" of maltreatment (e.g., Gelles, 1982; Justice & Justice, 1976; Meier, 1985; Milner & Ayoub, 1980). Most have resulted in lists of child, parent, family, and extrafamily characteristics and conditions thought to be associated with abuse and neglect. In Chapter 1 we saw that there are five broad categories of risk factors that increase the likelihood of a child being maltreated including: (1) personal characteristics and personal resources of the parents (e.g., low income, poverty, inability to empathize, increased stress, poor health and coping abilities, a history of maltreatment in the parents' background); (2) individual characteristics of the child (e.g., difficult temperament, unresponsiveness, excessive crying, prematurity, low birth weight); (3) characteristics of parent–child relationships and parent interactions with people outside the family (e.g., social isolation, coercive styles of interaction, marital discord); (4) both the immediate context and broader based events that stimulate maltreatment (e.g., job loss, intra- and extrafamily life crises); and (5) cultural and societal values and beliefs that support or encourage violence (e.g., attitudes toward physical punishment). As noted by Garbarino (1986), Meier (1985), and others (e.g., Belsky, 1980; Milner & Ayoub, 1980), any combination of the factors implicated as the "causes" of abuse or neglect increase the probability of episodes of child maltreatment.

There are a number of things noteworthy about the aforementioned factors when viewed from a prevention perspective. First, using a causal analysis framework, it is possible to begin to hypothesize about the temporal, causal, and mediational relationships among the risk factors themselves. Second, many of the consequences of the presence of risk factors are the same behaviors manifested by parents in response to the birth and rearing of a handicapped child (Fewell & Vadasy, 1986). Third, evidence from a number of sources, including the child abuse literature, converges on the point that many of the adverse effects associated with risk factors can be lessened or alleviated through provision of supportive experiences.

Consequences of Life Events

Stress, loneliness, social isolation, depression, physical and emotional distress, and other psychosocial disorders and dysfunctions are often the consequence of both normative life changes (McCubbin & Figley, 1983) and life crises (Figley & McCubbin, 1983). These various psychosocial reactions are often present in persons who engage in episodes of abuse and neglect (Ayoub, Jacewitz, Gold, & Milner, 1983; Causey, 1983; Collins, 1975; Kempe & Kempe, 1978; Milner & Wimberley, 1980; Perry, Wells, & Doran, 1983; Straus, 1980). Life events that produce episodes of stress, depression, and so on, are known to cause changes (disruptions) in the family social system (McCubbin, Cauble, & Patterson, 1982; McCubbin & Figley, 1983) that, in turn, increases the likelihood of maltreatment (Justice & Justice, 1976; Miller & Myers-Wall, 1983).

In their discussion of the causes of loneliness, Periman and Peplau (1984) make a distinction between predisposing factors and precipitating events that we have found useful in examining the temporal occurrences leading to the probability of child maltreatment. These investigators "distinguish between *predisposing* factors which make people vulnerable to loneliness and *precipitating* events that trigger the onset of loneliness" (p. 23). Substituting the term maltreatment for loneliness in this statement results in the assertion that there are "predisposing factors which make people vulnerable for maltreatment and *precipitating* events that trigger the onset of maltreatment."

Predisposing Factors

Predisposing factors for maltreatment include the characteristics of the parent(s), the characteristics of the child, characteristics of the situation, and cultural beliefs regarding violence (Garbarino, 1986). The extent to which different life events produce negative consequences depends, in part, on the nature of these predisposing factors. For example, both positive self-esteem and internal locus-of-control have been found to moderate stress reactions in response to different life events (Fisher, 1984; Lefcourt, 1981). Likewise, parental attributions about the intention of their childrens' behavior have been found to affect their reactions to aversive child behavior (Dix & Grusec, 1985); an antecedent condition that has been implicated as a cause of maltreatment (Steele & Pollack, 1968).

Examination of those factors known to contribute to child maltreatment (e.g., Garbarino, 1983, 1984, 1986; Meier, 1985) shows that many can be categorized as predisposing factors. These include poverty, low income, economic distress, depressed self-esteem, the inability to empathize, untimely or unwanted childbearing, a history of maltreatment in the parent's background, unrealistic parental expectations for their child, parental coping and problem-solving skills, attitudes toward and values about the use of physical punishment, etc. Any of these factors can predispose a person to engage in episodes of maltreatment.

Precipitating Factors

As noted by Garbarino and Stocking (1980), nearly 60% of the general population can be designated as having at least several of the predisposing factors of abuse and neglect, yet less than 10% of the general population actually engages in episodes of child maltreatment. Therefore, we must look elsewhere for the actual causes of maltreatment. Evidence suggests that different precipitating events increase the likelihood of abuse and neglect. For example, one of the most commonly mentioned events is excessive child crying that cannot be terminated through adult interventions (Meier, 1985). Such an event can easily precipitate maltreatment if certain predisposing factors (e.g., the child being a product of an untimely or unwanted pregnancy) are present.

Garbarino (1983), in a review of factors associated with maltreatment, found that the personal characteristics of both the parents and child can function as elicitors of abuse and neglect, particularly when social stress and social isolation characterize the family. It has been demonstrated in a number of studies that different life crises produce negative consequences (i.e., psychosocial disorders) which, in turn, increase the likelihood of child maltreatment (Justice & Justice, 1976). For example, Garbarino (1976) found that job-related stress was a major correlate of child abuse. Loss of one's job, another major life crisis, has also been found to be associated with child maltreatment (see Meier, 1985). Thus, the extent to which an individual's coping mechanisms are threatened by different life crises, stress as well as other dysfunctional behaviors are likely to be manifested, and the likelihood of maltreatment increased.

HANDICAPPED CHILDREN AND CHILD MALTREATMENT

A number of investigators have contended that a disproportionate number of handicapped and developmentally disabled children are victims of abuse and neglect (e.g., Briggs, 1979; Gil, 1970; Souther, 1983), although controversy continues over this assertion (Garbarino,

1986; Starr *et al.*, 1984). Starr *et al.* (1984), based on an extensive review and analysis of the literature, concluded that there is no "clear causal link between prior handicaps and abuse" (p. 62). While we would agree that a handicapping condition per se may not be an elicitor of abuse, we would argue that it does constitute a possible predisposing factor to the extent that behaviors associated with the handicap (e.g., excessive time demands) function as precipitating events that adversely affect personal well-being, family functioning, and other parental behaviors. This is the case because aberrations in behavior are more likely to occur among handicapped children causing stress, and thus predispose these children to maltreatment.

Parental Reactions to a Handicapped Child

The birth and rearing of a handicapped child often produces the same types of reactions that function as both predisposing factors and precipitating events associated with the increased likelihood of child maltreatment. Emotional and physical distress, depression, denial, grief, and anger are often the types of parental reactions manifested in response to the discovery of their child's handicap or disability (Gabel, McDowell, & Cerreto, 1983). Furthermore, the rearing of a handicapped child oftentimes has negative effects on family functioning which adversely influences marital relationships, parent–child interactions, and other types of intra- and extrafamily relationships. Disruptions in these relationships, in turn, often produces negative reactions, including increased stress levels, emotional and physical distress, marital discord, withdrawal, depression, and other psychosocial disorders (Blacher, 1984; Crnic *et al.*, 1983a).

In our own work on parental and family reactions to handicapped children, we have found that parents often manifest a host of negative reactions to the birth and rearing of a handicapped child depending upon the severity of impairment (see Dunst, 1985a). That is, the more severely retarded or handicapped the child, the more likely one will find that the child's handicap produces excessive time demands, family disintegration, negative parental attitudes, pessimism toward the child, and parental perceptions that their child's behavior is both troublesome and difficult. To the extent that these responses and reactions function as predisposing factors or precipitating events, the likelihood of episodes of maltreatment become greater.

The rearing of a handicapped child, particularly one that manifests difficult behavior characteristics (difficult temperament, poor feeding and sleeping patterns, behavioral disorders, etc.), often places excessive time demands upon the child's parents and other caregivers (Holroyd, 1985). Increased time demands have been a major factor implicated as a cause of negative parental reactions, including stress, emotional and physical problems, and disruptions in family functioning (Blacher, 1984). In a recently completed study in our Child Development Laboratory with 224 parents of handicapped, mentally retarded, and developmentally at-risk children (Trivette & Dunst, 1986), we found a particularly compelling set of correlations between parental ratings of excessive time demands and emotional and physical distress [$r = .63, p (.001)$], negative attitudes toward their child [$r = .53, p (.001)$], parental over protection [$r = 47, p (.001)$], family disintegration [$r = .44, p (.001)$], lack of family opportunities [$r = .54, p (.001)$], and parental perceptions of their childrens' behavioral difficulties [$r = .53, p (.001)$].

The results of the Trivette and Dunst (1986) study, the findings from other studies conducted at our program (Dunst, 1985a; Dunst & Leet, 1985; Dunst & Trivette, 1984; Dunst et al., 1986a, 1986b, in press; Trivette & Dunst, 1986), and other empirical evidence (e.g., Blacher, 1984; Fewell & Vadasy, 1986, Holroyd, 1985) as well as our clinical impressions (see e.g., Dunst, 1983; Dunst, Cushing, & Vance, 1985) have increasingly led us to the realization that the caregiving demands associated with the rearing of a handicapped child function as a major precipitating event that can adversely affect parent and family functioning, which, in turn, can produce the types of situational conditions that have been found to be associated with episodes of child maltreatment. *In fact, we view child maltreatment as one of a number of possible conditions that may result from the increased responsibilities and demands associated with rearing a handicapped youngster.*

Parental and Family Adaptations

Not all families of handicapped children manifest the same reactions in response to the birth and rearing of a child with developmental problems. The complex relationships between stress, coping, and adjustment has recently been examined in detail by Crnic et al. (1983a) as part of a model of family adaptation. The model views the family as a social system, considers those variables that affect adaptations to a retarded or handicapped person, and proposes how ecological influences mediate stress and coping associated with the presence of a retarded or handicapped child.

According to Crnic et al. (1983a), adaptations to the birth and rearing of a handicapped child vary tremendously, which suggests that ecological influences within and beyond the family unit account, in part, for the variance associated with differing reactions. These factors include, but are not limited to, social support (Dunst & Trivette, 1984; Trivette & Dunst, 1986; Dunst et al., 1986a, 1986b), locus of control (Sarason, Johnson, & Siegel, 1978), individual coping and problem-

solving mechanisms (Folkman, Schaefer, & Lazarus, 1979), SES and income (Nihira, Meyers, & Mink, 1980), self-concepts and personal beliefs
in self-efficacy (Gregory, 1981), and child characteristics (Beckman, 1983;
Dunst, 1985a). Beckman (1983), for example, found that the child characteristics most associated with negative parent and family functioning
were difficult child temperament, unresponsiveness on the part of the
child, and extra caregiving demands resulting from the child's handicapping condition. The correlation between extra caregiving demands
(excessive time demands) and negative reactions on the part of the
parent and family was .81 [p (.001)]. This latter finding provides yet
additional evidence that the time demands associated with the care of
a handicapped child function as a precipitating event that negatively
affects parent and family functioning. Thus, to the extent that time demands can be lessened and the consequences of other predisposing
factors and precipitating events alleviated, positive family functioning
should be promoted, and the possibility of negative outcomes prevented (or at least reduced).

Social Support and Family Adaptations

Social support has increasingly been found to buffer the negative
reactions associated with the birth and rearing of a handicapped child
(Blacher, 1984; Fewell & Vadasy, 1986; McCubbin et al., 1982; Patterson
& McCubbin, 1983). The role that social support plays in the promotion
of parents, family, and child functioning in households with young
children with developmental problems has been the focus of a series
of studies conducted in our Child Development Laboratory (Dunst,
1985a; Dunst & Leet, 1985; Dunst & Trivette, 1984; Dunst et al., 1986a,
1986b, in press; Trivette & Dunst, 1986). Dunst (1985a) recently summarized the major findings from these investigations. The results
showed that different types of support were significantly related to a
host of parent and family behavior characteristics, including emotional
and physical health, excessive time demands, and personal well-being;
family integration and family opportunities; parental overprotection and
overcommitment; and parent perceptions of child behavior difficulties.
In all instances, either satisfaction with provision of support or quantitative aspects of the parents' social network (network size, intrafamily
role sharing) were correlated with positive parent and family functioning. For example, in a study by Dunst and Leet (1985), the relationships
between family resources and both well-being and health were examined among 45 parents of preschool handicapped youngsters. Adequacy of resources was significantly associated with parental physical
health [$r = .50, p (.001)$], emotional health [$r = .46, p (.001)$], general
coping abilities [$r = .58, p (.001)$], coping with the child's handicap [r

TABLE 2.1. Correlations between the Independent and Dependent Variables

| | Dependent measures | | | | | |
| | Personal well-being | | Family integrity[c] | | | |
Independent measures	Emotional and physical health[a]	Psychological well-being[b]	Cohesion intrafamily relationships	Personal autonomy/ achievement	Family structure/ organization	Total scale score
Personal characteristics						
Mother's age	.06	.26***	.01	−.09	−.05	−.03
Mother's education level	.14	.23**	.07	.22*	.05	.23**
Father's age	−.20*	.03	−.05	−.01	−.10	−.01
Father's education level	.07	.19*	.18*(4)	.24**	.17*(1)	.31***(5)
Family characteristics						
SES	.17*	.30***(4)[d]	.13	.09	.07	.14
Income	.15	.18*	.26**(3)	.09	.08	.20*
Child characteristics						
Child sex (female = 1, male = 2)	.14	.01	.00	−.06	.01	−.04
Child age (months)	−.10	.08	.05	.11	.01	.12
Child DQ (developmental quotient)	.11	.01	.01	.10	−.02	.07

Social support measures

FSS satisfaction[e]	.49***(1)	.43***(2)	.30**(2)	.47***(2)	.14	.52***(1)
FSS total	−.04	−.11	.04	.12	−.14	.06
MSI role[f]	.04	.03	−.09	−.03	−.05	−.06
MSI total	.42***(2)	.48***(1)	.33**(1)	.39***(3)	.06	.44***(2)
Social network characteristics[g]						
Network size	.27***(5)	.28***(4)	.16	.39***(4)	.04	.36***(4)
Durability	.19*	.21*	−.02	.08	−.15	.01
Intensity	.29***(4)	.31***(3)	.11	.32***(5)	.01	.28***
Number of contacts	.31***	.27***(5)	.06	.49***(1)	.03	.28***
Number of roles	.33***(3)	.25**	.17*(5)	.28***	−.05	.40**(3)
Network density	−.02	−.05	−.04	−.04	−.02	−.05

[a]Questionnaire on Resources and Stress (Holroyd, 1985).

[b]Psychological Well-Being Index (Bradburn & Caplovitz, 1965).

[c]Family Environment Scale (Moos, 1974).

[d]The numbers in parentheses beside the correlation coefficients are the rank-orderings of the five highest/significant coefficients.

[e]Family Support Scale (Dunst, Jenkins, & Trivette, 1984).

[f]Maternal Social Support Index (Pascoe, Loda, Jeffries, & Earp, 1981).

[g]Psychosocial Kinship Network Inventory (Pattison, DeFrancisco, Wood, Frazier, & Crowder, 1975).

*$p < .05$, **$p < .01$, ***$p < .005$.

= .25, *p* (.05)], and stress management [*r* = .40, *p* (.005)]. In a recently completed study of 103 mothers of preschool developmentally delayed children (Dunst & Trivette, in preparation), the relationships between personal well-being, family climate, and social support were also examined. Both satisfaction with support and several social network characteristics (network size, intensity of relationships, number of contacts, and multidimensionality) were significantly related to both well-being and family climate (see Table 2.1). Moreover, the magnitude of the correlation coefficients were greater than for either the personal (parental age and education levels) or family (SES and income) characteristics variables. Taken together, the findings from these studies provide converging evidence to suggest that social support can proactively affect parental and family functioning and buffer parents from the negative reactions often associated with the birth and rearing of a handicapped child.

Social Support and the Prevention of Child Maltreatment

While observed associations between predisposing factors, precipitating events, and parental and family reactions may be interpreted in a number of ways, the model previously described provides a framework for hypothesizing the causal and mediational relationships between different parent, family, child, and extrafamily characteristics leading to either positive or negative outcomes (see Trivette & Dunst, 1986, for a description of a study that employed this type of conceptual and methodological framework). Figure 2.2 shows a causal/mediational model that depicts the temporal sequence of events that we suspect influence the extent to which the birth and rearing of a handicapped child is likely to have positive or negative consequences and, thus, decrease or increase the probability of episodes of maltreatment. The model views parent and family characteristics as determinants of intrafamily and informal support (Broadhead, Kaplan, James, Wagner, Schoenbach, Grimson, Heyden, Tibblin, & Gehlbach, 1983). Temporally, the establishment and maintenance of an informal support network is seen as occurring prior to the birth of a child and, consequently, should buffer any negative reactions to the extent that members of the parents' network provide the types of supportive experiences that strengthen parent and family functioning (Wandersman, Wandersman, & Kahn, 1980). The birth and rearing of a handicapped child is seen as a set of conditions that may have either positive or negative consequences depending upon existing intrapersonal and intrafamily resources, the adequacy of informal support, and the nature and types of formal support that a family receives as part of the care of their child (Crnic *et al.*, 1983b). The extent to which precipitating factors (e.g., excessive time

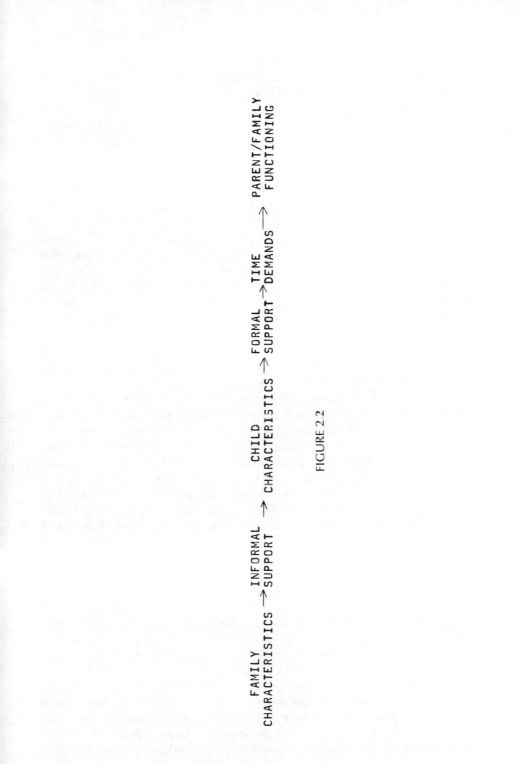

FAMILY
CHARACTERISTICS → INFORMAL
SUPPORT → CHILD
CHARACTERISTICS → FORMAL
SUPPORT → TIME
DEMANDS → PARENT/FAMILY
FUNCTIONING

FIGURE 2.2

demands) produce negative consequences is considered multiply determined by individual, family, and extrafamily influences (Belsky, 1980).

The plausibility of this model was tested with data collected from
214 parents of preschool-aged mentally retarded, physically impaired,
and developmentally at-risk children. The independent variables included in the analyses were family characteristics (SES and income),
intrafamily support (role division and role satisfaction), informal support
(satisfaction with provision of support from one's spouse/mate, rela-
tives/kin, own parents, friends, the church, etc.), child characteristics
(level of intellectual functioning and diagnostic group), formal support
(satisfaction with provision of support from professional helpers, early
intervention program, social agencies, child/family's physician, school/
day-care, etc.), and parental ratings of the time demands (Holroyd, 1985)
their child placed upon them. The dependent measures of parent and
family functioning included emotional and physical health, family integrity, and parental perceptions of child behavior difficulty (Holroyd,
1985). The data were analyzed by a series of hierarchical multiple
regression analyses (Cohen & Cohen, 1983) with entry of the variables
as specified in Figure 2.2. In each analysis, the increments in R^2 were
determined to discern the unique amount of variance accounted for
by the different independent measures.

The results of the analyses are shown in Table 2.2. With the exception
of the formal social support measure, nearly all the zero-order correlations between the independent and dependent measures were significant. The multiple regression analyses showed that all the independent variables, taken together, accounted for 42–51% of the variance
in the dependent measures. However, there was considerable specificity with respect to the differential contributions of the individual
predictor variables. As expected, time demands accounted for significant amounts of variance in all three dependent measures. The results
also showed that the severity of a child's handicap (i.e., children with
lower IQ scores) was likely to negatively affect both family functioning
and parental perceptions of child behavior. Of particular importance
were the findings pertaining to the moderating influences of intrafamily
and informal support. The aggregate of these measures accounted for
14 [p (.001)], 15 [p (.001)], and 10% [p (.005)] of the variance, respectively,
in emotional and physical health, family integrity, and perceptions of
child behavior difficulties. These results suggest that social support may
act as a moderating variable buffering parents from the negative reactions associated with rearing a handicapped child. What the results
do not tell us is whether the parent and family outcomes function as
intervening variables increasing or decreasing the likelihood of maltreatment, or whether or not the levels of well-being, family integration,
and parent attitudes can be affected by social support in a manner that

TABLE 2.2. Multiple Regression Coefficients (R^2) and Increments (I) in R^2 for Three Parent, Family, and Child Outcome Measures

Independent variables	Dependent measures								
	Emotional and physical health			Family integrity			Child behavior difficulties		
	r	R^2	I	r	R^2	I	r	R^2	I
Family characteristics[a]	.13*	.02	.02	.19***	.04*	.04*	.14**	.03	.03
Intrafamily support[b]	.25****	.10****	.08****	.33****	.16****	.12****	.07	.05*	.02
Informal support[c]	.29****	.16****	.06****	.24****	.19****	.03*	.29****	.12	.08****
Child diagnosis[d]	.17**	.19****	.03	.33****	.34****	.15****	.44****	.30****	.18****
Formal support[e]	.08	.19****	.00	.00	.34****	.00	.02	.30****	.00
Time demands[f]	.65****	.45****	.26****	.52****	.42****	.08****	.53****	.51****	.21****

[a]SES and income (the zero-order correlation is for income).
[b]Role division and role satisfaction (Parent Role Scale; Gallagher et al., 1982).
[c]Family Support Scale (Dunst et al., 1984).
[d]Developmental quotient.
[e]Family Support Scale (Dunst et al., 1984).
[f]Questionnaire on Resources and Stress (Holroyd, 1985).
*$p < .05$; **$p < .01$; ***$p < .005$; ****$p < .001$.

reduces the probability of negative consequences. It seems reasonable to speculate, however, that social support exerts beneficial effects by attenuating or preventing the types of reactions often associated with both rearing a handicapped child and maltreatment.

Both direct and indirect evidence from other sources support our contention that social support plays a buffering role in preventing child maltreatment. Hunter and Kilstrom (1979), in a study of individuals who themselves had been abused as children, found that if these persons had adequate provisions of informal support, they were less likely to engage in episodes of maltreatment with their own children. Similarly, Egeland and Brunnquell (1979) found that predisposing factors were less likely to be transformed into abusive patterns by mothers of children at-risk for maltreatment if the mothers had adequate provisions of support from the child's father and the mother's family. Colletta (1981) found that mothers who had adequate social support available to them displayed more positive behaviors toward their children, whereas mothers with inadequate support systems were more hostile and rejecting of their children. Dunst and Trivette (1986) found nearly identical results in a study examining the relationships between social support and styles of caregiver interaction in families of handicapped children. Converging evidence thus suggests that the effects of both the predisposing and precipitating factors associated with child maltreatment can be moderated by social support. The role that social support plays in preventing child maltreatment, along with the evidence to substantiate the claim that provision of support can have proactive influences, is extensively reviewed and analyzed by Garbarino and Stocking (1980).

PROMISING APPROACHES FOR PREVENTION OF CHILD MALTREATMENT

Like most social problems, child maltreatment is multiply determined (Belsky, 1980), and, consequently, requires multiple solutions. Like most sociological constructs, social support is multidimensional and cannot be viewed in a unitary manner (Hall & Wellman, 1985; Pearlin, 1985). Consequently, different types of "support" are likely to produce differential influences (Dunst & Trivette, 1984), and multiple approaches seem necessary in order to prevent the maltreatment of handicapped children. In this section, we briefly review several promising approaches for preventing child maltreatment with particular emphasis on the manner in which preventive interventions can support and strengthen families. Many of the approaches have been employed with families of nonhandicapped youngsters. It should be noted that none of the preventive strategies is mutually exclusive nor have they typically been conducted at the exclusion of other approaches.

Child-Focused Interventions

Handicapped children often display behavior aberrations (excessive crying, difficult temperaments, resistence to being consoled, etc.) that have been identified as precipitating factors associated with maltreatment. The "very difficult" child is very likely to manifest aversive behavior (Wolfe & Manion, 1984), constituting a source of stress for the family (Hetherington & Martin, 1979; Mash, 1984). A promising approach to preventing maltreatment is to decrease or extinguish the occurrence of the particular behaviors that the parents find "difficult" while at the same time facilitating more appropriate and adaptive behaviors.

Wolfe and Manion (1984), as part of the Parent/Child Early Education Program, describe the manner in which behavioral interventions are used to extinguish socially maladaptive behavior that parents find particularly aversive. In our own work with severely and profoundly retarded preschoolers, we have found that fostering a handicapped child's ability to interact with the environment in an adaptive manner often results in decreases in aversive child behavior (particularly crying and fussing) and increases in parental responsiveness to their children (Dunst et al., 1985). To the extent that handicapped children can be taught socially adaptive behaviors at the same time difficult behavior characteristics are extinguished, the possibility of negative reactions to the child ought to be decreased and the likelihood of maltreatment lessened. This type of preventive effort should prove effective to the degree that the interventions affect the family system in a manner that facilitates and strengthens positive parent–child interactions.

Parent-Focused Intervention

The inability to cope with and manage normative transitions (McCubbin & Figley, 1983) and life crises (Figley & McCubbin, 1983) often affect parental well-being and health in a negative manner. Poor coping and stress management are factors often associated with both episodes of maltreatment (Garbarino, 1983, 1984, 1986) and the rearing of a handicapped child (Crnic et al., 1983a). It would seem, therefore, that attempts directed toward enhancing coping mechanisms should prevent negative reactions associated with rearing a handicapped child and, in turn, reduce the probability of maltreatment.

Wolfe and Manion (1984) describe several procedures they employ in the Parent/Child Early Education Program for teaching problem-solving skills as a way of fostering coping and stress management behavior.

Interventions that emphasize enhancement of coping and personal management skills are most likely to be successful if they facilitate parents' abilities to see multiple solutions to single problems. This contention is based on the results of a study by Pearlin and Schooler (1982) who found that the "sheer richness and variety of responses and resources that one brings to bear in coping with life-strains . . . shields one's self from emotional stress" (p. 18). It would seem, therefore, that enhancement of coping abilities should function as a preventive interaction to the extent that such efforts facilitate and strengthen a parent's ability to deal with the types of demands often associated with rearing a handicapped child.

Parent–Child Focused Interactions

Disruptions in parent–child relations, particularly parental use of coercive styles of interaction, often set the occasion for episodes of maltreatment (Garbarino, 1986). A considerable body of evidence indicates that interactions between handicapped children and their parents tend to be characterized by both intrusiveness and directiveness (see Dunst, 1985b). It would seem, therefore, that efforts toward affecting changes in the parent–child dyad should promote more positive styles of interaction and lessen the likelihood of situational factors being transformed into maltreatment (Straus, 1980).

There are a number of promising approaches that might be used to support parents' acquisition of positive styles of interactions. Embry (1980), as part of the Practical Parenting Project, and Lutzker, Wesch, and Rice (1984), as part of Project "12-Ways," describe ecobehavioral strategies designed to increase parental responsiveness to positive child behavior and decrease responsiveness to negative child behavior. Expending large amounts of time responding to negative behavior while ignoring positive behavior sets the stage for episodes of maltreatment since this interactive pattern typically involves the use of physical interventions to control the child. Thus, to the degree that parenting behavior can be strengthened by teaching the skills to change their interactive patterns, the likelihood of maltreatment should be diminished. Both projects are noteworthy on two accounts. First, they both focus on the prevention of child maltreatment, and, second, the efficacy of project efforts have been empirically established (Embry, 1980; Lutzker & Rice, 1984).

A different approach that holds promise for affecting changes in parent–child relations is being conducted in our own program as part of the FAMILY PLACE project. FAMILY PLACE is a model-demonstration project for teenage mothers whose children are at-risk for developmental problems, including maltreatment. The project is designed to provide and mediate the provision of different types of support to these young women, with special emphasis on helping them acquire the necessary skills to meet the needs of both the child and the family. As part of their involvement in FAMILY PLACE, the teenage mothers participate in an 18- to 20-week work–study program in a preschool setting where the teenagers work with skilled caregivers (paid staff and parent volunteers) who are known to interact with children in a positive, facilitating manner. It is expected that these caregivers will model interactive behavior that the teenage mothers will adopt with their own children. (It should be noted that no more than two teenage mothers work together at any one time so they are less likely to model one anothers behavior and more likely to model the behavior of the caregivers whose styles we predict the teenagers will adopt.) The results of a study designed to validate our expectations showed that over the course of 18 weeks, the teenage mothers manifested significant increases in positive, facilitative styles of interaction together with decreases in both intrusive, coercive, and controlling interactive styles (Dunst, Vance, & Cooper, 1986). This rather simplistic, low-cost intervention suggests that opportunities to observe and interact with persons who display positive, nurturing behavior may be sufficient to affect changes in parent–child relations and function as a preventive intervention to the degree that alternative interactive behaviors are acquired (see especially Cochran & Brassard, 1979).

Child and Respite Care

The day-to-day care of a handicapped child often takes its toll on parents' well-being and health. Evidence from a number of sources (Dunst et al., 1986b; Trivette, 1982) indicate that the increased burdens associated with the care of a handicapped child is predominantly the sole responsibility of the mother and increases the day-to-day child care responsibilities placed upon her. Excessive child care demands can affect parents negatively (Beckman, 1983; Trivette & Dunst, 1986), which in turn can produce the types of reactions often associated with episodes of maltreatment. Intrafamily role sharing and provision of child care would seem important as preventive interventions in that it alleviates excessive time demands which, in turn, reduces the probability of negative effects on parental well-being and health.

The role that intrafamily role sharing plays in mediating positive influences comes from clinical experience in our program. As part of a parent support group, which was attended only by mothers, they continually discussed the fact that their husbands did not help with child care responsibilities. In order to obtain baseline information regarding role sharing, we had both the mothers and fathers complete the Parent

Role Scale (PRS: Gallagher, Cross, & Scharfman, 1981). The PRS includes 20 roles that are typically performed in households rearing a young child. Simply completing the scale functioned as an intervention. In several instances, fathers realized that they provided their wives little support and began helping with the care of the child. In a number of other instances, the mothers commented upon how much their husbands actually did do, which appeared to reduce interpersonal difficulties. These clinical findings suggest that attempts to affect changes in role sharing where mothers (or fathers) are primarily responsible for day-to-day care of the child should reduce time demands, promote positive functioning, and decrease the likelihood of child care demands being transformed into maltreatment (Dunst & Trivette, 1986).

The role that respite care plays in preventing child maltreatment is being examined in our program as part of Project PROACT. This model-demonstration project provides both in- and out-of-home respite care to families with handicapped children who have been identified as at-risk for maltreatment according to criteria established by Milner and Wimberley (1980) and others (e.g., Belsky, 1980; Garbarino, 1983, 1984). The model shown in Figure 2.2 is being used to test the effects of the respite care. Child care relief is expected to alleviate excessive child care demands which, in turn, is expected to have positive effects on parent well-being and health and parent perceptions of the extent to which they view their child's behavior as troublesome or difficult. Data collected thus far indicate that respite care has the hypothesized influences, and that parent and family functioning is positively affected by child care relief. Dunst (1983) describes one method that can be used to assess and intervene to decrease the time demands handicapped children often place on their families.

Meeting Basic Family Needs

Inadequacies in basic family resources often plays a role in producing child maltreatment (Garbarino, 1984). Dunst and Leet (1985) recently established the relationship between the inability to meet family needs in households with a handicapped child and the deleterious effects on parental well-being and health. Frequently, the human and economic costs involved in the rearing of a handicapped child exacerbate an already volatile situation and increase the likelihood of negative consequences, including maltreatment. Given this set of conditions, it would seem that attempts to mediate provision of support aimed at meeting basic family needs should alleviate many of the deleterious factors. Hartman and Laird (1983) describe a set of procedures that can be used for assessing family needs and conducting interventions designed to meet these needs. Their assessment/intervention strategy seem particularly useful since it uses a social systems framework for understanding the family's ecology and mediating linkages among persons and agencies for achieving intervention targets. In our own program, Project SHARE uses an informal bartering program for meeting the needs of low SES background families with handicapped children through the mediation of exchange of resources among the members of the SHARE organization.

Mobilizing Informal Support Networks

Many of the types of help and assistance that can be of benefit to handicapped children and their families are available from relatives, friends, and neighbors. Ballew (1985) and Pancoast (1980) describe how natural helpers can be mobilized in order to provide child care, decrease isolation, offer advice, affect changes in attitudes and beliefs, and otherwise serve as a resource that promotes well-being and health. The results of a study by Ballew (1985) suggests natural helpers enhance families' coping and problem-solving resources which reduce the probability of maltreatment. Thus, to the extent that mobilization of support from the members of the family's social network can function to alleviate any negative consequences associated with rearing a handicapped child and promote positive functioning, the conditions which function as predisposing and precipitating factors of maltreatment should be lessened (see especially Hartman & Laird, 1983).

IMPLICATIONS AND RECOMMENDATIONS

The evidence reviewed in this chapter provides converging support for the contention that different types and forms of social support can be used to promote parental well-being, family integrity, and other positive intra- and interpersonal outcomes. The data that we presented indicated that the negative consequences and reactions often associated with the birth and rearing of a handicapped child can be lessened or alleviated in situations where families benefit from the help and assistance received from the members of their social support networks. Based on available evidence, it would seem that a safe environment for handicapped children includes one in which adequacy of resources and support promotes rather than impedes family adaptations to the handicapped child. The evidence raises a number of issues as well as has major implications in terms of promotion of parental and familial well-being and prevention of child maltreatment.

1. *Prevention versus Treatment.* If we are ever to reduce or eliminate child abuse and neglect, we must make a firm commitment to prevention efforts designed to alleviate the negative consequences resulting from both the predisposing factors and precipitating events associated with maltreatment. This will require the use of interventions that promote and strengthen family functioning as a means to prevent volatile situations.

2. *Proactive versus Deficit Approach.* Prevention efforts must be proactive rather than deficit in their orientation. Proactive approaches focus on supporting and strengthening families through enhancement of positive intra- and interpersonal functioning. Risk factors associated with the likelihood of maltreatment should not be viewed as inherent parent or family deficits but rather as a result of ecological forces affecting parent and family functioning. Accentuating the positive, while avoiding blame, will go a long way toward proactive prevention of the maltreatment of handicapped children.

3. *Social Systems Perspective.* Prevention efforts must take a broader based, social systems perspective of child maltreatment. The conditions that transform risk status into abuse or neglect are complex and thus require a conceptual orientation that can help to explain the myriad of factors that contribute to episodes of child maltreatment. A social systems perspective of child maltreatment can provide this type of framework.

4. *An Ounce of Prevention Is Worth a Pound of Cure.* Successful prevention efforts are likely to be those that involve adequate allocation of financial and human resources in order to carry out prevention trials. Enough is known about both the predisposing factors and precipitating events associated with the probability of maltreatment to identify those families with handicapped children at-risk for negative outcomes. The establishment of social policies that support prevention efforts are needed if the elimination or the reduction of child maltreatment is to occur on a broad scale.

Besides shifts in conceptual perspectives and establishment of social policy which supports prevention efforts, there are several major recommendations and conclusions that can be made in order to establish safe environments.

5. *Managing the Difficult Child.* The stresses and strains associated with the care of a handicapped child who displays difficult-to-manage behaviors can be beyond the capacity for any one family to handle. Because difficult behaviors can precipitate episodes of maltreatment, it is extremely important to deal with these aversive situations in a preventive manner. Professionals should be alert to situations where parents find their handicapped child's behavior difficult or troublesome

and suggest the use of interventions designed to alleviate the stress-producing situation. Parents should seek advice and assistance from persons who can provide the type of support that will make difficult-to-manage situations more manageable and tolerable. They should also bear in mind that seeking help is not a sign of poor parenting but is rather an indication of a "positive step" toward strengthening oneself and one's family.

6. *Coping with the Demands of Rearing a Handicapped Child.* Rearing a young child in today's complex society is difficult enough. Rearing a handicapped child often adds to this difficulty and can tax one's ability to cope with other added responsibilities. Feeling trapped and seeing no way out is a sign of trouble. If a parent feels this way, (s)he is likely to benefit from efforts designed to explore alternative ways for coping with these demands. The adage that "two heads are better than one" is especially applicable here. Different people with different perspectives see different solutions to problems. Talking to friends, relatives, the clergy, the child's teacher, etc., can often open new avenues for dealing with the demands of rearing a handicapped child.

7. *Emphasizing the Joys of Child Rearing.* No matter how handicapped a child, no matter the parents' background or education level, each and every individual has strengths and assets that bring to bear on interactions with others. We should look for the positive things handicapped children do, be proud of their accomplishments, and emphasize the positive at every opportunity. Moreover, parents should recognize their parenting strengths and use them when interacting with their child. Professionals who work with handicapped children should support and strengthen parent and family functioning by building upon child and parent capabilities without always attempting to rectify weaknesses. Taking a "positive stance" should make rearing a handicapped child a more enjoyable and rewarding experience.

8. *Fostering Intrafamily Support and Role Sharing.* Mothers are often the ones who assume primary responsibility for the care of their handicapped child while still performing other household duties. Consequently, there is a need for others to be sensitive to the added responsibilities involved in the care of a handicapped child and an effort made to assist the primary caregiver with his or her duties and responsibilities. Provision of intrafamily support as well as more equal distribution in role responsibilities involving child care and household chores will help "spread the load" with respect to the care of a handicapped youngster. In single-parent households and those where role division is not feasible (e.g., due to work schedules), parents and professionals should explore alternatives for easing day-in and day-out

responsibility placed upon the shoulders of the primary caregiver. Reciprocal provision of support between the members of the parents social network is often an excellent way of facilitating intrafamily support and role sharing (e.g., an older sibling watching their brother or sister in exchange for a parent taking them to a movie).

9. *Active Attempts toward the Reduction of Excessive Time Demands.* Our assertion that excessive time demands function as a major precipitating event causing negative consequences in family functioning suggest that different types of respite and relief should alleviate or at least reduce some negative reactions associated with the day-to-day care of a handicapped child. Various options are open to accomplish this goal. These include in- and out-of-home respite services, use of one's personal social network for provision or exchange of child care, specialized day-care centers and public school programs, short- and long-term respite care facilities, and drop-in day-care and parents' night out programs. Most parents of young children use baby-sitters in order to pursue personal interests, go out to a movie or dinner, or engage in other social events. Because handicapped children frequently have special needs that require care by specially trained persons, babysitters may not be an option for certain families. Professionals who work with families of handicapped children should be sure to inform parents about the types of respite and childcare available to them, and if not available, consider the possibility of establishing such services. (Many families in our program have established informal baby-sitting cooperatives as one way of ensuring the availability of emergency and as-needed childcare.) Parents should be aware of and recognize instances when excessive time demands may be taking their toll and "take time out" by using child-care programs to obtain respite, get other things done, or simply have time to oneself.

10. *Meeting Basic Family Needs.* The extent to which personal well-being and family integrity are maintained is, in part, determined by whether basic family needs are met. Poor housing and living conditions, inadequate health care, lack of financial resources, etc., can all function as predisposing factors that affect the likelihood of maltreatment. Prevention activities need to include efforts designed to meet basic family needs in order to eliminate these factors as correlates of abuse or neglect. Professionals should bear in mind that asking families to fulfill professionally prescribed recommendations (e.g., conducting therapy sessions), when basic needs are going unmet, can actually add to the family's stresses and strains and exacerbate a potentially volatile situation. Professionals need to "be sensitive to the bigger picture" and order priorities in terms of the family's point of view. Parents who find themselves being asked to do things that simply add to already existing demands should be prepared to discuss with professionals how they

feel and explain why they need to address other concerns before they are able to deal with these additional demands.

11. *Mobilization of Personal Social Networks.* Inasmuch as a strong and active personal social network has been found to be associated with the lower probability of maltreatment, and families of handicapped children often have less support available to them compared to families of nonhandicapped children, efforts to mobilize and strengthen personal social networks is strongly indicated. Efforts toward this end should foster linkages that address specific family needs that result in promotion of positive family functioning. A "rule of thumb" worth following is for professionals never to do for families what members of the family's informal network can do (e.g., providing transportation). To do so circumvents the family's personal social network and decreases opportunities to build supportive relationships that are likely to last a lifetime.

12. *Maximizing the Use of the Existing Community Resources.* Maximizing the use of existing community resources can go a long way toward meeting family needs and alleviating the negative consequences that function as precipitators of maltreatment. Increasing parents' knowledge of resources as well as teaching parents how to go about accessing them on behalf of their child and family should result in needs being met, and in turn should decrease the probability of risk factors being transformed into maltreatment. This seems especially necessary when working with families of handicapped children since child and family needs (e.g., medical treatment, counseling) cannot always be met by less formal support systems. Parents should query professionals about what services are available to the children and families, ask why certain services are not available, and mobilize efforts to establish services when they are needed but unavailable. The adage that there is "strength in numbers" should be considered when advocating for needed services and resources.

13. *Supporting and Strengthening Families.* A fundamentally important consideration as part of the prevention of child maltreatment is the effects of supporting and strengthening families. According to Attneave (1976), proactive interventions focus on "restoring control of function of the natural (support network) rather than a professional assuming complete responsibility" for meeting needs (p. 221). Likewise, Hobbs (1975), discussing intervention efforts from a social systems perspective, noted that the goal of intervention is to strengthen normal socializing agents and agencies and not to supplant or replace them. Thus, supporting and strengthening families should be an empowering experience (Katz, 1984; Rappaport, 1981) that permits greater adaptations to both normal life changes and life crises. This is especially im-

portant in work with families of handicapped children where usurpation of decision making and creation of dependencies often occurs as part of parental involvement with professionals (Dunst, 1985a).

Attention to the preceding recommendations as well as those prescribed by others (see especially Garbarino & Stocking, 1980, Epilogue) should contribute to the establishment of safe environments for handicapped children and ultimately result in the prevention of child maltreatment of these special needs children. This should occur if prevention efforts support and strengthen families. Since many handicapped children are at special risk for maltreatment, the need for preventive interventions is strongly indicated. The probability of preventing abuse and neglect seems an attainable goal for one major reason: Handicapped children are typically involved in early intervention and other treatment programs designed to optimize their learning opportunities. Many programs now provide services beginning at birth or at the time a handicapping condition is identified. Involvement in these types of programs set the occasion for prevention trials to the extent that staff take a broader-based, social systems perspective of handicapped children and their families, and efforts are taken toward supporting and strengthening them. The approach described in this chapter can be used as a blueprint for building the types of social support networks that can prevent maltreatment.

chapter 3

THE ROLE OF
SIBLINGS AND PEERS

Susan M. McHale
Wendy C. Gamble

INTRODUCTION

In the two decades since the move toward deinstitutionalization began, handicapped children have spent an increasing amount of their time in the company of nonhandicapped children. Both at home with brothers and sisters and in mainstreamed school environments with peers, children with physical, sensory, and mental handicapping conditions are being exposed to experiences with nondisabled children that 20 years ago, in the heyday of residential care, would have seemed unlikely and possibly inappropriate.

In fact, one important impetus behind the normalization movement was a recognition of the important role other children play in normal social and cognitive development. In mainstreamed classroom settings, for instance, nonhandicapped children are expected to serve as social reinforcers and models of appropriate behavior for disabled children. In addition, educators initially thought that becoming part of the mainstream should result in more positive self-concepts and increased self-confidence in handicapped youngsters. Finally, educators believed that early and regular contact with disabled children at school and involvement with disabled siblings at home would have significant effects on nonhandicapped children, including reducing stigma associated with handicapping conditions, fostering attitudes of acceptance and feelings of empathy toward disabled individuals on the parts of nonhandicapped youngsters, and increasing children's tolerance for differences between themselves and other persons (Bricker, 1978; Gottlieb, 1981).

Not surprisingly, the evidence available to date provides a mixed picture of the outcomes of mainstreaming, in general, and of the developmental consequences of social relationships between handicapped and nonhandicapped children, in particular. Probably the most general conclusion that can be reached from this body of research is that the goals of moving handicapped individuals back into family and community settings are not and cannot be met by simply changing children's places of residence or schooling. Moving handicapped children into the mainstream of society is a first step. However, such programs will require additional supports if they are to achieve these goals for handicapped children and society at large and, if they are to avoid unintended negative consequences. One of these potential negative outcomes is that the psychological and physical well-being of disabled children may be at risk when the stresses, frustrations, and fears associated with regular or transitory contact with these youngsters are not balanced by supports for coping with the unique challenges that these children may present. Evidence that families with handicapped children may be experiencing greater stress—without sufficient means of coping with such stress—can be found in the higher divorce and suicide rates among parents of retarded children (Price-Bonham & Addison, 1978) and the increased rate of child abuse by parents who have handicapped children (Embry, 1980).

The research literature on child abuse, with few exceptions (e.g., Straus, Gelles, & Steinmetz, 1980), tends to focus on adult perpetrators. In keeping with this focus on adult offenders, little attention has been paid to the question of whether and in what ways handicapped children are mistreated by other youngsters. On the contrary, the research literature on mainstreaming emphasizes social advantages accruing to disabled children via contact with nondisabled youngsters. Consequently, our discussion about potential abuse of handicapped children by siblings and peers is largely speculative.

The focus of this chapter is on handicapped children's relationships with nondisabled youngsters and their potential effects on children's well-being and development. We examine both sibling and peer relationships, emphasizing the unique characteristics of these relationships as contrasted with adult–child relationships, and both the potential developmental consequences of disabled children's experiences with other youngsters as well as the processes through which these outcomes may arise. We then turn to a consideration of the conditions under which children may develop more positive relationships with nondisabled youngsters, concluding with suggestions for possible intervention goals and strategies.

INTERPERSONAL RELATIONSHIPS BETWEEN CHILDREN

Differences between Adult–Child, Peer, and Sibling Relationships

Most of what we know about children's social relationships comes from studies of parents (usually mothers) and children and the focus most often pertains to how interpersonal relationships affect children's development. That is, development of psychologists have been more interested in interpersonal relationships as influences on individual development rather than in longitudinal studies of developing relationships in their own right. Investigators also have been interested in how individual developmental changes may affect children's relationships, but these studies tend to focus exclusively on within-individual changes (e.g., children's conceptions of friendship) rather than longitudinal changes in, for instance, the interactions or activity patterns of a dyad (such as a friendship or brother–sister pair). Consequently, when it comes to studying handicapped children's relationships with siblings and peers, there are few normative data available against which to gauge the quality of relationships between disabled and nondisabled children.

In making a case for the move beyond the family unit in studies of social influences on children's development, Hartup (1978) identified the egalitarian nature of child–child interaction as one unique feature of peer relationships. That is, unlike in interaction with adults, when status and competencies are unequal, peer interaction requires that children learn to compromise and work out their differences, because no one child necessarily has authority or power over the other. In investigating children's moral development, Piaget (1932) noted that children's perspectives are more similar to one another from a developmental standpoint. Consequently, children may learn and change more as a result of listening to a peer's perspective than by accommodating to the perspective of an adult (which may be highly discrepant from the child's own ideas). For the child who is mildly retarded or whose perspective is already different from others because of a physical or sensory handicapping condition, peers may be an especially important resource. Finally, peer interactions in the context of play, in particular, appear to differ from adult–child exchanges. That is, whereas play involving adults and children may be goal-oriented (e.g., the adult stacks blocks for the purpose of building a tower or a castle), children's play most often takes place simply for the fun of it. In peer play—especially imaginary play—children may have a greater opportunity to practice social, problem solving, and physical activities, with few constraints on getting things right. These distinctions mean that peer interaction may have unique consequences for children's development and highlight important differences between peer and adult–child interactions and activities.

Dunn (1983) has described sibling interactions as falling somewhere on the continuum between the egalitarian interchanges of peers and the status-based exchanges of adults and children. Like Hartup, Dunn notes that the interactions of peers involve behavioral *reciprocities*. That is, children's behaviors are likely to elicit matching behaviors from their peers. In contrast, exchanges between adults and children tend to involve *complementary* behaviors, such as would be seen in teacher–student exchanges, for instance. Interactions between siblings often are characterized by the older child acting as the leader and the younger child as the follower (Lamb, 1978; Samuels, 1980). In these instances siblings adopt the complementary role patterns of adult–child interactions. In certain contexts, however, siblings may revert to egalitarian interactions—and in so doing they exhibit the reciprocal role patterns of peers. In fact, as Dunn (1983) and others have noted, the sibling relationship is often the first experience children may have with reciprocal role behaviors. It also is likely to be the first chance children have to play the adult role of shaping or leading interactions with a less socially and cognitively competent younger sibling. With their siblings, youngsters also may have their first experience in acting as "disciplinarians," possibly even practicing mentally or physically abusive strategies they have seen their parents employ.

The Potential Consequences of Handicapping Conditions

Depending on the nature of children's handicapping conditions, they may be limited in terms of the nature and contexts of their social experiences with other youngsters. In his research on the structure and adjustment of families of handicapped children, Farber (1960) noted that the handicapped child usually assumed the position of the youngest sibling in the family regardless of that child's absolute or relative chronological age. The implication is that others relate to the handicapped child by adopting the complementary patterns of adult–child exchanges, due to the disabled child's dependent status. In these instances, disabled children may miss out on the important social experiences of egalitarian peer interactions and also may fail to obtain the "leadership" experience that being an elder sibling entails.

Beyond this, siblings or classmates may find it necessary to continually adopt more adultlike roles such as caregiver or disciplinarian with disabled children who may be older, larger, and stronger than they. Nondisabled children are likely to be ill-prepared to deal with such a situation and may react by withdrawing from contact with a disabled child or by experiencing feelings of frustration, anger, and resentment when they are unsuccessful at controlling a disabled child's inappropriate behavior. Other children may respond by using physical means to control or punish a disabled youngster. These responses may stem from their anger or frustration with that youngster's aversive behavior or, as we have noted, from their observations of the "discipline strategies" used by adults around them. Some writers have suggested that "normal" feelings of sibling rivalry are exacerbated when children take stock of the amount of parental time and attention and family financial resources a handicapped sibling's care demands, as well as the extent of involvement in household task and child care responsibilities that is required of nondisabled siblings when one child in the family has a handicapping condition (Farber, 1960; Grossman, 1972; Powell & Ogle, 1985). We will consider further some of these possible limitations in handicapped children's relationships with other youngsters when we discuss the results of research on sibling and peer effects on development. First, however, we turn to a consideration of the potential for conflict in disabled children's relationships with siblings and peers.

Conflict in Children's Relationships

The sibling relationship involves more aggression than any other family relationship, according to the results of survey research (Straus, Gelles, & Steinmetz, 1980). Those who are concerned with family violence tend to focus on child and spousal abuse and, consequently, may find it interesting to note that one of the most frequently reported reasons for children being brought to hospitals for emergency treatment is aggression perpetuated by siblings. Parents' concern about sibling rivalry is acknowledged by parent educators whose childcare manuals contain advice about how to deal with this problem (e.g., Dreikers & Grey, 1968). Parents and professionals may fail to regard "sibling abuse" as pathological, however, because: (1) They consider such aggression as normative, for instance, that children are "just going through a stage"; (2) they think children are not strong enough to inflict severe harm; (3) they believe they ultimately can control such bouts of aggression (by using physical force themselves if need be); and (4) perhaps, most importantly, because these aggressive exchanges, generally speaking, occur between equals. As others have noted (e.g., Garbarino, Guttmann, & Wilson, 1986), the inequality in strength and status is one of the most unpalatable components of child and spouse abuse. Because sibling (and peer) aggression often does not entail undue differences in status or power, such activities may be taken less seriously.

The precipitants of sibling aggression are unknown. In a recently published report of case studies of severe sibling aggression, Green (1984) suggests that poor parenting leading to emotional disturbance may be one basis of pathological levels of aggression exhibited by one sibling toward another. Discussing family constellation and personality development, Adler (1938) sees sibling rivalry as a natural consequence of children's competition for a limited amount of parental attention and finite family resources. Children, themselves, will work to minimize this competition by finding their own niche in the family ecology, one that brings with it a unique set of rewards (Adler, 1938). Thus, one child may become the family "scholar" and another the family "artist." When parents' rewards are distributed *only* to children who assume certain roles, and when the competition for those rewards is extreme, a child may assume the role of the family's "black sheep" and, in this case, seek only negative kinds of attention. As such, according to Adler (1938), sibling rivalry can be seen largely as the result of parental mismanagement. To avoid this problem parents are told to "put all children in the same boat" rather than taking sides in a controversy, to spend time alone with each child, and to attend to and reward the unique abilities and achievements of each child (Dreikers & Grey, 1968).

Children's personal characteristics also may put them at risk for abuse by siblings and peers. A severely handicapped child who requires extensive care may drain family members' energy and emotional resources, and in such cases siblings may be called upon to provide care and supervision for the child. When these demands become burdensome or when children are too young or inexperienced to know how to handle these responsibilities, they may react with frustration and aggression. In addition to physical characteristics, disabled children's behavioral style or temperament may put them at risk for abuse. In our research, for instance, we have found that handicapped children who also display more conduct problems (hyperactivity, aggression, uncooperative behavior) are treated with more hostility by their siblings. These data are only correlational and, as such, the direction of this effect is unclear. Furthermore, a handicapped child's difficult behavior is not an excuse for abusive treatment. These findings suggest, however, that it may be important to work with disabled children to extinguish inappropriate and disruptive behavior before leaving them in the care of other children. In addition, programs for siblings or peers that teach them how to handle such behaviors in more positive ways may be an effective means of preventing maltreatment.

An additional perspective on the origins of sibling conflict stems from a social learning model. From this perspective children learn to interact in aggressive ways by observing parental aggression, for instance, in a parent–child or spousal relationship. A number of investigators have noted that authorization or power-assertive discipline styles by parents—characterized by harsh and punitive techniques of behavior control—are associated with increased aggressiveness and lowered moral development in children (Steinmetz, 1979). Straus and colleagues (1980) have explicitly linked spousal and child abuse to violence between siblings. Their survey data reveal a strong positive correlation between extreme forms of sibling aggression and the incidence of aggression in other family relationships.

Social learning mechanisms also may play a role in sibling aggression when children learn (either in the sibling, parent–child or peer contexts) that they can get their own way by escalating the intensity of their aggressive or aversive behavior. These coercive behavior cycles, described by Patterson (1980) in regard to parent–child interactions, may be applied to sibling interchanges as well. In families with handicapped children, the coercion may work in either of two directions: The handicapped sibling may quickly become a tyrant when the family norm (perhaps because of parents' feelings of guilt) is to give in to that child "because she is blind" or "because he is crippled." Anecdotal evidence from preadolescents and adolescents attending a support group for siblings of handicapped children suggests that, at least from these siblings' perspectives, this norm characterizes many families (McGowan, personal communication). Alternatively, when a child is lacking basic physical or mental capabilities, submitting to the demands of an assertive sibling may constitute the pattern of their sibling relationship. In this case, the nonhandicapped child learns that being aggressive and demanding will cause the sibling to capitulate, and the handicapped sibling in this case becomes the "victim."

The extent of *physical aggression* in sibling relationships may arise because brothers and sisters spend a good deal of time together unsupervised by their parents (or other adults). As we noted earlier, the rate of physical aggression by siblings is about four times higher than that of any other family relationship. Survey research by Straus *et al.* (1980), for instance, shows that 40% of children are kicked, bitten, or punched by their siblings during a given year, almost 20% are beaten up, and .03% are attacked by a sibling who uses a knife or a gun. As Straus and colleagues note, this .3% figure may seem fairly small, that is, until it is applied to the national population—the figure then becomes about 109,000 children who are assaulted with deadly weapons by their brothers and sisters in a given year. When these researchers calculated the number of children who had ever in their lives been assaulted, the projected figure increased to 1.5 million. The proportion of these abused siblings who are handicapped is unknown.

Even less is known about physical aggression toward disabled youngsters perpetrated by children outside the family. During regular school hours children may be supervised sufficiently, such that abusive incidents are minimal. Children may not fare so well, however, at the bus stop, on the playground at school, or in the neighborhood. Even more worrisome to parents and even siblings of disabled children are the *teasing* and *ostracizing* that occurs in school and in the neighborhood (Powell & Ogle, 1985). Recent research suggests that by 20 months of age, normally developing children already have figured out effective means of teasing their older brothers and sisters (Dunn & Munn, 1985). Our own research suggests that children with handicapped siblings do *not* tease their brothers and sisters more frequently than other youngsters do; on paper-and-pencil questionnaires mothers and children in both families with handicapped and with nonhandicapped children rate this as a "sometimes"-occurring event (McHale & Gamble, 1985). Few hard data are available on peer aggression toward disabled youngsters at school, although most adults have been privy to the kinds of name-calling school children direct toward their peers. Labels such as "retard" or "dumbbell," however, may be even more harmful when a child actually is attending a special class.

In addition to teasing, ostracism by peers may involve what might be called *scapegoating,* that is, more organized attempts by a group of children to target and poke fun at a single child. For instance, we were told about a mildly retarded girl attending junior high school who was the object of repeated "jokes" by a group of boys in the school. These boys would take turns sending love letters, telephoning, and accosting this girl in the halls at school to ask her out on dates and tell her how attractive she was (she actually was *not* attractive). Her older sister was very distressed by these activities, but because the boys involved were among the most popular in the school, she did not know what she could do to stop them.

An even more active form of abuse of handicapped children by their peers (and siblings) is *exploitation.* An item on the Adaptive Behavior Scale (Lambert, Windmiller, Tharinger & Cole, 1975), for instance, is concerned with whether a handicapped child will "do anything to make a friend." One mother we interviewed described her mentally retarded child's behavior as ranging from giving away his lunch to giving away his clothing or his toys. Sexual exploitation may occur via similar processes as youngsters strive to gain acceptance from their peers or, due to their cognitive deficiencies, when they fail to anticipate or comprehend the motives of other youngsters.

Finally, handicapped children may be harmed by experiencing *rejection* from their peers, that is, simply by being ignored or tacitly excluded from peer or sibling activities. Studies of handicapped children's status in school suggest that this more passive kind of response to handicapped youngsters may prevail. Although parents and teachers may find it difficult to accuse youngsters of being abusive when they ignore or exclude a handicapped child from their activities, we might argue that a system—such as the school—which allows disabled children to be isolated and ignored is not a healthy environment for a handicapped child.

In sum, because of their handicapping conditions, some children may be more frequent targets of both physical and emotional maltreatment by other youngsters. To some extent, this mistreatment may be similar to that exhibited in so-called normal sibling or peer relationships. On the other hand, their disabled status often may make children more vulnerable to *physical aggression, ridicule, exploitation,* and *rejection* by other youngsters. At this point there are no empirical data on these possibly elevated rates of mistreatment, although these experiences may have important consequences for disabled children's well-being and development.

Investigations of peer influences on child development have focused mainly on academic performance (i.e., as a function of participating in mainstreamed classrooms) and social behavior. In the following section we review the mechanisms through which children are thought to influence handicapped children's development and well-being. We then discuss research findings documenting the effects of siblings and peers on children's development, and, finally, consider individual and contextual characteristics which may mediate those effects.

CHILDREN'S INTERPERSONAL RELATIONSHIPS AND CHILD DEVELOPMENT

Mechanisms of Influence

We noted earlier that peer and sibling relationships have several properties that distinguish them from adult–child relationships and that are thought to have important developmental consequences. The egalitarian nature of peer interaction may be one of the most important aspects children's social experiences, because it provides a prototype for many important relationships in adult life (e.g., with friends, spouse, work associates). Children's sibling relationships are unique in that this is the longest relationship most individuals have, lasting from childhood through old age. In addition, experiences with siblings occur across a variety of contexts and give children a chance to practice a variety of social roles (leader, follower, status equal). As noted, disabled children may miss these important socialization experiences when they have insufficient contact with other youngsters or when situations are not arranged to optimize their experiences. For instance, some handicapped children never may participate in a peer activity in which they are capable of being involved on an equal basis.

Advocates of mainstreamed school programs have emphasized the role of peers as models and sources of social reinforcement. Children may learn appropriate social behavior and also can acquire academic skills by modeling behaviors exhibited by peers in a naturalistic environment or when peers are trained to display specific behaviors to be modeled (Apollini, Cooke, & Cooke, 1977). Both peers and siblings also can be taught to use reinforcement contingencies to shape and to maintain appropriate social behaviors of handicapped children (Hingtegen, Saunders, & DeMeyr, 1965; Strain, Kerr, & Ragland, 1979).

Such strategies may be employed by child tutors working with their peers or siblings, for instance, on academic tasks (Miller & Miller, 1976; Schreibman, O'Neill, & Koegel, 1983; Young, 1981). Finally, as has been noted, peers and siblings, in particular, serve as sources of identification and role models for other youngsters (Bank & Kahn, 1982; Hartup, 1978). In addition, sibling relationships and friendships outside the family may help children fulfill important affiliative needs.

Effects on Development

Research on nonhandicapped children demonstrates the important influences that peers have on normal development (Hartup, 1978). In interacting with other children, youngsters learn the social arts of compromise, sharing, and cooperation; they also learn how to handle aggressive exchanges. As noted earlier, peer interaction also may be a significant basis for the development of social understanding. That is, children may find it easier to see the world from peer's perspective, to comprehend peer's intentions, and to understand the emotional states of peers because other children's perspectives, although somewhat different are likely to be less discrepant than those of adults (Hartup, 1978).

In contrast to these efforts to study peer influences, systematic research on siblings' effects on children's development is in its early stages. Possibly because of researchers' emphasis on parent–child relationships, most information about sibling effects pertains to family constellation and birth order, with researchers attempting to document differences between children from large versus small families or between firstborn, middle, and lastborn children. The nature of sibling influences, per se, is not the focus of concern in these investigations. Rather, when differences are found they generally are explained as somehow emanating from parents (e.g., firstborns are more achievement-oriented because they spend more time with parents and are more likely to use adults as role models). Nonetheless, investigators recently have shown an increasing interest in the unique role siblings play in one another's development (e.g., Dunn, 1983; Furman & Buhrmester, 1985; Lamb & Sutton-Smith, 1982). Furman and Buhrmester note that, together with friends, siblings socialize youngsters regarding the norms of the peer culture, teaching one another about such things as dress and dating. These researchers also note that youngsters receive most of their information about sexual matters from siblings and peers.

Siblings in families with handicapped children have been the subject of research since the 1960s when the family sociologist, Bernard Farber, investigated the functioning of families of retarded children (Farber,

1960; Farber & Jenne, 1963). Farber's work, as well as later research efforts, however, have concentrated almost exclusively on the well-being of *nonhandicapped* children in these families. Although investigators in this field initially expressed great concern about the adverse consequences of growing up with a handicapped child, research conducted during the past decade has revealed few differences between children with handicapped versus those with nonhandicapped siblings. Family structure, the family's social and financial resources, and the interpersonal dynamics within the family, however, do appear to affect the ways in which children respond to their handicapped brothers and sisters (McHale, Simeonsson, & Sloan, 1984; Powell & Ogle, 1985). In contrast, little is known about how nonhandicapped children affect the development of their handicapped siblings.

Some studies have revealed that relationships between handicapped and nonhandicapped brothers and sisters are somewhat *more* positive than those between nondisabled siblings (McHale, Sloan, & Simeonsson, in press; Miller, 1974; Ogle, 1982), with children treating disabled siblings more kindly and expressing less negative affect toward them. As suggested earlier, disabled children also seem to engage in somewhat different activities with their siblings. Miller (1974) found that activities between disabled and nondisabled siblings tended to be more instrumentally oriented, whereas those between nondisabled siblings were more often expressive.

In our work we have collected information on siblings' daily activities with one another via telephone interviews (Gamble & McHale, 1985; McHale & Gamble, 1985). These interviews were conducted on five occasions, during the evening, shortly before children's bedtimes, and the children were asked to report in a structured way on their activities with their younger mentally retarded or nondisabled "control" siblings during the day of the call. Results revealed no differences in the overall number or duration of siblings' activities together. The only significant difference was that children with disabled siblings spent more time on caregiving tasks (including baby-sitting and teaching the younger child new skills) than did children with nondisabled siblings. These findings are consistent with Miller's (1974) results in regard to the increased incidence of instrumental (caregiving) activity by siblings or handicapped children. On the other hand, the children in our sample were equally likely to engage in such activities as playing, watching television, eating dinner, and going on outings with their handicapped and nonhandicapped siblings.

What consequences differential sibling activities may have on disabled children's development is unclear. On one hand, one might argue that nondisabled children are missing out on some of the egalitarian interactions usually involved in child–child relationships because of their dependent status. Alternatively, children may be responding in a realistic way to the needs of their disabled brothers and sisters.

Some work suggests that nondisabled children can serve an important function in fostering appropriate behavior in disabled siblings (Miller & Cantwell, 1976; Miller & Miller, 1976). Children have been trained in behavioral strategies of reinforcement and modeling which they, in turn, can use to successfully elicit appropriate responses and eliminate aversive behaviors of their handicapped siblings (Schreibman et al., 1983; Weinrott, 1974). These findings are consistent with those of other investigators who have employed peers as behavior change agents for disabled children in school contexts (e.g., Young, 1981). Investigators who employ such strategies note that the advantage of training children—either siblings or peers—is that reinforcement contingencies are applied in naturalistic contexts and may be more readily generalizable. Moreover, once children realize that they can control some of the aversive behaviors exhibited by disabled children they may be more likely to engage voluntarily in activities with those children (Weinrott, 1974).

The effects of children outside the family on handicapped youngsters' development also have been the subject of research efforts. Although the goals of mainstreaming disabled children into school classrooms with nondisabled peers have not been fully realized, some work suggests that even without explicit training, contact with nonhandicapped peers can have important therapeutic effects on disabled youngsters. As we noted earlier, the goals of integrated classroom settings mandated under federal legislation (PL 94-142) were to promote academic and social competencies of handicapped children via modeling of and social interaction with nondisabled peers. Evaluations of the effectiveness of mainstreamed classrooms for meeting these goals, however, have not met with clear-cut results. In terms of academic achievement, some studies reveal no differences between the performances of disabled children in integrated versus those in special classrooms (e.g., Budoff & Gottlieb, 1976; Kaufman, Agard, & Simmel, 1981). Other studies with just an experimental group (compared to control groups) reveal positive gains and advantages for children in integrated programs (Ipsa & Matz, 1978) as compared to those in special classes (Rodee, 1971, cited in Gottlieb, 1981). In contrast some studies have uncovered poor academic outcomes for disabled children in mainstreamed settings (Meyers, MacMillan, & Yoshida, 1980). In terms of the processes of change, peer tutoring programs have been found to be effective in promoting school-related skills in handicapped children (McHale, Olley, Marcus, & Simeonsson, 1981; Young, 1981). In general, however, the academic achievements of disabled children in integrated settings largely seem to be due to the effectiveness of the classroom teacher in carrying out a structured curriculum and to the availability of resources, personnel, and facilities outside the classroom.

In regard to handicapped children's socioemotional functioning, the results of recent studies are equivocal. Studies of preschoolers in structured integrated settings reveal gains in social interaction and play (e.g., Apollini et al., 1977). Studies of school-aged handicapped children's social behavior suggest that integrated children's social behavior is the same (e.g., Pastor & Swap, 1978) or better than that of segregated children (e.g., Gampel, Gottlieb, & Harrison, 1974; Gottlieb, Gampel, & Budoff, 1975). In keeping with these results, Budoff and Gottlieb (1976) report that mildly handicapped children who are mainstreamed like school better than do those in segregated classrooms. Children with lower IQs who are physically handicapped, however, may prefer special classrooms. Finally, in studies of handicapped children's self-concepts, when differences are found they tend to favor mainstreamed children (e.g., Carroll, 1967), although other studies reveal no group differences (e.g., Budoff & Gottlieb, 1976).

For those children who have experienced a minimum of normal peer contact, interaction with nonhandicapped agemates may be particularly beneficial. Both Lord (1984) and McHale (1983), for instance, found that providing autistic children in special classrooms with play experiences with untrained nonhandicapped peers resulted in increases in the frequency of the social behavior and play of the autistic youngsters. In explaining the possible basis of these gains, McHale (1983) cited the persistence of the nonhandicapped children in engaging the autistic children in interaction and the repetitive (versus goal-oriented) quality of the children's play, which allowed autistic children to practice simple play routines to be used in later play sessions. These peer interactions were egalitarian in the sense that the nonhandicapped children could not force the autistic children to engage in particular activities (because they were neither larger, stronger, nor of higher "status"). Thus, play was built around autistic children's spontaneous behavior, possibly making such activities more appropriate to the children's developmental level and increasing the likelihood that the autistic children would remain involved in these activities.

In contrast to these positive results, studies of handicapped children's acceptance by nonhandicapped peers reveal somewhat negative outcomes. That is, contrary to the expectations that underlie the move toward mainstreamed school programs, children who have contact with handicapped peers in their classrooms view these peers as negatively or more negatively than they do handicapped peers in special classrooms (e.g., Goodman, Gottlieb, & Harrison, 1972; Gottlieb, Cohen, & Goldstein, 1974). In general, handicapped children are not so well accepted as nonhandicapped children regardless of their placement. More detailed analyses have revealed that the amount of contact between disabled and nondisabled youngsters and the context of the children's contact may make a difference (Corman & Gottlieb, 1978). For instance, when the context is play as opposed to academic activities, young children report highly favorable attitudes toward their disabled peers (McHale & Simeonsson, 1980).

Although research on this issue has yet to be conducted, negative attitudes toward handicapped children that arise in mainstreamed school settings may lead to aggression, ostracism, exploitation, or rejection by nonhandicapped youngsters. In the final section of this chapter we review the effects of intervention strategies designed to promote positive attitudes and behaviors on the parts of nonhandicapped children toward their disabled peers and siblings. First, however, we turn to a discussion of factors that may influence the nature of handicapped children's interpersonal relationships with other youngsters.

Factors Affecting Disabled Children's Social Relationships

Handicapped children's relationships with other youngsters are tremendously variable. In fact, we have suggested elsewhere that relationships between handicapped children and their siblings may be characterized by more variability than are those of nonhandicapped children—with the former group displaying both more positive and more negative relationships (McHale et al., in press).

What factors account for such variability? Researchers investigating sibling relationships have explored a number of possible mediators which may apply to relationships between disabled children and their peers, as well. These factors include characteristics of the disabled child and characteristics of the family and, presumably, the school environments.

The nature and severity of a child's handicapping condition will have a major impact on the family's daily life. Children who cannot walk or who need constant supervision place tremendous demands on all family members, and their care may easily drain the energy, time, and financial resources of families. In one study, the extent of caregiving demands for developmentally disabled infants, in itself, accounted for 66% of the variance in predicting family stress and problems (Beckman-Bell, 1980). The findings of other work suggest that children who are nonambulatory and/or incontinent provide the most stress for family members. A number of studies have compared sibling (and family) relationships of children with different disabling conditions, and the few and inconsistent results of these efforts suggest that diagnostic label, per se, probably is not the best predictor of others' reactions to a disabled child. Rather, individual characteristics including functional behaviors or temperament may be more significant (Simeonsson & Bailey, 1983). Clearly, these characteristics will be of greater importance to those who spend more time with the disabled child. Some writers have suggested that the adjustment problems of eldest female siblings in families with disabled children are due to their extensive involvement in sibling care. As such, these girls may be the most affected by the competencies and temperamental characteristics of the child.

Neither may a linear relationship between the severity of a handicapping condition and others' reactions to a disabled child provide the most accurate picture: When a child's disability is mild or undefined, other youngsters may react to that child more negatively (Simeonsson & McHale, 1981). This seems to be the case particularly in higher socioeconomic contexts when, perhaps, the disabled child's behavior violates social expectations with little or no apparent basis for those violations. In these cases, rather than attributing delayed or inappropriate behavior to a disabling condition other youngsters may conclude, for instance, that a child is "bad" or "stupid."

Additional factors that mediate the effects of a disabling condition on social relationships include the age of the handicapped child, family size and socioeconomic status (in the case of siblings), the availability of services that reduce a child's responsibilities toward a handicapped sibling or peer (such as respite care and babysitting services in the case of siblings or possibly resource rooms and teachers in the case of peers at school), and finally, the attitudes of adults whom youngsters see interacting with the disabled child. The literature provides some suggestions about the directions in which these factors operate, although how they operate is largely speculative at this point.

Some evidence suggests that, in the case of siblings, family size and socioeconomic status interact to affect children's reactions to their disabled brothers and sisters (Farber, 1960). When there are sufficient financial resources, having more children in the family means that the burdens and responsibilities of each individual are reduced. Farber (1960) suggests that families of different social backgrounds react differently to the birth of a handicapped child: Families of lower socioeconomic status experience an "organizational crisis" when they must generate sufficient resources to provide for a disabled child's needs; when families are of higher socioeconomic status their reaction instead has been termed a "tragic crisis," a concept that reflects family members' difficulty in resolving their violated expectations in regard to the disabled child's life achievements. Outside the family context in the world of peer relationships, socioeconomic status also appears to make a difference, with some investigators suggesting that children with disabilities are better accepted by youngsters from lower as opposed to upper social class backgrounds (Corman & Gottlieb, 1978).

In the case of both siblings and peers, the attitudes and behaviors of significant adults such as parents and teachers affect the way these youngsters react to handicapped children. By modeling positive attitudes and behaviors toward a disabled child, by communicating openly about both handicapped and nonhandicapped children's needs and concerns, and by accepting the child and his handicapping condition, adults can facilitate more positive relationships between peers and siblings (Powell & Ogle, 1985; Shores, 1981). We will discuss specific techniques that have been employed by adults to foster positive attitudes and behaviors in children in the final section of this chapter. Before considering these and other strategies for intervening in child–child relationships, one additional point is in order. That is, our consideration of sibling and peer relationships has been discussed thus far without regard for the developmental status of the nonhandicapped children involved.

Just as the level of the disabled child's functioning makes a difference for her interpersonal relationships, so too do the cognitive, social, and emotional levels of nonhandicapped peers and siblings affect the way they understand and treat a handicapped child. In terms of social behavior, for instance, most children become increasingly proficient at initiating and maintaining social interactions as they grow older. Although adults generally must direct the course of social interaction with infants, toddlers, and young preschoolers, by the school-age years most children are adept at sustained social interactions and are quite capable of altering their own behavior to conform to their playmates level of understanding (e.g., Guralnick & Paul-Brown, 1977; Shatz & Gelman, 1973). Developing cognitive abilities enable youngsters to comprehend the points of views of others with increasing accuracy and sophistication as they move into adolescence—an ability that presumably helps them get along better with others.

Although increasing social understanding may make children more sympathetic to the handicapped child's plight, their developing mental abilities also may make them less likely to include handicapped youngsters in their activities. If we consider, for example, the kinds of play activities in which children engage, we see that they change fairly dramatically between the preschool and school age years. Whereas preschoolers spend much of their time involved in pretend play, older children seem to enjoy games with rules, such as card games or board games. One difference between these two kinds of activities is the specificity of the rules that govern children's behavior in the two contexts: whereas a broad range of activities is possible in imaginary play—because "it's just pretend"—one of the prominent features of the games school-age children play is their rules. Other children place a high premium, not only on winning a game, but winning when playing by the rules. Due to these higher performance standards, a disabled child, especially one with a mentally handicapping condition, may have a harder time being accepted by her peers during the school-age years.

As youngsters develop their abilities to think in abstract and hypothetical ways, the way they see others also changes (Selman, 1976). For instance, although young children describe others as well as their relationships with others in concrete terms (e.g., "Johnny has brown hair, and we play soccer together") by adolescence, youngsters see their social world quite differently (e.g., "John is a caring and sensitive person; he would stand by me through thick and thin"). What this means is that for young children, the primary characteristic of a disabled person may be her handicapping condition, whereas, in the case of teenagers, other qualities of the individual may be recognized and appreciated.

Another change in children's cognitive abilities pertains to their understanding of cause and effect. Older children may be able to understand, at least in part, the causes of another child's disability. Younger children who are not yet capable of logical reasoning, however, are more inclined to "blame the victim." Consequently, they tend to believe that such things as their own sickness, a hospital stay, or their parents' divorce are caused by their own "naughty" behavior. Similarly, preschoolers may be more likely to believe that a handicapped child has caused his or her own disability. For instance, young children may believe that a handicap is a punishment for an individual's being "bad." We should point out there that this belief is not limited to children—many adults seem to retain too many remnants of this immature style of thinking. Our point is only that such ideas may be more understandable and expected in the case of young children.

Although their increasingly sophisticated mental abilities may make youngsters more understanding of handicapped persons as they approach adolescence, their greater awareness of others also may have negative consequences: Youngsters may feel increasingly embarrassed about their sibling's behavior and concerned about whether their brother's or sister's condition will reflect upon their own status with their friends. To the extent to which peer norms involve rejection of what is different or "weird," youngsters may feel more uncomfortable about being seen with their sibling in public or about inviting friends to their home as they approach adolescence. Some researchers have suggested that adolescents with disabled siblings may have a particularly difficult time when it comes to dating: They may feel awkward in explaining their sibling to a boyfriend or girlfriend and uncomfortable about having a date visit them at home due to their worries about their sibling's behavior (Powell & Ogle, 1985).

To complicate matters, with increasing maturity, youngsters' leisure activities center more often outside the home, making inclusion of a handicapped sibling or peer more difficult. One mother of 16-year-old twins—one with spina bifida who was confined to a wheelchair and one nondisabled—explained that when her daughters were young other children would come over to watch television or play games in which both girls could participate. In recent years, however, her nondisabled daughter seemed to prefer socializing with her friends who could drive—an activity that excluded her disabled sister. This mother revealed that she herself was her disabled daughter's "best friend"—as she seemed to be the only one who did not mind spending her time engaged in activities her daughter could undertake or taking the trouble to transport her daughter and her wheelchair when she was going out.

At school, as well, when peer groups solidify into cliques around the time of adolescence, conforming (for instance, in appearance and in athletic, social, and academic abilities) to the high standards of the group becomes particularly important. This orientation to peers, in fact, seems to peak in early adolescence (Garbarino, Guttmann, and Wilson, 1986). To the extent to which adolescents' identity is tied to the composition of their peer group, group membership must serve to enhance each teenager's feelings of status. Including a disabled youngster as an equal may undermine feelings of self-esteem which may be fragile at this age.

In short, we are likely to find that different issues arise in the context of disabled children's peer and sibling relationships at different points in development. Unfortunately, there are no longitudinal studies that examine youngsters' developing attitudes and behaviors toward handicapped siblings and peers, nor are there systematic cross-sectional data that address this issue. In fact, although investigators have examined such phenomena as individuals' changing conceptions of friendship, the developmental consequences of peer popularity, and longitudinal changes in individuals' behavior toward others, little is known about the development of peer and sibling relationships even among nonhandicapped youngsters. Clearly such matters constitute an important focus for future investigation.

PROMOTING POSITIVE RELATIONSHIPS BETWEEN HANDICAPPED AND NONHANDICAPPED CHILDREN

As we pointed out earlier in this chapter, one of the premises behind mainstreamed school programs—the "social contact" hypothesis (Corman & Gottlieb, 1978)—held that placing handicapped and nonhandicapped children in the same classroom would enhance the social and cognitive skills of disabled children via their interactions with nondisabled peers. As teachers soon discovered and as parents observed at home, simply placing children in the same classroom or moving a child from institution to home did not ensure positive interactions between handicapped children and either their siblings or peers (e.g., Allen, Benning, & Drummond, 1972; Devoney, Guralnick, & Rubin, 1974). Neither did social integration, in itself, foster the goals of cognitive and social growth on the part of the disabled children (see Guralnick, 1978). For this reason, a number of intervention strategies have been developed that are aimed at changing nonhandicapped youngsters' behaviors and attitudes toward disabled children. Table 3.1 provides a summary of these approaches; Appendix A includes a list of programs that have been developed for siblings and peers as well as addresses for where to obtain these materials.

Curricular or programmatic approaches to fostering social integration include, most importantly, a careful choice of the context or activities in which integration occurs. Involving a small number of disabled and nondisabled children in special projects or recreational activities such as planning a carnival or playing on a bowling team is one effective strategy for fostering social interaction and positive attitudes of nonhandicapped children toward disabled peers (Aloia, Beaver, & Pettus, 1978; Chennault, 1967; Johnson, Johnson, DeWeerdt, Lyons, & Zaidman, 1983; Rucker & Vincenzo, 1970; Stainbeck, Stainbeck, & Jaben, 1981). The development of such activities for use with severely handicapped and nonhandicapped students is described by Brown, Branston, Baumgart, Vincent, Falvey, and Schroeder (1979). An alternative approach is to design activities in which nonhandicapped children are given a special invitation to become involved in activities with handicapped children in the capacity of teacher helpers (e.g., McHale, 1983; Poorman, 1980). Other programmatic considerations for fostering social integration include the nature of the classroom's physical layout and equipment (Hoben, 1980; Twardosz, Cataldo, & Risley, 1974), and encouragement and reinforcement by adults (Guralnick, 1978; Hoben, 1980).

To promote handicapped children's acceptance in the regular classroom and to enable them to profit from their instruction in that context, these children must be prepared for their mainstream program. For instance, giving students experience with materials used in the regular classroom and with instructional styles employed (e.g., amounts and forms of teacher attention and feedback) may aid in the children's adjustment (Simpson, 1980). In addition, disabled children may be provided with training in social skills through modeling reinforcement, role playing, and coaching techniques so that their behavior is more in keeping with the expectations of nondisabled peers (Gresham, 1982; Russo & Koegel, 1977).

TABLE 3.1. Strategies for Promoting Positive Relationships between Handicapped
          and Nonhandicapped Children

Interventions directed at the contexts of social interactions
  1. Involve handicapped and nonhandicapped children together in intrin-
     sically enjoyable projects or recreational activities.
  2. Define the interaction context as one in which nonhandicapped children
     serve as "teachers" or "helpers" of handicapped children.
  3. Choose activities in which handicapped children's limitations are least
     relevant or apparent.
  4. Use reinforcement strategies to maintain a high level of appropriate social
     interaction.
  5. Optimize the physical environment in terms of available materials and
     room arrangement or the location of resource rooms and special class-
     rooms at school.

Interventions directed at nonhandicapped children
  1. Educate children about the nature of specific disabilities (through puppet
     shows or role playing various handicapping conditions).
  2. Train children in behavior management skills to apply toward disabled
     siblings or peers and coping skills to resolve frustrations arising relative
     toward disabled youngsters.
  3. Establish counseling or support groups in which children can work
     through their negative feelings—such as jealousy or resentment—and
     learn ways to both emotionally and instrumentally cope with a disabled
     child (usually directed at siblings).

Interventions directed at handicapped children
  1. Use behavioral strategies to train children in social and adaptive behavior
     prior to their involvement in peer or sibling activities.
  2. Give children experiences in the contexts or with the materials that will
     be employed in social interactions with other youngsters.
  3. Train children in areas that are consistent with their competencies and
     that are highly valued by the peer culture (e.g., a nonambulatory child
     may become adept at video game or computer skills; a blind child may
     learn to sing or play guitar).
  4. Teach children to present a physically attractive appearance by helping
     them choose clothing and attractive hairstyles, by teaching them about
     personal hygiene, and by ensuring that they receive sufficient exercise
     and an appropriate diet.

Interventions directed at adults
  1. Train parents and teachers to promote social interactions between hand-
     icapped and nonhandicapped siblings and peers.
  2. Establish parent education programs for fostering positive sibling rela-
     tionships.

Handicapped children are not the only ones who need to be prepared for mainstreamed classrooms. Unless professionals attend to the
attitudes and potential reactions of nondisabled youngsters, one of the
primary goals of the mainstreaming movement, promoting positive societal attitudes toward individuals who are handicapped, cannot be
achieved. Investigators have described several attempts to promote

positive attitudes toward handicapped children (e.g., Schroeder, 1978; Westervelt & McKinney, 1980). All of these programs provide children with an understanding of specific handicapping conditions and the limitations they impose on a child. In addition, however, they offer nonhandicapped children opportunities to appreciate what they have in common with a disabled peer, regardless of the nature or extent of his or her handicapping condition. Like teachers, parents, and other family members, children need to be taught that a handicapping condition is only one characteristic of a child, and not necessarily the most important characteristic, at that.

Finally, in addition to the children involved in these interpersonal relationships, significant adults, such as parents and teachers, can be trained to promote social interaction and positive relationships between disabled youngsters and their siblings and peers. A curriculum entitled the Social Competence Intervention Package for Preschool Youngsters (SCIPPY) was developed recently for the purpose of training teachers to promote social interaction between disabled and nondisabled children (Day, Powell, & Stowitscheck, 1981). The procedures are based on social learning principles, and in this program, teachers are trained to model, prompt, and praise children for social interactions. Program evaluations have revealed that teachers trained in these strategies can promote increases in peer interaction. A similar program has been designed for parents to facilitate interactions between siblings (Powell, 1982; Powell, Salzberg, Rule, Levy, & Itzkowitz, 1983). These efforts need to be expanded for use with preadolescent and adolescent youngsters.

Although many parent education programs acknowledge that sibling rivalry is a central concern for parents, very few offer special techniques for dealing with sibling issues. An exception is Dreikers and Grey's (1968) approach to parent education, a child-rearing guide that is based on an Adlerian model of personality development. As we mentioned earlier, Adler sees sibling rivalry—and the extent to which parents play into the "natural" competitiveness among siblings—as one fundamental basis for children's self-concepts and subsequent personality formation. Siblings are inclined to compare their accomplishments and their treatment at the hands of their parents. Consequently, it is incumbent on parents to treat children as fairly as possible in the sense of spending time with each child, recognizing each child's unique characteristics, and not taking sides in sibling conflicts (Dreikers & Grey, 1968). Dreikers further recommends that the logical consequences of sibling rivalry be shared equally among children involved; thus, for instance, when there is an argument over a toy or play material, both children should do without unless they can reach a compromise. Of course, the use of any one strategy depends on the cognitive skills of the children involved, but the approach as a whole will provide parents with a perspective on their role in sibling relationships. Along these lines, Powell and Ogle (1985) recently published an excellent volume on siblings of handicapped children that is directed to parents and professionals. They review the findings of research on the adjustment of siblings of handicapped children and examine a variety of means for how parents can promote the social and psychological well-being of nonhandicapped children in the family as well as foster positive relationships with handicapped siblings.

CONCLUSIONS

As we noted in the beginning of this chapter, the goals of the normalization movement—namely, the well-being of handicapped children and attitudes of acceptance by society at large—cannot be met simply by moving disabled children from institutions back into family and community settings. Rather, the children themselves as well as those with whom they come into contact—peers, siblings, and adults—first must be prepared to cope with the challenges pertaining to a handicapping condition that are likely to arise. Our review of the literature suggests many potential positive consequences for disabled children who spend their time with nonhandicapped siblings and peers. It is up to parents and concerned professionals, however, to establish optimal conditions for promoting positive relationships between children. This preventive orientation is a key to any overall strategy aimed at creating and maintaining safe environments for handicapped children.

chapter 4

THE ROLE OF THE EDUCATORS

James Garbarino
Karen J. Authier

INTRODUCTION

In industrial society there has existed a relatively well-defined inter-dependency among child–family–school–community. The family produces children, who depend on the family to provide the means of survival. The family depends on the school to teach its children the skills necessary for them to become competent, self-supporting adults. The school depends on the family to support and reinforce its goals and methods. The community depends on the family and school to cooperate in providing productive, law-abiding citizens. The school depends on the community to provide financial support for its efforts.

While this interdependency always has been an imperfect interactional system, there seem to be new pressures, internal and external to the system, which threaten the sense of trust that has developed around that reciprocity. Some of those pressures for and threats to interdependency are related to the separate, but often related, problems of child maltreatment and handicapped children. In the past the community system of interdependencies was very limited for a family with a handicapped child. The handicapped child depended on the family for survival. The family often was required to meet that need on its own or sent the child outside the community to an institution supported by the state. In many cases neither the school nor the community regarded the handicapped child as their responsibility. The child's handicap frequently made the child and family ineligible for inclusion in the mutual interdependency system available for nonhandicapped children and their families.

Only minimal attempts were made to provide special school programs within the communities in the early 1900s. However, following

World War II, many communities developed special education programs for some categories of mentally retarded children (Bijou, 1983).
However, it was the passage and implementation of the Education for
All Handicapped Children Act of 1975 (Public Law 94-142) that succeeded
in adding handicapped children to the web of child–family–school–
community interdependency. The accompanying moves toward
"mainstreaming" and deinstitutionalization have both opened opportunities for and increased pressures on families and communities.

In the past, child maltreatment, like the rearing of a handicapped
child, was regarded as a family problem. Societal support for physical
punishment both by parents and by educators made it easy to overlook
excesses of "discipline" (Miller, 1983). An attentive teacher might be
nurturing in addition to providing academic instruction if there was
concern about a child's treatment by parents, but the school had no
official role. In some extreme cases, the school and community, for
example, police and public welfare department, might intervene to
protect a child from maltreatment, but most cases were frequently
overlooked or ignored. Within the last several decades, schools and
communities have taken greater responsibility for reporting and intervening in situations of child maltreatment. What once was a family
problem was redefined as a social problem by the Child Abuse Prevention and Treatment Act of 1974 (Select Committee on Children,
Youth, and Families, 1984).

The role of the school in prevention of child maltreatment, in contrast
to its role in identification, has been ambiguous (Halperin, 1979). There
are mixed reactions in most communities to the idea that provision of
education for parenthood is part of the school's responsibility for turn-
ing children into competent adults. In reviewing changes in expectations among families, schools, and communities in relation to child
maltreatment and to handicapped children, it seems clear that the role
of the educator in those areas cannot be considered without also addressing the role of both the family and the community.

The mandate for school responsibility for education of handicapped
children was made quite clear and specific in Public Law 94-142, although, to be sure, controversy flourishes as to the specific requirements. While the general mandate for involvement of schools in addressing the problem of child maltreatment is clear, the specifics of
the mandate are not so well-defined. A legitimate question can be
raised: Where do schools fit into the complex and difficult problem
of child maltreatment? To answer that question, we can begin with a
brief look at how recent literature deals with the role of schools. Even
a cursory review reveals several dominant themes which can be seen
in a series of illustrative statements drawn from a variety of sources.

Because schools are concerned with the *whole child,* seeking help for the child in trouble is quite compatible with educational objectives (American Humane Association, 1971, p. 3).

Educators and others who work directly with children have an excellent opportunity and a grave responsibility to identify and properly report suspected cases of child abuse or neglect (Soeffing, 1975, p. 129).

American education is potentially a major resource for helping abused children and their families. But this potential has rarely been tapped and, as yet, has never been fully utilized (Education Commission of the States, 1976, p. 3).

Although school personnel are generally mandated to report suspected abuse or neglect, the requirement is widely disregarded. . . . There are seldom clear-cut channels for reporting and the extent of the school's involvement is uncertain. Yet few professionals are more genuinely concerned about children (Delaney, 1976, p. 342).

The school system must be convinced, pressured, or even coerced to initiate parenting and early child development courses and skill learning experiences for every elementary, junior, and senior high school student (Helfer, 1976, p. 370).

Where else may we find the legally and socially sanctioned abuse of children? I point to the institution which, after the family, is the most important socializing agent in America, namely the school (Zigler, 1976, p. 7).

These diverse conclusions about the role of schools in the maltreatment of children are echoed throughout the body of literature dealing with this topic (Broadhurst, 1975, 1977; Gil, 1969; Kibby, 1975; Martin, 1973; Nordstrom, 1974; Paulson, 1976; Reskow, 1973; Richards, 1973; Sanders, 1975; Schmitt, 1975; Shanas, 1975; Wald, 1976). When combined they suggest a tension between two views of the role of schools, namely, as part of the problem or as a key to the solution. This tension is itself a complex phenomenon rooted in the ongoing love–hate relationship between reformers and schools. If there is one common theme to the extensive reformist critique of American education it is that of "unfulfilled potential." The issue of child maltreatment and the schools is no different in this respect from the issues of moral development, cooperation, reading, or redressing social inequalities.

There is at least one way in which the problem of child maltreatment presents a somewhat different picture regarding the schools from that of many other issues: It is deadly serious. Without denying the genuine importance of other concerns, one confidently can assert that the issue of child maltreatment is the bottom line in any discussion of child care and the "quality of life." This factor forces us to do our best to understand both the potential and actual roles of schools in child maltreatment. Moreover, it creates a real urgency in our attempts to close the gap between them.

As with other tasks related to integration of handicapped children into the schools, the educator's role with respect to maltreatment of handicapped and nonhandicapped populations is similar in some ways and different in others. The maltreatment issues can be approached from a "mainstream" point of view while still attending to the special needs of handicapped children.

The Child Abuse Protection and Treatment Act of 1974 preceded by one year the Education for All Handicapped Children of 1975. Now more than a decade later the two movements that produced those pieces of legislation are entering their adolescence independently but with greater awareness of each other's existence. Not only has Public Law 94-142 added an additional unserved population of children to the schools but has done so at a younger age than nonhandicapped children through preschool handicapped programs. As noted in a previous chapter (Garbarino, Chapter 1), some of these children are handicapped as a result of abuse, while others are at increased risk for abuse because of their handicapping condition.

THE ROLE OF SCHOOLS IN THE HUMAN ECOLOGY OF CHILD MALTREATMENT

There are at least four serious issues regarding the role of schools in child maltreatment that must be addressed for handicapped as well as nonhandicapped children: (1) What is the responsibility of schools to identify and report suspected maltreatment? (2) Are schools culpable as perpetrators of or as accessories to the fact of maltreatment? (3) Are schools in a position to significantly affect the causes for maltreatment in the home (or in other extramural settings)? (4) Can schools realistically be expected to contribute directly to the prevention or treatment of child maltreatment? Of our options at this point, the most useful is to deal with each of these issues in a manner that compares our current situation with that which provides us with the future role of the school in dealing with the problem of maltreatment. We can begin by presenting brief answers to the questions posed and then proceed to a more general discussion of the role of schools in maltreatment of handicapped children.

Identification and Reporting

There is a legal mandate for school personnel to report suspected child maltreatment (Katz, Ambrosino, McGratni & Sawitslsy, 1976), although this responsibility is often not met in practice (Delaney, 1976).

There are efforts by both local demonstration projects (Broadhurst, 1977) and national policy initiatives (Education Commission of the States, 1976, 1977; Council for Exceptional Children, 1979), to remedy this situation. For all children, there are a variety of factors, including the lack of clearly defining maltreatment and a particular reluctance to intervene in family privacy, that stand as a roadblock to these efforts.

There are additional practical problems in applying the mandate to handicapped children, who may be limited in their ability to communicate information about an abusive episode. Identification may be complicated by the fact that some behaviorally impaired and mentally retarded children engage in self-abusive behaviors (Menolascino & McCann, 1983), and that some physically handicapped and mentally retarded children may be prone to accidental injury. Sorting out cases of accidental from possibly nonaccidental injury to any child is difficult, and is particularly so when the child is handicapped. Identification of neglect also poses unique dilemmas when the child is handicapped. Care of a handicapped child may require careful and regular attention to medical procedures or administration of medication. Is the parent neglectful when those demanding and burdensome regimes are not executed properly or faithfully?

The issue of sexual abuse may also be problematic. Handicapped children may require greater assistance with personal care routines at a later chronological age then nonhandicapped children. Lifting or positioning of a handicapped child may result in occasional touching of sexual parts of the body. When is the touching accidental or required (e.g., in toileting, diapering, or positioning), and when is it exploitive? It is apparent that questions may be more easily raised than can be answered.

Culpability as Perpetrators or Accessories

This issue revolves around the definition of maltreatment. If we use the narrowest possible definition (intentional bodily harm that violates community standards), schools are rarely culpable as perpetrators. However, if we use a broader definition that sees violence against children as intrinsically abusive and refusal to provide service as inherently neglectful, many schools are directly culpable for maltreatment. The use of corporal punishment as a prerogative of school officials has been upheld by the U.S. Supreme Court, to the acclaim of many educators. At the same time, there is evidence that many schools refuse to provide service to many children and youth who deviate from the normal, either by being in some way educationally handicapped or by exhibiting antisocial behavior (Children's Defense Fund, 1974). While the Education for All Handicapped Children Act clearly defined the right to education for all handicapped children, there is ongoing squabbling and haggling in individual cases regarding the limits of the school's responsibility and suitability of placement.

These facts demonstrate that many schools are culpable for abuse and neglect if a broad rather than narrow definition is adopted. By the same token, some schools engage in various forms of psychological or emotional maltreatment, once again to a degree dependent upon the definition employed as a basis for evaluation (Garbarino 1977a, 1977b).

As accessories to the fact of maltreatment, the case against schools is less equivocal. The very poor record of schools as reporting agents is testimony to this. Here, as in many other areas, it seems that school leadership (specifically the principal) sets a tone or defines the norms. The variability of school performance as reporting agents suggests this, and firsthand interviews with principals and child protective service officials reinforce it.

More broadly, despite their concern for children, schools are typically very passive with regard to parental and community standards concerning child care, particularly with respect to neglect. This passivity is reinforced by the overwhelming focus of professionals in the area of child maltreatment with infants and preschool children with seemingly little attention paid to older groups. This professional neglect parallels community noninterest. For example, while a great deal of attention is given to the development of day care for young children, little systematic effort has been directed at adequate extramural care for school-age ("latch-key") children (Harris, 1977). Schools generally do not define their mission as including the active pursuit of minimal care for their children once they leave the school building. There are, of course, many notable individual exceptions to this overall institutional pattern, but these exceptions only serve to sharpen the contrast between our definition of what a school is and how its responsibility for children is understood.

Can the Schools Help?

One can hardly pick up a journal dealing with educational issues in the 1970s without reading something dealing with "the limits of education." If schools were seen as the *deus ex machina* of reformist visionaries in the 1960s, they are now seen as marginal institutions by a substantial proportion of the professional community—and perhaps by the general public as well. It is in this climate that the question "can schools help?" must be addressed. Given that there is increasing concern about the ability of the schools to master their core tasks—teaching basic academic skills—there are grounds for doubting that they can realistically be asked to do more.

Forgetting for a moment the general issues of potency and appropriateness, what could schools do to help? They could become resources for reducing the social isolation of families and the cultural support for violence against or neglect of children that are necessary conditions for maltreatment. The forces working against this will be discussed later. The schools could also emphasize educational efforts that provide both parent education and life management skills. As we shall see later in our discussion, that only sporadic efforts are being made in these areas that are particularly relevant to the maltreatment of handicapped children.

Can We Expect Schools to Help?

Can we realistically expect schools to contribute directly to the prevention or treatment of child maltreatment? If we are speaking about school-initiated efforts on any broad scale, the answer is probably NO. Schools seem hard pressed to do what they see as their fundamental goal—teaching basic academic skills. Most schools are preoccupied with day-to-day discipline and management of their academic programs. Except for specific individuals who develop a special commitment and/ or expertise, or special grant programs that permit the addition of staff, schools seem unlikely to take the initiative. The one general exception seems to be the work of the Education Commission of the States' Child Abuse and Neglect Project (1976, 1977). It remains to be seen what effect this meta-institutional project will have on the day-to-day operations of schools.

Perhaps the more likely source of change is the application of community influence to the task of making schools a key component of prevention and treatment (Zigler, 1976). As will be shown later in our discussion, there are at least three points at which this extramural influence may be particularly useful: parent education, use of the student–teacher relationship as a resource in identifying developmentally dangerous conditions in the home, and use of the school facility as a center for providing services to families.

These three conclusions can only be properly understood after a more detailed examination of the interplay between the potential and the actual roles of schools in the maltreatment of children. This reverses the customary order of presentation—to have the conclusions precede the complete analysis. However, only by assessing where we stand— or could stand—can we see the relevance of various ideological, structural, and operational characteristics of schools.

THE ROLE OF SCHOOLS IN THE HUMAN ECOLOGY OF CHILD MALTREATMENT

What is the role of schools in the cultural support for violence against children? In practice, the schools present a mixed picture. As many observers have noted, American schools tend to reflect local values more than they actively seek to shape them. Where local support for violence is strong, this may be a fatal liability for children. Gastil (1971) has found that there are regional differences in homicide rates linked to cultural and historical influences. Schools appear to echo and reinforce the use of force in interpersonal relations.

Zigler (1976), among others (Gil, 1970), has criticized American education for their support of the use of physical force against children (generally in the form of corporal punishment). Growing concern for the lack of discipline in schools in both public and professional circles may serve to exacerbate the problem, as the challenge of "disorder" is responded to by a culture that offers fundamental support for violence.

Schools have an important role to play in defining social reality through what they model and what they reinforce both for children and parents. Example remains the best teacher, even in the area of parent education. When schools present a model of abuse and/or neglect the overall quality of life for children must suffer. The many "latchkey children," estimated to number approximately 2 million (National Academy of Sciences, 1976), are a prime example of such neglect. Left unsupervised by parents (usually because of work), these children need the attention of schools (directly or indirectly) to return nurturant control to their lives. This need often goes unmet, however (Harris, 1977). (For some examples of schools that are meeting the need see Coolsen, Seligson, & Garbarino, 1985.) Unsupervised children are prey to a host of antisocial forces and developmental problems. Schools should lead the way in providing a model for adequate care.

Perhaps most disturbing of all developments in American education is the apparently growing sense that schools are getting out of control. It is this sense of lack of control that permeates families involved in maltreatment. How do schools respond to "difficult" or "special" children? In many cases they resort to behavior that parallels the behavior of families in such situations, that is, by using coercion or by neglect. The recent report of the Children's Defense Fund on "Children Out of School in America" (1974) makes this point quite persuasively: Schools tend to neglect if not abuse socially, psychologically, and physically deviant children. In this, schools are both victim and victimizer (Garbarino, 1976a). In a society that increasingly demands minimal academic competence, we cannot afford to permit children to experience such institutional neglect.

Where do schools fit into the problem of isolation from support systems? Primarily, there is the role of the school as itself a support system. As Gray, Cutler, Dean, and Kempe (1977) have noted, in America the child generally has no official enduring relationship with the state from the time he/she leaves the hospital until their entrance to school. During that 5-year period, the child depends totally upon parents and whatever other persons have access to and interest in the child (through the family). Gray et al. (1977) have reported experimental results showing the effects on maltreatment of powerful support systems. Among a high-risk group of families ($N = 50$), a very low incidence of abuse occurred in the 2 years after birth when the family was involved with a powerful support system (an active visiting nurse program). Among a control group not receiving these special services, nearly 50% were involved in some form of maltreatment in the 2-year period. At birth, health-care institutions have a natural "in" with families. Schools assume that natural role later.

As identification of handicapping conditions and referral to appropriate educational programs occur at an earlier age as a result of the thrust of federal mandates and encouragement (Select Committee on Children, Youth and Families, 1984), the school is often in a position to become a support system to the family during that critical period of family crisis following identification of a handicapping condition. Because care of a handicapped child imposes burdens on time, energy, and financial resources, the family with a handicapped child is often more isolated than other families. Since the Education for All Handicapped Children Act lowered the age for involvement with the school to age three, the school and health care systems share access to many families with handicapped children who may be isolated otherwise. Through the school, parents may become linked to other families with similar problems with the potential for development of mutual support systems. The schools can provide practical instruction to parents regarding techniques and methods of care and management of the handicapped child.

While there is potential for great assistance and support via the school, the reverse is also a possibility. Indeed, many parents may experience relationships with the school that increase the potential for abuse if the school serves as an added source of stress in family life. Parents also may perceive the school as critical, uncaring, or uncooperative in the interactive process necessary for planning the child's education (Knitzer, 1982).

Do schools provide the feedback and resources that are the *sine qua non* of support systems? Two recent reviews lead one to doubt that they do (in general) as a matter of policy and routine practice, that is, as part of the American cultural definition of what a school is (Broadhurst, 1975; Fowler & Stenlund, 1976). Indeed, there are grounds for believing that American schools systematically opt for the role of academic specialist as opposed to family support system (Garbarino, 1976a, 1978). The list of possible support system functions for schools is long (Garbarino, 1976a) and includes long-term enduring teacher–family relationships initiated prior to the start of a child's school enrollment. At the very least, it requires an active policy and program to assess the quality of life for the schools' families and to cooperate with other agencies such as Child Protective Services in treatment, that is, preventing a recurrence of maltreatment once it has been initially identified. Isolation is the greatest danger facing children. Schools have a legal, moral, and historical mandate to ensure that each and every child has a direct and enduring relationship with adults or groups of adults that have an interest in the child's welfare. The school is the child's natural link to the community. The role of student is the closest a child comes to being a citizen of the state, for it is as a student that the child enters into a direct, formal relationship with "officials" of the community.

Recent developments such as those spearheaded by the Education Commission of the States (1976) are promising in this regard, at least in the realm of policy. Demonstration programs (Broadhurst, 1977) provide working examples of how to translate these policies into practice. The key in the long run, of course, is the degree to which the school is internally and externally defined as a family support system in which responsibility for the welfare of families is a central mission, and not merely a peripheral concern.

What can schools do about the underlying conditions for child maltreatment? A fundamental problem underlying the maltreatment of children is the intersection of stress (both personal and social) and inadequate support and social control.

To cope with the underlying conditions, a systematic effort must be undertaken to accomplish three goals. First, the small minority of families beyond the reach of conventional rehabilitation and treatment models must be identified. These families [estimated to be between 10 and 20% of those involved in abuse and, thus, approximately 0.1–0.2% of the general population, according to Kempe (1973)] cannot or will not provide adequate care for children. Based on their experience, Kempe and others recommend immediate action to terminate parental rights in such cases. Schools can play a role in identifying such families, in supporting the agencies charged with responsibility for terminating these rights, and (perhaps most importantly) in assisting children and foster or adoptive parents. As has been noted in several recent studies, foster care in America is itself sometimes abusive or neglectful (Mnookin, 1973). Schools can take an active role in assisting the thousands of children who are removed from their families because of maltreatment. These children require all that the school can offer in the way of stable, nurturant, interpersonal relationships.

Second, a universal program of training in parenting and life management skills can be developed and implemented. The role of the schools in this must, of course, be substantial. Part of this, however, is a redefinition of priorities. The role of schools in socialization to adulthood should be recognized more explicitly and with greater attention to its implications for program, curriculum, and structure (Garbarino, 1978). Basic academic skills are, of course, an important part of the competence needed for effective life management, but they are not the whole story. Education with a life course perspective highlights the need to facilitate the development of coping skills to reduce the likelihood that pathogenic stresses will accumulate and ultimately precipitate maltreatment.

Caregiver incompetence is a situationally defined problem of role learning and performance. It seems all but self-evident that parent education should play a role in primary prevention of child maltreatment. Although there are dissenting voices (e.g., Jayaratne, 1977), most professionals agree that a systematic program of parent education would be an effective preventive strategy (Zigler, 1976).

Such a program, however, must include practical apprenticeship experiences as well as (and probably much more importantly than) conventional classroom instruction (Bronfenbrenner, 1970). Instruction and apprenticeship must include content and experiences related to the care of handicapped children. Such an approach has the additional effect of providing: (a) children to practice on and thus provide day care for, and (b) exemplary models to portray good parenting. Both of these are beneficial in that they may be expected to enhance efforts at prevention by offering families needed support (Gil, 1970; Zigler, 1976) and increasing the effectiveness of adult life management skills, which is really the crux of the matter. If schools focus on the task of socialization to adulthood, they can aid substantially in the development of needed life management skills. There are hopeful signs that schools, students, and parents are responding positively to parent education courses where they are offered (Meier, 1976). Children with handicaps also must be included as participants in any parent education courses. Some recent reviews of the literature suggest that children of mentally retarded parents may be more at risk for abuse and neglect (Schilling,

Schinke, Blythe, & Barth, 1982). Many handicapped children are potential parents and must be included in prevention efforts aimed at the next generation of parents and children.

Third, schools can join with other agencies to cushion the stresses upon families which tend to accompany change. Justice and Duncan (1976) found that families involved in abuse were going through periods of major life changes—in residence, income, family composition, work schedules, health, marital relations, etc. These changes can generate stresses that are pathogenic. The presence of a handicapped child is an additional significant stress factor for families. Schools can take the lead in helping families cope with stress. This function serves the interest of the school because it improves the lot of children and enhances the school's ability to perform its primary academic mission (Garbarino, 1976a). While providing this kind of service directly is but one aspect of the larger issue of support systems addressed earlier, stimulating the community to assume this responsibility highlights a somewhat different area: child advocacy.

Although schools are, in principle, the natural allies of children, child advocacy has been problematic for educators who see children's rights as a threat to their authority and obligations. Nonetheless, one of the most important roles to be played by schools is as advocates for children, for their right to a secure and nurturant environment, which implies that schools become active (and some already are) in prodding the larger community to support this same basic right. Involvement in community-wide child abuse and neglect councils, in legislative action on behalf of children, and in public education on behalf of child protective services can all be part of the advocate role.

CONCLUSION

Handicapped children are first and foremost children. The educators' concern for the maltreatment of handicapped children can be regarded both as a "mainstreaming" issue (an issue shared with the population of children as a whole) and a special issue (an issue with unique ramifications for special populations of children). Both approaches are important and necessary.

The maltreatment of children and youth is a prime social indicator of the overall quality of life for families. If we view abuse and neglect from an ecological perspective, the cultural origins of the problem are apparent. The maltreatment of children requires a social context that will permit it, specifically one that offers support in law and custom for violence against children and that permits and even encourages isolation of parent–child relations from potent prosocial support systems.

Schools in principle, could have an important role to play in the human ecology of abuse and neglect. By modeling nonviolent interpersonal relations, particularly nonviolent social control, the behavior of present and future generations could be shaped. By acting as a support system (feedback and resources for families of handicapped children), the school could be a force to break down the dangerous barrier of isolation where it exists and build social networks where the opportunity is present.

Schools could work cooperatively with other community agencies to identify the very small minority of adults who have no business being in the role of parent. Schools could provide support systems to the foster care system that assumes responsibility for children removed from their parents, and which desperately needs help and close scrutiny to meet its responsibilities. By embarking on a program of parent education and life management skills training, schools could aid in the cause of primary prevention, particularly if such programs involve apprenticeship experiences in which modeling and direct service could occur. Finally, by assuming an active stance of child advocacy, schools can support individuals and agencies throughout the community. The evidence makes it clear that America's children need advocates wherever they can find them (Meier, 1976). When children live in a world of abnormal rearing, they require active allies if they are to survive physically and psychically. Schools have a natural place in the lives of children and thereby in the human ecology of child maltreatment. It is the responsibility of all concerned to ensure that schools play that role to its fullest. With this in mind we can return briefly to the issues with which we began this discussion of the role of schools in child maltreatment.

Based on the foregoing analysis, it is apparent that the discrepancy between the actual and potential positive contribution of schools to prevention, identification, and treatment is substantial. The task before us is to help schools meet those obligations they already have in law, policy, and custom and to provide incentives for the more visionary potential functions of schools to be realized.

chapter 5

THE ROLE OF
RESIDENTIAL INSTITUTIONS

James K. Whittaker

INTRODUCTION

In the first chapter of this volume, Garbarino summarizes the as-yet inconclusive evidence on the etiology of abuse and neglect and identifies five broad areas of risk for children and youth. These include: (1) inadequate parental resources, (2) behavioral characteristics of the child, (3) factors particular to the relationship between a child and adult that produce a deteriorating pattern of interaction, (4) factors immediate to the situation that stimulate abuse/neglect, and (5) cultural/societal values or institutions that encourage maltreatment or permit it to occur. He concludes that handicapped children and youth may be at special risk because of any or all of these five factors and, that since handicapped children and youth are more likely to be in out-of-home placement at some point in their lives, the identification, prevention, and remediation of maltreatment in residential settings deserves special attention.

This chapter briefly will examine what is known about the incidence of maltreatment in out-of-home, group care placements: residential institutions, group homes, shelter facilities, and the like.* Second, the ecological paradigm which undergirds this volume will be examined for its special implications for residential settings vis-à-vis prevention of maltreatment of handicapped children. Third, a variety of intrainstitutional and extramural factors potentially relevant to the prevention of maltreatment will be examined. The final section of the chapter consists of practical suggestions for parents, child- and youthcare staff, and citizen advocates.

*No particular attempt will be made to identify issues specific to foster family care, although much of the material covered here as well as in Chapter 2 by Dunst and Chapter 3 by McHale will be relevant.

MALTREATMENT OF HANDICAPPED CHILDREN IN RESIDENTIAL SETTINGS: A BRIEF OVERVIEW

Estimates of population figures for handicapped children in residential settings are 100,000 (the Urban Institute, 1975). For example, two surveys from the early 1980s in the child welfare sector estimate that approximately 25% of the children in out-of-home care are handicapped (U.S. Children's Bureau, Child Welfare Research Note, 1, 1983). These surveys show as well that approximately three-fourths of children enter care for family-related reasons and that three-quarters of these are for abuse and neglect. Finally, these same surveys indicate that for children receiving out-of-home care, approximately 70% are in foster family homes and 30% are in residential institutions.

While the recently completed census of children and youth in residential facilities by Donnell Pappenfort and his colleagues at the University of Chicago specifically excluded facilities for the mentally and physically handicapped, it is, nonetheless, relevant to the focus of this volume in that we know handicapped children are represented liberally in residential settings other than those specifically for the mentally retarded and developmentally disabled, and that therefore the changing characteristics of those settings will be relevant to planning for the prevention of maltreatment (Dore, Young, & Pappenfort, 1984; Pappenfort, Young, & Marlow, 1983). For purposes of this brief review, the following trends from the Pappenfort census of 1981, which, essentially, updated an earlier census conducted in 1965 are as follows (Pappenfort, Kilpatrick, & Roberts, 1973):

- While the number of residential group care facilities has increased markedly since 1966, there has been a decline in the number of children and youth in care.
- The rate in growth in numbers of facilities has been concentrated in the category of juvenile facilities for children and youth considered delinquent or status offenders and in mental health facilities.
- Facilities in all categories have declined in size over the past 16 years. In 1966, less than 50% of the facilities surveyed had fewer than 26 children and youth in residence. The majority of all facilities surveyed in 1982 were of that size.
- Among the facilities surveyed in 1982, the number of children were divided almost evenly among public and private facilities. Slightly more than one-third of all children were in juvenile justice facilities, one-fourth were in mental health facilities, and about one-fifth were in child welfare facilities. The remainder of children were in short-term care facilities.

In all, there appears to be approximately 125,323 children in group care in 3914 facilities in 1981, which decreased from 155,905 in 2138 facilities in 1965. The drop in placement figures reflects a decline in the rate of group care placement: from 19.9 per 10,000 youth in 1965 to 17.3 for 10,000 in 1981 (Pappenfort et al., 1983).

In short, for residential settings other than those specifically for the mentally retarded and developmentally disabled, the trend seems to be: fewer children in smaller facilities being placed at a slower rate than in the mid-1960s. In addition to difficulties in obtaining accurate population figures for children and youth in residential settings, accurate statistics on incident of abuse and neglect in those settings remain difficult to ascertain. A major federally funded conference on institutional maltreatment held in 1982, began with the following caveat:

> The full extent of child abuse and neglect in residential institutions in this country is not known. In part this is so because institutions do not lend themselves to public monitoring. There are only meager data on the type, incidence, and severity of such maltreatment and there are no definitive statistics (Corrigan, 1982, p. 2).

Since the late 1970s, the National Center on Child Abuse and Neglect has been active in addressing the problem of institutional abuse and neglect by focusing on several priority areas: developing reporting, investigative, and corrective procedures for institutional maltreatment; developing model state legislation; development and demonstration of improved systems for ensuring child protection in institutions; sponsoring research on needs and resources for child protection in residential settings and cosponsoring special conferences on the prevention and treatment of institutional abuse and neglect (Corrigan, 1982, p. 3). The fruits of these efforts, which continue apace, have yielded: training materials for residential staff (Harrell & Orem, 1980); reports of specialized conferences and compilations of relevant readings (Child Abuse and Neglect in Residential Institutions, 1978; Washburne, Van Hull, & Rindfleisch, 1982); research on child maltreatment in institutional settings (Rindfleisch, 1984); materials specific to sexual abuse of children in residential settings (Navarre, 1980); and materials for citizen review of children's residential facilities (Goldman, Drew, & Aber, 1980). In addition, concern with maltreatment of children and youth in residential settings has been reflected in recent standards and guidelines for such settings (Child Welfare League of America, Standards for Residential Child Care, 1985: Oregon Association of Treatment Centers, 1985; Residential Child Care Guidebook, 1980), as well as in specialized volumes on inspecting children's institutions (Inspecting Children's Institutions—National Coalition for Children's Justice, 1977), on adolescent abuse (Adolescent Maltreatment, 1980; and Garbarino, Schellenbach, & Sebes, 1986), as well as on issues specific to defining, identifying, and preventing institutional maltreatment (Hanson, 1982). In short, where limited materials existed only a few years ago, thanks largely to the leadership of the National Center on Child Abuse and Neglect, there now exists a variety of resources for the citizen, supervisor, and trainer interested in addressing the problem of institutional abuse and neglect.

What are the forms of maltreatment to which handicapped children in residential settings are subjected? Garbarino, citing the work of Rindfleisch (1984) and others, identifies three forms of maltreatment: (1) *institutional abuse* (corporal punishment, misuse of psychotropic drugs, prolonged isolation, mechanical restraint); (2) *institutional neglect* (failure to provide specific services, e.g., treatment services, negligence in the administration of psychotropic drugs, and failure to notify the placement agency when a child's continued residence is detrimental to him/her); and (3) *wrongful abrogation of rights* (including tampering with mail, racial or other improper segregation, restrictions on visitation and family contact, and interference with a youth's ability to consult with outside agents) (in press, pp. 17–18). Gil provides another threefold categorization including: (1) *physical abuse;* (2) *program abuse* (e.g., "when programs within a facility are below normally accepted standards; have extreme or unfair policies; or rely on harsh, inhumane, or unusual techniques to teach or guide children" [1982, p. 10]); and (3) *system abuse* ("that not perpetrated by any single person or program, but by the immense and complicated child care system, stretched beyond its limits and incapable of guaranteeing safety to children in care" [1982, p. 10]). While some have argued that the fact of placement itself is an act of system neglect, most would agree that in all streams of service there will continue to be a need for some residential provision. It is toward the prevention of maltreatment of handicapped children and youth in such settings that the remainder of this chapter will be directed.*

THE ECOLOGY OF HUMAN DEVELOPMENT AND THE INSTITUTIONAL ENVIRONMENT

Central to this volume and to the understanding of child maltreatment contained herein is a view of human development and behavior as the result of the complex interplay of proximate and distal environments with the developing child and his/her family. This perspective as developed and articulated by Bronfenbrenner (1979), Garbarino

---

*Material specific to the legal aspects of institutional abuse/neglect, the development of model state reporting laws, and the interface between child protective services and residential childcare institutions is covered in chapter by Howerton (Chapter 6), Melton (Chapter 9), and Authier (Chapter 12).

(1981), and others (Whittaker, Gilchrist, & Schinke [in press]) has come to be known as the "ecological perspective or paradigm." Bronfenbrenner's characterization of human development captures the idea of organism–environment interplay:

> [It is] the progressive, mutual accommodation between an active, growing human being and the changing properties of the immediate settings in which the developing person lives, as this process is affected by relations between these settings, and by the larger context in which the settings are imbedded (1979, p. 21).

Central to Bronfenbrenner's definition is the notion of *reciprocity:* an active, dynamic individual moving and reshaping the environment even as he or she is acted on by it. "Environment" is here conceived of as a set of "nested concentric structures" each influencing the other and, ultimately, the developing child. The *microsystem* refers to the immediate setting(s) directly experienced by the developing child—the family, the day-care center, the play group, and so on. *Mesosystems* refer to relationships or links between microsystems in which the developing child directly experiences reality: the connections between home, school, and neighborhood, for example. Central to Bronfenbrenner's theory is that the stronger and more varied the links between these microsystems, the more powerful the impact on the individual. *Exosystems* refer to "one or more settings that do not involve the developing child as an active participant, but in which events occur that affect, or are affected by, what happens in the setting containing the developing person" (1979, p. 25). Examples include the workplace of the parents, a school class attended by an older sibling, and the activities of the local school board. Finally, *macrosystems* reflect the broad ideological and institutional patterns of a particular culture underpinned by belief systems, values, and so on. Bronfenbrenner refers to macrosystems as the "blueprints" for society that determine the shape, character, and relationship to each other of dominant institutions—schools, the workplace, hospitals, and the like. The term *macrosystem* connotes the societal "blueprint" as it presently exists and as it *might* exist in some future form. For each of these levels of environment, Garbarino poses key questions with respect to *sociocultural risk* and *opportunity*. Risk refers to "dangers to development that come from outside the individual child in the way his or her world is organized (1981, p. 17)."

The ecological paradigm contains a fundamental implication for all human service programs, namely, that a requisite for effectively protecting children and strengthening families is an accurate understanding of child behavior and family functioning in relation to the various levels of environment that affect both and are, in turn, affected by both. Holahan, in exploring the importance of the ecological paradigm in mental health, identifies two implications for that sector:

> The *environmental* emphasis of the ecological view supports environmentally-oriented interventions directed towards strengthening or establishing methods of social support. . . . The *transactional* emphasis of the ecological perspective fosters individual-oriented interventions directed toward promoting personal competencies for dealing with environmental blocks to achieving personal objectives (1979, p. 6).

Thus, the core activities in a residential program for special needs children should include: (1) building more supportive, nurturant environments for residents through various forms of environmental helping designed to increase "social supports"; and (2) improving the child's (and family's) competence for dealing with both proximate and distal environments through the teaching of specific "life skills."*

In the arena of residential services, we have abundant empirical evidence to support both of these prescriptions. Convincing evidence of the pervasive and severe deficits in life skills exhibited by children and youth referred for mental health services as opposed to a matched sample of nonreferred controls is offered by Achenbach and Edelbrock (1981).

Using as a primary measure the Child Behavior Checklist (CBCL), these investigators found significant differences between the referred and nonreferred groups in over 20 social competency items and 118 common behavioral problems. Similarly, clinical surveys of children entering residential care indicate marked behavior problems and competence deficits, including, among parents, an inability to control their own child (Fitzharris, 1985). Clearly, these studies and others provide empirical validation to the growing trend in many residential settings toward the teaching of life skills to both youth and parents. In the area of social supports, recent reviews of residential outcome studies in such sectors as child welfare, juvenile justice, and mental health clearly point to the centrality of the postplacement environment as the salient factor in predicting youth outcome. Several studies clearly demonstrate that presence or absence of a supportive community environment (family, neighborhood, school) is a more important determinant of postinstitutional adjustment than any of the following: severity of presenting problem(s), caseworker and teacher judgments of improvement, status at discharge, and type of treatment offered (Whittaker & Maluccio, in press; Whittaker & Pecora, 1984). Moreover, there is some evidence that work at the institution–community interface is not limited to aftercare but is best thought of as beginning prior to and continuing

*For nominal and operational definitions of "social supports," "life skills," and related constructs, see Whittaker, Gilchrist, and Schinke (in press).

during and after placement ends (Taylor & Alpert, 1973). These limited outcome studies are consistent with the wider and growing body of literature showing the preventive and ameliorative effects of social supports for a range of life problems and stressors (Cohen & Syme, 1985; Dunst, Chapter 2, this volume; Gottlieb, 1981; Whittaker, Garbarino, & Associates, 1983).

Whittaker defines an ecologically focused residential program as follows:

> [It is] a specifically-designed environment in which the events of daily living are used as formats for teaching competence in basic life skills. The living environment becomes both a means and a context for growth and change, informed by a culture that stresses learning-through-living (1979, p. 36).

"Teaching formats" include things like rule structures, daily routines, play and activities, group discussion, and treatment, as well as more individualized education, counseling, treatment, and support programs for children and parents. The central figures in such a residential program are the child/youth care worker, who may alternately be called "educateurs" (Hobbs, 1982); "teaching parents" (Phillips, Phillips, Fixsen, & Wolf, 1974); "teacher counselors" (Hobbs, 1982); or "child care counselors" (Trieschman, Whittaker, & Brendtro, 1969). In the area of developmental disabilities, Project TEACCH in North Carolina exemplifies many of the features of ecologically oriented residential services described previously (Schopler & Reichler, 1976). This model program includes a dual emphasis on skill training and social support facilities, with a high degree of parent involvement and community outreach.

What is the importance of all this for our topic at hand: prevention of the institutional maltreatment of handicapped children? It is simply, that the best prevention for institutional maltreatment—in any of its previously described forms—will be the presence of a clearly articulated and well understood statement of philosophy for the residential setting which is actualized in (1) active teaching of life skills to residents through a variety of formats and (2) building community supports through linkages to family, neighborhood, and other caregivers who are potential sources of social support to the youth and his family. The obstacles to obtaining such richness and variety in residential programming are many, and any current assessment of residential provision would indicate that we are far from the mark. It is true, nonetheless, that however important are improved reporting systems or specific program initiatives such as specific training in handling violent and disruptive behavior, they must be viewed as necessary but insufficient elements in an overall strategy to prevent institutional abuse. Lack of a clear philosophy, mediocre programming, inadequate staff training and evaluation, and lack of bridges to the external community all, eventually, will weight the probabilities in favor of increased abuse and neglect.

INTRAINSTITUTIONAL FACTORS AND THE REDUCTION OF ABUSE AND NEGLECT: CREATING THE INFRASTRUCTURE FOR A SAFE ENVIRONMENT

How does one refocus and retool the various elements in a residential milieu with the goal of preventing maltreatment? Here, the training guide of the National Center on Child Abuse and Neglect (NCCAN) (Harrell & Orem, 1980) provides an excellent overview of both the factors that predispose toward maltreatment and the critical elements in program to both deal with maltreatment that has already occurred, as well as prevent its recurrence. These elements include:

1. *Systems to facilitate the reporting and investigation of maltreatment*
   - Who reports?
   - Where to report?
   - What to report?
   - How and when to report?

The chapter by Helen Howerton (Chapter 6), director of NCCAN, as well as Chapter 9 on legal issues by Melton, updates information in the training guide on model reporting statutes and procedures. Thomas (1982, p. 26) provides an excellent summary of the child's rights in residential placement beginning with the right to continued developmental opportunity:

- All children have the right to protection and nurturance, . . . preconditions to personal development.
- All children have the right to achieve basic developmental goals consistent with their individual abilities: . . . individualization, . . . socialization, . . . cognitive preparation.
- All children have the right to achieve corrective interventions to overcome impediments to developmental progress. . . .

Thomas goes on to delineate specific procedures for formulating and implementing treatment plans and offers, as well, a useful set of guidelines for the use of control procedures (1982, pp. 30–31). These latter supplement the earlier work of Russo and Shyne (1980) on coping with disruptive behavior in residential settings.

Model Institutional Policies to Ensure Residents' Rights, Individualized Treatment Plans, and Family Involvement

Both the NCCAN guide (Harrell & Orem, 1980) and Thomas (1982) offer specific suggestions for formulating institutional policies in these arenas; other examples of model institutional policies may also be found in *Children without Homes* (1978). Other useful sections in the NCCAN guide offer suggestions in such areas as: staff selection, training, and support child self-reporting and the use of ombunsmen; procedures for citizen review and institutional advocacy (1980, pp. 37–46). Rather than reiterate these materials here, the interested reader is referred directly to NCCAN or its numerous distribution networks for current information on training materials, model reporting statutes, and guidelines for citizen involvement. For purposes of this chapter, I would like to focus, briefly, on three related considerations in an overall strategy to prevent institutional maltreatment: the function of *training;* the function of *evaluation;* and the issue of *staff peer supports.*

Despite advances in some regional and state projects (Alberta Association of Child Care Workers, 1985), *training* for direct care residential staff remains a patchwork in most areas of the country in all streams of care. The most ambitious federally funded effort at developing a basic training course for residential care workers suffered from the failure to adopt the systematic dissemination strategy advised by the developer. Consequently, while materials have been available, dissemination has been spotty at best. This, despite the fact that virtually every review of the problem of institutional maltreatment cites lack of adequate staff training as a critical need. Clearly, if the kind of resident rights outlined earlier by Thomas (1982) are to be realized, systematic, thorough, and ongoing staff training must be an integral part of the agency's program—particularly where handicapped children are concerned. Similarly, if the concept of the milieu as an arena for teaching competencies in basic life skills—through the purposive use of rules, routines, activities, group and individual treatment, and the like—is to be implemented, training must become the primary support system for staff (Whittaker, 1979). What characterizes exemplary training programs for residential care staff, and do such models exist in practice?

Fortunately, the answer to the second question is YES: model training programs for residential care staff in group homes (Fixsen, Phillips, & Wolf, 1978; Phillips *et al.* 1974), specialized forms of foster care (Hawkins & Breiling, in press), and residential facilities for the developmentally disabled (Wetzel & Hoschouer, 1984). What characterizes such training models? First, they are *behaviorally specific,* that is, oriented to specific behavior which staff must demonstrate. Second, they are *directly related to the treatment–education goals of the residential* setting. Wetzel and

Hoschouer (1984, pp. 161–200), for example, provide detailed schema for assessing resident skills in a wide range of self-care and social skills areas and outline procedures for both teaching such skills and monitoring progress. Finally, such model training programs tend to be *criterion based,* that is, they require staff to actually demonstrate the relevant behavioral skill to a certain level of proficiency *before* advancing to the next stage of training. For example, at Boys Town in Nebraska, a national leader in the development of youth care training programs, fully three-fourths of the time allocated to training of new staff is spent in role plays, behavioral rehearsals, and other forms of active teaching as opposed to 25% in didactic lectures. Other groups and associations, like the Alberta Association of Child Care Workers (1985) have developed basic training materials for residential care staff suitable for use within the institution or a community college setting. Successful completion of the basic sequence is tied to initial appointment and advancement in the provincial youth care system. Clearly, much work remains to be done to develop training materials along the lines of the previously cited criteria, which are directed toward the *total* role and function of the residential care staff—as teacher, therapist, and care giver—not merely at one or another aspect of the residential care task (e.g., developing more effective techniques for managing disruptive, bizarre, and violent behavior). In the final analysis, the best check on the kinds of disruptive and provocative behaviors that often occasion abuse is the presence of a rich, creative, and challenging residential program.

Closely related to successful training is *evaluation* as a central component in a system designed to reduce the probability of institutional maltreatment. Fortunately, the last decade has witnessed a tremendous growth in the development of practitioner-oriented, "user friendly" systems for monitoring, tracking, and providing corrective feedback to both staff and residents (Bloom & Fischer, 1982). Various forms of single-subject designs, "consumer" evaluations (from youth, staff, parents, referring agencies, for example), as well as various forms of critical incident reporting provide useful data to on line staff and supervisors and can indicate progress of individual youth in care, as well as on staff performance. Some agencies, like Boysville in Michigan, are experimenting with computerized intake systems for residential care that provide continuous measurement of progress toward treatment goals.

A final element in the infrastructure for successful residential care, *staff support,* includes the variety of organizational factors that are essential requisites to effective residential programming. These include: adequate salary and fringe benefit programs, employee assistance programs, peer consultation, supervision, availability of external consultants, and the like. Model residential programs like the Boys Town Family

Teacher model, as well as nonresidential services, like Homebuilder's intensive in-home family services, have concentrated a great deal of time and attention in the formation and maintenance of a supportive staff culture—believing, as they do, that such a culture is every bit as important to effectiveness as the particular change technologies they are using with youth and families. Residential child and youth care is a demanding, undervalued, and underpaid occupation. Ultimately, efforts to prevent institutional maltreatment will be strengthened by supporting state, national, and provincial childcare work associations who are struggling to improve pay, training, and working conditions for child and youth care workers. Some state associations of voluntary residential agencies, like the California Association of Services for Children, offer excellent models for building coalitions between provider, childcare worker and advocacy associations. Finally, recent scandals in group day care in California and New York indicate the need for thorough staff screening prior to employment in the residential care setting. While much work remains to be done in this area, preliminary studies by Haddock and McQueen (undated) show promise in the development of a battery of instruments designed to provide early identification of institutional caretakers with potential for abuse of a client.

EXTRAMURAL FACTORS AND THE REDUCTION OF INSTITUTIONAL MALTREATMENT

Many factors external to the residential environment can help to prevent the occurrence of child maltreatment. Three will be briefly discussed here: the *function and forms of family involvement; strategies for community liaison;* and *citizen review.* As the previously cited outcome research clearly indicates, a supportive family environment is critical to successful community reintegration from residential placement. Having parents involved as full and active partners in the total placement process—from preplacement through aftercare—will significantly improve the chances for community reintegration where that is desirable and reduce the potential for institutional maltreatment by making the parents active, questioning participants in the residential experience. Parents of handicapped children have given poignant, and often eloquent, expression to the vagaries of working with professionals (Turnbull & Turnbull, 1984). In the area of residential care, parents have often been kept at a distance from the life of the institution for a variety of reasons which I have outlined elsewhere, including:

Economic Disincentives. The cost of family work, particularly aftercare, often must be borne by the residential center. Many agencies are thus prevented from providing the kind of family outreach work—including work with siblings and neighborhood peers—that they would like to.

Geographical Isolation. Since many centers draw on a far-reaching catchment area, some extending across state lines, families are often inaccessible for regular involvement. A related difficulty is that many of the large institutional settings are located in rural areas at considerable distance from their clients' communities and often without public transportation.

Sociocultural Differences. In his study of adolescent delinquents in a large institution, Polsky (1962) notes some of the problems that occur when the goals, cultural values, social class, and life experiences of the therapist are not shared by the client population. Such a lack of correspondence may extend to other areas as well— ethnic and minority heritage, for example—and may act as a barrier to full family participation.

Limited Definition of Parental Involvement. Many programs offer parents a single role—that of client or patient—if they are to be involved in the process of their child's treatment. Such a conception is based on the belief that the parents themselves are troubled, disorganized, and in need of treatment—all of which may be true. In fact, recent studies (Bernstein, Snider, & Meezan, 1975; Fanshel & Shinn, 1977) indicate that a high percentage of children entering placement do so primarily because of parent-related difficulties. But that offers parents only a single vehicle for involvement (clinical treatment) and may overlook the numerous other possibilities for growth and change available to them, for example, parent education and family support groups. Furthermore, even the most troubled families are not incapacitated all the time and may participate, on occasion, in other aspects of the program as volunteer parent supporters. In short, parents may require extensive professional help in individual or conjoint treatment; they also may be quite able and willing to help the program—despite their difficulties.

Guilt over Causation. Many parents feel that they alone are responsible for their child's difficulties and may be reluctant to enter into a relationship with a professional for fear of being judged or criticized. In some ways, as Schopler (1971) has suggested, parents of troubled children have become "scapegoats"—perhaps because the specific factors that cause a particular child to have problems are still largely unknown.

Fear of Failure. In most instances, the parents have tried to alter their child's troublesome behavior and have failed. Their feelings of helplessness and frustration are often rekindled as they view their potential involvement in a helping relationship—particularly if they are required to be the teachers, therapists, or mediators of reinforcement for their own child. In such cases, we may be asking parents who already feel overburdened and defeated to take on yet another responsibility for their child's care—with no meaningful adjustments in other parts of their lives. A related problem concerns the parents who have made an accommodation to their child's bizarre, disruptive, or withdrawing behavior and—despite their realization of the necessity of change—may be reluctant to alter old coping patterns.

Overwhelming Life Circumstances. Many families of children entering group care are beset by a host of problems: family disorganization, absence of a parent, inadequate finances, poor health, legal difficulties. Such multiproblem constellations affect families across class and socioeconomic lines, but the poor have fewer resources available for adequate coping. No amount of skilled treatment can make up for an absence of the basics: adequate income, health care, decent housing, and education. Thus, the residential center must adopt new formats for family helping, including social brokerage and advocacy (Whittaker, 1981, pp. 70 72).

Over the past several years, a variety of formats have been identified for involving parents and families in the residential placement, including: specialized forms of family therapy; parent support groups; parent education, and parent involvement in the residential milieu (Whittaker, 1981). The variety of these approaches illustrate the fact that effective work with families consists of many different forms of helping including support, education, nurturing, counseling, respite, and, occasionally, family treatment. Dunst (this volume, Chapter 2) and others have written of the special stresses and strains attendant to having a special-needs child in the family. Dunst describes a multimodal early intervention program with many implications for family involvement in residential settings. Barsh, Moore, and Hamerlynck (1983) describe an innovative program for enhancing and extending the support network of families with a developmentally disabled adolescent that shows similar promise for transfer of intervention technology. Others have developed models of family treatment specific to the event of community reintegration of the institutionalized adolescent. Finkelstein (1981) describes a family work program in what was traditionally a child-focused residential treatment center. This typifies a trend in many residential settings— for example, Eastfield Children's Center in San Jose, California and the Walker School in Needham, Massachusetts—toward active involvement with parents before, during, and after placement. The field of special-needs adoption offers many relevant examples of practice technologies designed to aid the placement of a handicapped child in an adoptive family—much of which is relevant to the residential center (Cole, 1985). The growing literature on the interface between professional/lay helping offers many insights to the development of a broad-gauged family work program for handicapped children in residential care (*Programs to Strengthen Families*, 1984; Whittaker, Garbarino, and Associates, 1983). Finally, the growth and vitality of all manner of support and action groups for parents of handicapped children offers a useful template for sectors of service (like foster family care, for example) where parent organization is much less evident. Much needed is research on specific programs—like TEACCH with the University of North Carolina and the Oregon Association of Treatment Centers where parent involvement in treatment planning and decision making has been present from the start.

Closely related to family involvement is the matter of building effective *community linkages* between the residential centers and the other major systems that impact the child: neighborhood, peer groups, school, employment, church, and the like. Whittaker (1979) conceptualizes these links as the ecology of child treatment (Figure 5.1). Hobbs' (1982) pioneering work in Project RE-ED developed the role of "liaison" counselor essentially to work the boundaries between the residential setting and the community. This "liaison" concept has been further explicated by Hobbs (1982) and others. Catalano and Hawkins (1985) describe a model program (Project ADAPT) for aiding the community reintegration of youth from a state training school which includes skills teaching, liaison work, and family counseling. Some school districts, for example, in Sacramento, California, are experimenting with detached workers whose function it is to facilitate the school reintegration of youths returning to the community from foster and residential care. Other means of building community ties include development of volunteer and "special friend" programs, consultation links, and inclusion of residents in community youth services. Evidence cited earlier suggests the importance of community links in building supportive communities conducive to the reintegration of youths returning from residential placement. Such links may work in two ways: first, by aiding in the "normalization of services" through and by their extension into the broader community (Wolfensberger, 1972; Flynn & Nitsch, 1980) and, second, by increasing the community's tolerance for persons with special needs.

A third element important to the prevention of institutional maltreatment is the integration of *citizen review* and oversight into the operation of residential institutions. Such review may take many forms, such as the formal citizen review boards for children in care developed

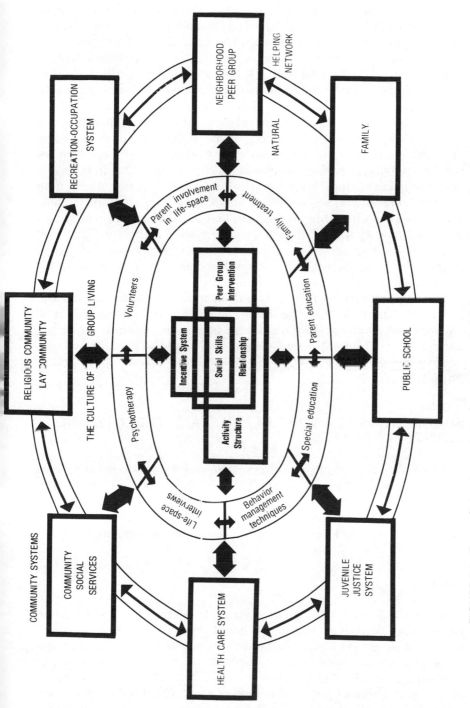

FIGURE 5.1. Group living in context: the ecology of child treatment. From Whittaker, 1979.

in South Carolina and elsewhere. The Massachusetts Office for Children (Goldman *et al.*, 1980) and the National Coalition for Children's Justice (*Inspecting Children's Institutions*, 1977) have developed handbooks for citizen review of children in residential facilities, and other advocacy organizations, like the Children's Defense Fund, have produced other studies which are designed to be useful to citizen advocates approaching the substitute care system (*Children without Homes*, 1978; Knitzer, 1982). Some agencies have developed more informal mechanisms such as community advisory boards and, at the state level, umbrella organizations like the Washington Alliance for Children, Youth and Families combine service-providing agencies and citizen advocates in the same organizational structure. Elsewhere, as in Ohio, the citizen organization most concerned with the condition of children in placement remains a separate structure. One mechanism that holds great promise for individual advocacy for children in the care system is the "guardian and litem," or court-appointed special advocate program primarily designed to train citizen advocates to represent the child's best interests in dispositional proceedings involving abuse and neglect. This program has well-established training protocols and organizational maturity. Without too many changes, it could be readily adapted as a requirement for all children and youth entering residential placement. In short, no better antidote to institutional maltreatment exists than the presence of concerned, knowledgeable, and committed citizens asking "naive" questions.

SUGGESTIONS FOR YOUTH CARE STAFF, PARENTS, AND CITIZEN ADVOCATES

There are many excellent sources of helpful suggestions for parents of handicapped children and professionals who work with them (Turnbull & Turnbull, 1984). The following pages contain suggestions particularly relevant for parents, child and youth care workers, and citizen advocates concerned with prevention of institutional maltreatment.

Parents

1. Resist the efforts of anyone—friend, relative, professional—to define placement as a "failure." It is not. Families with special-needs children have a right to expect the resources of a group home or other residential setting for purposes of respite, specialized treatment, or continuing care throughout the course of their child's development. It is neither a sign of personal failure or weakness if temporary or extended placement is what is in the best interest of your total family.

Although you share responsibilities with other caregivers, you remain central to your child's continuing need for love, support, encouragement, and hope.

2. Ask any prospective residential placement about both their philosophy and structure for parent participation: How are parents viewed by staff? What kinds of decision making are they involved in? Who participates in treatment–educational planning? Is there an organized parent group? Is contact with your child restricted by time or place? Is home visiting encouraged? Are counseling and/or support groups available? Is there a parent or a child in care whom you might talk with about the program?

3. Children do not come with problems/needs in neatly defined packages. Sometimes, problems get parcelled out to so many specialists that no single person has overall responsibility for the child's well-being in care. Seek and demand a central person who will be your primary contact within the residence for *any* concern that might arise. Arrange for and expect regular communication with that person.

4. Seek out other parents of children in care—including those whose children have returned to the community—and ask for specific and candid feedback on staff competencies, quality of care, and other special concerns.

5. Trust your gut feelings. You know your child better than anyone else. If you suspect he/she is being subject to maltreatment or questionable practice, do something about it. Know to whom and how suspicions of maltreatment should be reported. Familiarize yourself with your local advocacy network and know your legal rights as a parent. Above all, act quickly to protect your child and others in residence by reporting all suspected abuse/neglect as soon as you become aware of it.

Child and Youth Care Staff

1. Read *The Miracle Worker*, then replace it in your library—on the fiction shelf. You will do better thinking of yourself as but one member of a team of caregivers for special-needs children. Your primary job is to nurture, challenge, support, and teach the children in your care, not "rescue" them from evil parents or uncaring systems.

2. You face a tough, demanding, and infrequently rewarding job as a child–youth care worker. Seek and demand support from your administration: adequate and relevant training, periodic respite, and a decent wage. None of these things will be easily wrung from tightened budgets. Organize yourselves within and across agencies to carry the message of the cruciality of your work into the potential arena.

3. Be a careful monitor of your own emotions and behavior. Learn what types of behavior are likely to make you "lose your cool," and take steps to see that you have help when those situations are likely to occur. In child–youth care, there is no virtue in being the Lone Ranger: Seek out help from colleagues when you are faced with a difficult child-management situation. Work to build the kind of culture of support that allows you to intervene when you see a colleague struggling with a noisy, violent, provocative child.

4. Do not reason from "cure to cause": because some children respond well to a warm, caring relationship, do not assume that the root of their problem is the lack of such relationships with parents. View parents as allies, not adversaries. They have faced all of the challenges and frustrations you have—along with guilt and questioning. Your "success," in large measure, will depend upon your ability to help maintain a climate of support within the family.

5. Pay attention to your own mental health and well-being. Take and enjoy "time off from the kids." Have a part of your life clearly separate from the agency. Enjoy such respites from your work and, in so doing, realize the powerful help and support you can offer to parents who have full-time responsibilities for care.

Citizen Advocates

1. Do not presume malevolence, lack of caring, or characterological defects among institutional staff. They are people, like yourselves. Look for institutional policies and practices that create or maintain the conditions that occasion maltreatment. Treat staff with respect. Do not lose your sense of humor.

2. Do not routinize your visits to residential centers: Try to work evenings and weekends into your schedule whenever possible. Talk directly with residents and with care staff: Do not be confined to the administrator or supervisor's office. Ask naive questions, and do not stop until you get satisfactory answers.

3. Know the limits of your authority, and work within them.

4. Join forces with other advocacy groups, professional associations, and provider groups to raise "private troubles" into public social concerns. Learn the political process, and understand the local media.

5. Question accountability of youth care staff, supervisors, and administrators and elected officials. Set a high standard of expectations for care, nurturance, education, and treatment of children in care, and work to see that it is enforced. Keep yourself informed about exemplary programs and practices in other parts of the country. Maintain independence of thought. Challenge conventional professional wisdom.

chapter 6

THE ROLE OF THE FEDERAL GOVERNMENT*

Helen V. Howerton

INTRODUCTION

How is the federal role determined when dealing with the problem of abused and neglected handicapped children? As is the case in all social problems, the federal government's role is defined by at least three factors. First, it reflects the basic mandates and constraints of the Constitution and Bill of Rights—for example, to ensure equal protection under the law and refrain from abridging freedom of religion. Second, it manifests the particular ideology of the political parties in power, in Congress, in the executive branch, and in the federal court system. Third, and most specifically, it reflects the laws that are enacted and sustained to direct and enable action. Of course, this third element reflects the first two. It is the third element, the statutory foundations for the federal role and their interpretation, to which this chapter is addressed. In the context of this book, we are concerned with legislation affecting *children,* who have been or are vulnerable to *abuse or neglect,* and who are *handicapped or disabled.* It is not intended that this chapter be exhaustive in its coverage but rather that it highlight legislation which is relevant to current thinking on the topic.

Traditionally, parents have been the protectors of their children. This thesis has remained unquestioned both historically and across ideological lines. Public awareness and concern for maltreated children preceded both the development of federal legislation and state involvement in the protection of children. The need for public intervention can be traced to the 19th century when societies for the prevention of cruelty to animals began to address themselves to abused and ne-

*The interpretations and opinions expressed in this chapter are those of the author and do not necessarily reflect the views of any agency of the federal government.

glected children as well. Federal attention was evidenced in the First White House Conference on Children, held in 1909, and in the legislation which followed the establishment of the United States Children's Bureau. This public agency was charged with investigating and reporting upon "all matters pertaining to the welfare of children and child life among all classes of people" (Childrens Bureau Act of 1912). Child labor and high rates of infant mortality were among its earliest concerns. The use of children in the labor force was common, often as a means of economic survival of the family. Common concern for the health and safety of children, and their protection from industrial and mining accidents, absolved the family from responsibility. Similarly, the reduction of infant mortality could be seen as a cause for common concern. Thus, appropriate prenatal and postnatal care, sanitation, nutrition, proper medical care, and other factors which contributed to infant survival also were generally accepted as a public good. Such public intervention to protect children from exploitation in labor, or to reduce infant mortality were not apt to be viewed as intrusive into family life.

The results of war, which left widows and orphans behind, the Great Depression, infectious diseases, and early mortality justified public intervention to protect and provide for vulnerable children. The Social Security Act of 1935 and its subsequent amendments provided supportive services for young children and their families. These included: federal financial support for dependent children to protect them from the hardships of poverty; institutional care to house orphaned, abandoned, and handicapped children; foster family care to provide emergency and short-term care for children in a home setting; crippled children's services to provide specialized medical care; and maternal and child health services to provide needed medical services, immunizations, and preventive health care.

Many of these programs following the Great Depression have continued for half a century. The Second World War, the entry of women into the labor force, and other factors which contributed to the expansion of these programs, some might argue, led to their distortion and misuse. In the 1960s to the mid-1970s large numbers of children were placed in foster care and remained in these temporary placements for inordinate amounts of time. Corrective action by the Congress, evidenced by the passage of the Child Welfare Act of 1980, P.L. 96-272, sought to safeguard children against the failures of the systems that had been designed to protect them. By virtue of this Act, States were required to inventory all children in foster care, to review the cases of all children in foster care at six-month intervals, and to take steps to achieve permanency planning for children removed from their own homes.

The Child Abuse Prevention and Treatment Act, P.L. 93-247, was first enacted in 1974. It recognized increasing numbers of children who were being maltreated, mainly by parental figures. More recent amendments to that Act, in 1978 and in 1984, expanded the definition of abuse and neglect to include sexual abuses against children. In addition, they offered further protections for disabled infants and for children abused by out-of-home caretakers. Under this Act and the rules published by the Department of Health and Human Services, January 26, 1983, states must receive reports and provide for prompt investigation of reports of known or suspected child maltreatment.

The number of child maltreatment reports received by public child protective service agencies increased from 669,000 in 1976 to over 1.7 million in 1984. (American Association for the Protection of Children, 1986). Less than one-half of the reported cases, about 42%, are said to be substantiated; however, criteria for substantiation vary among the states and the extent to which cases are fully investigated, or investigated at all, is unknown. Many of the unsubstantiated cases receive services, although the reasons for providing such services are not reported nationally. The number of spurious reports or truly unfounded cases is not known. Some argue that child maltreatment is overreported, and that agency procedures are overly intrusive into family life. Others believe that the vulnerability of children justifies public intervention for their protection. The balance between constitutional and ideological support for "family privacy" and "parental rights," on the one hand, and the need for protective intervention in the interest of vulnerable children, on the other, is not a new issue but one that is receiving increasing attention.

The greater vulnerability of handicapped children to maltreatment and the consequences of maltreatment which may result in handicapping conditions argue for public intervention on behalf of children who are at risk of maltreatment. The shifting public perception of handicapped or disabled children more as "community responsibilities," and less as the "parents' problems" reinforces the thesis. "Mainstreaming"—bringing those with disabilities out of institutions and home care and into public view—has helped to change attitudes. Recent benchmark publications, such as *The Unexpected Minority: Handicapped Children in America* have as their theme that the disabled have been, in many ways, treated like racial minorities before the advent of civil rights—segregated, misunderstood, and mistreated (Gliedman and Roth, 1980). As the handicapped become integrated into our communities and more visible in daily life and in the media (i.e. television), the public's perception of their "differentness" wanes and they increasingly become the subject of general civil rights protection.

The handling of the "Baby Doe" case, in which the decisions of parents and doctors concerning the treatment of a handicapped newborn was subjected to public scrutiny, serves to illustrate these efforts. At one time such decisions were strictly private; the "Baby Doe" case became painfully public. "Baby Doe," an infant with Down's syndrome, from whom available surgical treatment to repair a detached esophagus was withheld, did not survive.

On April 30, 1982, following the child's death, the White House sent a memorandum to the Attorney General and the Secretary of Health and Human Services (HHS) on the enforcement of federal laws prohibiting discrimination against handicapped persons. In this memorandum, the Secretary of HHS was instructed to notify health care providers of the applicability of section 504 of the Rehabilitation Act of 1973 to the treatment of handicapped patients. On May 18, 1982, the Secretary of HHS issued a notice to approximately 7000 hospitals, which were receiving federal financial assistance, noting that:

> Under Section 504 it is unlawful for a recipient of federal financial assistance to withhold from a handicapped infant nutritional sustenance or medical or surgical treatment required to correct a life-threatening condition if: (1) the withholding is based on the fact that the infant is handicapped; (2) the handicap does not render the treatment or nutritional sustenance medically contraindicated.

Interim rules issued on March 7, 1983 under section 504 concerning the provision of medical services to handicapped infants were invalidated by the United States District Court in the District of Columbia on procedural grounds. Proposed rules issued on July 5, 1983 revised the requirements and added provisions concerning child protective service agencies; an appendix of standards and examples were also added. The Final Rule published on January 12, 1984, following the comment period and based on HHS' interpretation of section 504, also established procedures for investigating reports of the withholding of such treatment which would have permitted on-site investigations, when necessary, by the Office of Civil Rights, DHHS. In June 1984, a federal court invalidated those regulations and enjoined the Department from further investigation of such cases. On appeal to the United States Supreme Court, the section 504 rules were again invalidated on June 9, 1986.

Some argue that this decision will not affect the protection of handicapped infants since amendments to the Child Abuse Prevention and Treatment Act (the Act), P.L. 98-457, enacted on October 9, 1984, requiring states to establish procedures to receive and respond to reports of medical neglect including instances of withholding of medically indicated treatment (including appropriate nutrition, hydration, and medication) from disabled infants with life-threatening conditions, provide the necessary protections. However, while the Act's provision is similar in subject matter to the section 504 regulations, differences can be noted in certain important aspects.

Section 504 prohibits discrimination in *any* program or activity receiving federal financial assistance. Requirements under the Act affect only those funds available to the states authorized under its provisions. The incentive for the states to comply with the section 504 regulations would be much greater than that for compliance with the requirements of the Act. Section 504 regulations would have required notices to be posted advising the public of the applicability of the section 504 regulations; the Act's provision does not. Although section 504 provided for a telephone "hotline" to report suspected violations of the law and potential federal investigation of complaints, no such stipulation is provided in the Act. The Act defines the withholding of medical treatment, whereas section 504 regulations did not. Nevertheless, the Child Abuse Prevention and Treatment Act does require that state child protective service agencies develop procedures to assure protection for handicapped infants.

This joining of the federal government's mission to prevent child abuse and its increasing role in providing for handicapped children suggests the need to review the statutory bases for this link. In large measure, federal laws, programs, and policies concerning child maltreatment and disabled persons have proceeded along separate, but parallel, courses. Fortunately, not all children who are maltreated are disabled; nor are all who are disabled maltreated. Nevertheless, the intersection of these two populations is sufficient to warrant attention— if not in federal legislation—perhaps, more importantly, in the implementation and translation of existing legislation into practice at the state and local levels.

FEDERAL LAWS, PROGRAMS, AND POLICIES CONCERNING CHILD MALTREATMENT AND DISABLED PERSONS: SEPARATE BUT PARALLEL COURSES

Federal statutes for child protection, education, maternal and child health, mental health, health and social services, and the rights of the disabled have evolved separately. Nevertheless, they offer the potential for a powerful array of prevention and treatment services on behalf of children and the handicapped when they are well orchestrated in practice.

The protection of children from maltreatment by parental figures, and, more recently, child care providers, is addressed specifically in the Child Abuse Prevention and Treatment Act, P.L. 93-247, as amended. For more than a decade, since its enactment in 1974, the federal government has played a significant role in serving as a catalyst to mobilize the nation's social service, mental health, medical, educational, legal, and law enforcement resources to address the challenges of child abuse and neglect.

Traditionally, the legal and political principles governing the regulation of the relationship among family members emphasized family autonomy, with only an occasional severe case of child maltreatment coming to public attention, usually as a result of the death of a child and viewed as an isolated act of a deviant individual(s). Because of this view, there was little emphasis on child abuse prevention, and the collective response, as evidenced by legal processes, was limited to the punishment of offenders (Nelson, 1979).

The case of Mary Ellen Wilson in 1874 is generally credited with focusing public attention on child abuse and neglect and serving as the impetus behind the formulation of child protection societies that became the forerunners of modern child protection efforts. Mary Ellen was approximately 10 years old when her mistreatment, including beatings and confinement, was brought to the attention of the Society for the Prevention of Cruelty to Animals. The founder of the Society initiated court action on the child's behalf. On the basis of this action, Mary Ellen was brought to court and became the focus of public attention. In the aftermath, the attorney who brought this action formed the New York Society for the Prevention of Cruelty to Children (NYSPCC), which, within 10 years, acquired police powers and became a significant force in the reception, care, and disposition of child neglect cases in New York City (Thomas, 1972).

The organization of the NYSPCC was followed by the establishment of similar societies in other cities between 1874 and 1900. By 1900, 161 societies in the United States had formed to protect children or animals or both. The general emphasis of these societies was child "rescue," with legal actions brought on the child's behalf when abuse or neglect was suspected. Beyond the initiation of court action, few private resources were available for the placement of maltreated children. Thus, most children were referred to institutions where they were placed together with juvenile offenders (Thomas, 1972).

Prevention societies began to decline in the 1900s and were, with rare exception, defunct or decimated by the end of the Depression. They were victims of their own unwillingness to provide services to "rescued" children, and suffered from the lack of badly needed funding. However, it was also during this time that federal involvement in the problem of child maltreatment began. Until 1909, responsibility and interest in child welfare was entirely within the province of state and local governments, which regulated the activities of private charitable organizations. But with the first White House Conference on Children in 1909 and the subsequent establishment of the Children's Bureau, the federal government took its first steps toward making the welfare of children a legitimate national concern.

At the first White House Conference on Children, the concept of protective services rather than the law enforcement approach to child maltreatment, which had been gradually evolving, firmly took root. The Conference promoted the idea that a child should not be removed from his (or her) own home solely due to impoverished conditions and that services and economic programs should be designed to protect that home rather than to prosecute the parents and remove the child (Thomas, 1972).

The Sheppard-Towner Act, passed in 1921, was the first federal grants program for children. Essentially a maternal and child health program, it was administered by the Children's Bureau until the legislation expired in 1929, when it was subsequently reenacted as part of the Social Security Act. Before the passage of the Social Security Act in 1935, the federal government's interest in child welfare was limited to the issues of child labor and maternal and child health. With the enactment of this legislation and the establishment of programs funded thereunder, federal involvement in child advocacy issues expanded to include a program specifically designed to stimulate child welfare services throughout the nation. Programs addressed various child-related concerns, such as Aid to Dependent Children and Crippled Children's Services.

Specifically, the Social Security Act of 1935 offered federal funds to the states on a matching basis for the support of needy children in their own homes when one parent was disabled, absent, dead, or serving time in prison. The Act also fostered the growth of protective programs for children in each state by providing federal funding for institutional or foster care for dependent, neglected, or predelinquent children.

Child abuse and neglect as a specific child welfare issue emerged with the recognition of physical abuse as a medical condition. With the invention and use of x-rays, physicians began to observe the clinical signs now considered standard signs of physical abuse. In 1946, Dr. John Caffey, a pediatric radiologist, first called attention to the common association of blood around the brain resulting from blows to the head (subdural hematoma) and fractures in various stages of healing in infants (Caffey, 1946). Based on the fact that parental explanations of the causes of these injuries did not match the clinical findings, medical professionals began investigating the injuries and case histories of infants admitted after emergency treatments. Several prominent medical leaders, including D. C. Henry Kempe, a Denver pediatrician, sponsored a symposium on child abuse in 1961. This work lead to the recognition and use of the term "battered child syndrome."

During this time, social workers were continuing their interest in child welfare. From 1955 through 1959, the American Humane Association (AHA), a private charitable organization specializing in research in child and animal protection convened semiannual meetings of child welfare experts. These experts included representatives of the Children's Bureau, then a division of the Department of Health, Education and Welfare (HEW). At a meeting in 1956, the AHA presented findings of research on the status of state child abuse and neglect laws and services (Nelson, 1984).

Recognizing the need for interdisciplinary cooperation, the Children's Bureau called a conference of appropriate professional groups in 1962 to promote better understanding of the issues surrounding child maltreatment. The principal recommendation of this group was that a model child-abuse reporting law be drafted for use by the states.

Throughout the 1960s, interest in child abuse and neglect legislation increased. The 1962 amendments to the Social Security Act "required each state to develop a plan to extend child welfare services, including protective services, to every political subdivision." A model law on the reporting of abuse and neglect promulgated in the same year provided the language adopted by most of the states within the following 2 years. By the end of the decade, many states introduced or reformed existing laws to require reporting by certain professions and to lift legal liability for unsubstantiated reports (Nagi, 1977).

The problem of child abuse and neglect achieved prominence at the national level in the 1970s. During 1973, several witnesses from different disciplines testified before the Subcommittee on Children and Youth on the subject of child abuse. It was estimated that 60,000 children were abused each year in this country. Representatives of the Department of Health, Education and Welfare (DHEW) testified that, despite the size of the problem, not one person in the federal government was assigned full-time to work on child abuse. Witnesses also testified that limited funding of existing child welfare programs through the Social Security Act resulted in a lack of focus on child abuse and neglect in programs at the local and national levels. (Hearings of the Subcommittee on Children & Youth, 1974). In 1973, DHEW assigned the task of coordinating the efforts of the National Institute of Mental Health, the Public Health Services, the Office of Education, and the Rehabilitation Services Administration in regard to this problem to the Office of Child Development.

The Child Abuse Prevention and Treatment Act of 1974, as Amended

P.L. 93-274, the Child Abuse Prevention and Treatment Act (The Act), enacted in 1974, established the National Center on Child Abuse and Neglect within the Children's Bureau, then located in the Office of

Child Development, DHEW, now known as the Administration for Children, Youth and Families, Office of Human Development Services, Department of Health and Human Services. The Act was amended in 1978, extended in 1981, and again amended and extended in 1984. Its underlying purpose has been to assist agencies and organizations at the national, state, and local levels in their efforts to improve and expand child abuse and neglect prevention and treatment activities. Four major functions are specified under the Act: (1) generating knowledge and improving programs; (2) collecting, analyzing, and disseminating information; (3) assisting states and communities in implementing child abuse programs; and, (4) coordinating federal activities related to child maltreatment.

Under the Act, the National Center makes grants to states to assist them in developing, strengthening, and implementing prevention and treatment programs. Eligibility criteria for state grants include: consistency in substance of state definitions of child maltreatment to those included in the Act; statutory or administrative provisions specifying who shall report known or suspected abuse; immunity provisions for persons reporting; procedures for prompt investigation by a child protective service agency or other properly constituted authority; provision for receipt of reports by an independent body of allegations of abuse or neglect involving an institution or facility of the agency normally receiving reports; emergency services to protect children in need of immediate protection; assignment of a guardian ad litem for the child in judicial proceedings; a system of services to deal with child abuse and neglect cases throughout the state; and, provisions to assure confidentiality of information obtained in the handling of child maltreatment cases (DHHS, Final Rule, January 26, 1983). Amendments to the Act, particularly in 1984, have expanded the definition of child abuse to include sexual abuse and exploitation, and medical neglect of the "Baby Doe" type; and have expanded the definition of perpetrators to include abuses in out-of-home child care settings. The amendments will also affect state eligibility. Final Rules governing these provisions have not been published at this writing.

In 1974, only three states had child protection statutes that met the eligibility requirements specified by the Act; by 1977, 42 states had achieved full or conditional eligibility for the state grant. Today, less than a handful of states are not eligible, or have not applied, for state grants. Thus, while the federal government has not promulgated standards, as such, the majority of states have accepted standards implied by the law itself. This is significant as state grants under the Act have been rather modest in amount. In the main, these funds have not been used to offset the costs of providing services but rather to improve the service system. Child protective services are supported through state revenues, and provisions under the Social Security Act—Title XX Social

Service Block Grants, and Title IVB Child Welfare Services provisions. The success of the Child Abuse and Neglect Prevention and Treatment Act state grant program has been enhanced by increased public awareness and recognition of the need to protect vulnerable children in the population.

A second major sphere of activity under the Act is its discretionary grants program. Between 1975 and 1986, under the auspices of the Act, approximately 650 research or demonstration grants have been made to public or private nonprofit agencies nationwide. Federal leadership has been augmented by the tremendous response from the field in competing for these grants. The projects, many multidisciplinary in nature, have touched on almost every aspect of child maltreatment, prevention, intervention, clinical treatment, and service improvement. Social service, medical, educational, legal and law enforcement professionals, the courts, service providers of every type, parents and other private citizens have participated in the program. Areas of concentration have included, among many others, early intervention to prevent maltreatment and its consequences, intervention programs to protect developmentally disabled children and those in institutions, and the use of parent aides and respite care to increase the use of volunteer and paraprofessional support for families under stress.

A Clearinghouse on Child Abuse and Neglect Information[1] required under the Act has been in operation since 1975. It has been an important adjunct to the National Center for the acquisition and dissemination of child abuse and neglect materials and has been a major resource of professional and programmatic information for the field—accessing journal literature, technical reports, completed and ongoing research and demonstration studies, program descriptions, training curricula, state laws, selected court case decisions, consumer publications, and audiovisual materials; preparing bibliographic and other materials; and, providing supportive services to enhance the exchange of information among professionals, policymakers, practitioners, and concerned others. Its computerized database includes materials dating back to 1965 and is maintained on DIALOG File 64 (available to the public through DIALOG Information Services, Inc., a subsidiary of Lockheed Corporation).

Another important mechanism for providing federal leadership is the Advisory Board on Child Abuse and Neglect. The Board, mandated under the Act, is charged with coordinating federal efforts to prevent and treat child abuse and neglect. Twenty-eight members from different federal agencies and 15 members from the private sector meet pe-

[1]Clearinghouse on Child Abuse and Neglect Information, P.O. Box 1182, Washington, D.C. 20013.

riodically to inform, realign, and enhance their respective programs. The Board reports on its efforts annually to the Secretary of HHS; and, in consultation with the Board, the Secretary reports to the Congress biannually on efforts made to achieve coordination.

"Challenge Grants" for Child Abuse and Neglect Prevention

On October 12, 1984, provisions for federal challenge grants to encourage states to establish and maintain trust funds or other funding mechanisms to support child abuse and neglect prevention activities were included in the Fiscal Year 1985 continuing appropriations bill, P.L. 98-473. Prevention activities specifically encouraged by the law include: increased public awareness about child abuse and neglect through statewide educational and informational seminars; greater professional and group involvement in recognizing and dealing with child maltreatment; broader dissemination of information to the public, organizations, and agencies dealing with abuse and neglect problems; and, more community-based programs, of which two types were suggested—those designed to strengthen the parent(s), child, and family; and, intervention programs to promote prevention among at-risk families. There are a number of examples including: educational programs on parenting, prenatal care, perinatal bonding, child development, basic child care, care of children with special needs, coping with family stress, personal safety and sexual abuse prevention training for children, and self-care training for latchkey children; and, programs relating to crisis care, aid to parents, child-abuse counseling, peer support groups for abusive parents and their children, lay health visitors, respite or crisis child care, and early identification of at-risk families.

Five million dollars of federal matching funds, appropriated in Fiscal Year 1985, were made available to states with established trusts or other funding mechanisms, including state appropriations, targeted for prevention activities. First established in Kansas in 1980, Children's Trust Funds are mechanisms used to raise money for prevention programs. Typically, funds are generated by surcharges on marriage licenses, birth certificates, or divorce decrees; or by specially designated refunds of state income tax. Since 1980, more than 30 Children's Trust Funds have been developed across the country. Their significance lies in the greater involvement of the citizenry both in promoting prevention activities and in raising funds to support them.

LEGISLATION RELATED TO THE HANDICAPPED

The *Summary of Existing Legislation Relating to the Handicapped* published by the U.S. Department of Education in August 1980, updated in 1983 and 1985, is the source of much of what follows in this section. It lists nearly 60 laws of relevance for the handicapped in the areas of education, employment, health, housing, income maintenance, nutrition, rights, social services, transportation, and vocational rehabilitation. The discussion here will highlight legislation of most concern to children, particularly those who may be disabled or vulnerable to maltreatment. Much of the Congressional concern expressed in legislation affecting disabled children occurred during the same era as legislation concerning child maltreatment. The National Defense Education Act of 1958 to prepare children for the coming of the Space Age, and the Mental Retardation Facilities and Community Mental Health Centers Construction Act of 1963 specific to the mentally retarded during the Kennedy Administration (arising, in part, from the President's personal experience with his mentally retarded sister, Rosemary) occurred somewhat earlier than tandem actions of the mid-1960s and 1970s. Legislative activity in education affecting all children, with special provisions for the handicapped, and statutes particularly bearing on the right of the disabled were enacted at about the same time as the Child Abuse Prevention and Treatment Act discussed above.

The Elementary and Secondary Education Act of 1965, as Amended

The Elementary and Secondary Education Act (ESEA) of 1965 (P.L. 89-10), as amended, contains ten titles addressing practically all aspects of educating children at the primary or secondary levels. However, Titles I and IV of the Act have the most direct bearing on handicapped children.

Title I authorized federal aid to support supplementary educational services to children from low-income families who were considered to be "educationally deprived." In the legislative history of the Act, Congress defined "educationally disadvantaged children" to include handicapped youngsters. Under the Act, handicapped children included those who are mentally retarded, hard of hearing, deaf, speech impaired, visually handicapped, seriously emotionally disturbed, orthopedically handicapped or health impaired, deaf-blind, or those with a specific learning disability. Approximately 90% of the school districts across the country are eligible to participate in the program. Comprehensive educational programs are also authorized for children enrolled in state-operated and -supported schools. Funds are distributed by a formula based on the number of eligible handicapped children, and the state's average per capita expenditure for children enrolled in elementary and secondary schools or the national average per pupil expenditure, whichever is higher.

Innovative and special educational developmental programs to improve local educational practices were authorized under Title IV of the Act. The 1967 amendments to the Act required states to use at least 15% of the funds available for special programs and projects to improve education for handicapped youngsters. Subsequent amendments to the Act have maintained this 15% set-aside requirement.

The Education of the Handicapped Act, as Amended

The Education of the Handicapped Act is the primary source of federal aid to state and local school systems for instructional and support services to handicapped children. This Act originated in 1966 as Title VI to the ESEA to assist in the education of handicapped children. Title VI also created a National Advisory Committee on Handicapped Children, and mandated the creation of the Bureau of Education for the Handicapped within the Office of Education. The Bureau was responsible for administering programs and projects relating to the education and training of the handicapped, including programs and projects for training teachers and conducting research in special education.

The Elementary and Secondary Education Amendments of 1970 (P.L. 91-230) established a new authority entitled the "Education of the Handicapped Act" to consolidate a number of previously separate federal grant authorities relating to handicapped children under one act.

The Education Amendments of 1974 (P.L. 93-380) authorized sharp increases in funds to assist in educating handicapped children in public schools, and to help states meet the legislatively imposed "right to education" mandates. These amendments also provided procedural safeguards for use in identifying, evaluating, and placing handicapped children, ordered that such children be integrated into regular classes whenever possible, and required assurances that testing and evaluation materials would be selected and administered on a nondiscriminatory basis.

In 1975, the Education for All Handicapped Children Act (P.L. 94-142) expanded Part B, the state grant program, into a multibillion dollar federal commitment to assist state and local educational agencies to provide appropriate educational services for handicapped children. A new allocation formula was established entitling states to receive funds based on the number of handicapped children (ages 3 through 21) receiving special education and related services, and the average per pupil expenditure in public elementary and secondary schools. Federal fiscal participation was to increase from 5% in Fiscal Year 1978 to 40% in Fiscal Year 1982 and succeeding fiscal years. Special conditions were placed on how the school-aged population was to be counted for this purpose. Federal funds controlled by the state education agency and distributed to local agencies according to an approved state plan in

Fiscal Year 1976 and 1977 would later be distributed to local agencies according to established percentages. By Fiscal Year 1979, 75% of the federal funds had to be passed through to local education agencies.

Preschool Incentive Grants to encourage the provision of special education and related services to preschool handicapped children, aged 3 to 5, were made available to supplement basic state grants. In 1983, the age range was altered to include children from birth to age three at the state's discretion.

Under P.L. 94-142, individualized educational programs must be developed, and reviewed at least annually, for each handicapped child. It must include a statement of the child's current educational performance, annual goals and short-term instructional objectives, services to be provided and the extent to which the child will be able to participate in regular educational programs, and the projected initiation date and duration of services. Due process safeguards specified in the 1974 amendments were retained and provisions were added to protect handicapped children and their parents, including an opportunity to examine all relevant records regarding identification, evaluation, and educational placement of the child; written notice of these actions including the right to be notified in one's native language; and, an opportunity to present complaints. In addition, provision was to be made for impartial due process hearings on complaints received from parents or guardians with the right to be represented by counsel, to present evidence, cross-examine and compel the attendance of witnesses, and to receive a statement of factual findings and decisions.

In contrast to the Child Abuse Prevention and Treatment Act which protects the right of children to be free from physical or emotional harm or threatened harm, the Education for the Handicapped Act protects the right of all children, particularly those who are handicapped, to a free and appropriate education.

Provisions for Centers and Services, Training, and Research

To enhance and facilitate services to handicapped children, the Elementary and Secondary Education Amendments of 1967 established regional resource centers for special education teachers, centers and services for deaf-blind children, and expanded earlier programs for production and distribution of educational media, teacher training, and research. These provisions were extended and incorporated into the Education of the Handicapped Act in 1970.

The regional resource centers were intended to assist teachers and other school personnel through the evaluation of educational materials and the development and dissemination of specific educational strategies for use with handicapped children. Centers and services for deaf-blind children authorized in 1967 provided for diagnosis and evaluation;

education, orientation, and adjustment for deaf-blind children; consultative services for parents, teachers, and others working with deaf-blind children; and, training for teachers and related specialists in research and demonstration activities.

Teacher training for work with the handicapped was initially authorized under the National Defense Education Act of 1958 (P.L. 85-926) and expanded in 1963 under the Mental Retardation Facilities and Community Mental Health Centers Construction Act (P.L. 88-164), and in the 1965 and 1967 amendments to that Act. The Elementary and Secondary Education Act Amendments of 1967 (P.L. 90-247) expanded teacher training to include information and dissemination programs. The authorization for these activities was continued with little change in the Education of the Handicapped Amendments of 1977 (P.L. 95-49).

Similarly, special education research and demonstration projects were originally authorized under the National Defense Education Act of 1958 (P.L. 85-926), and extended and expanded under the Mental Retardation Facilities and Community Mental Health Centers Construction Act of 1963 (P.L. 88-164) and in its 1965 amendments. In 1967, the Elementary and Secondary Education Amendments (P.L. 90-247) added authority for intramural research and support for extramural research to private, as well as public, educational or research institutions or organizations. Research and demonstration projects specific to learning disabilities authorized in 1969 under the Elementary and Secondary Education Act (P.L. 91-230) were later incorporated into the Education of the Handicapped Act (P.L. 95-49).

Recent Amendments to the Education of the Handicapped Act

On December 2, 1983, P.L. 98-199 was signed to revise and extend the Education of the Handicapped Act, and for other purposes. The new amendments: set the yearly spending ceiling for the state grants program, a permanently authorized program; change the age range of children who may receive special education and related services to include birth to 3 year olds at the state's discretion; establish grant authority for projects to help handicapped youth make a successful transition from public school to adult life; establish a new grant authority to earmark 10% of the funds set aside for personnel development every year to be used for parent training projects; adjust regulatory requirements for implementing the Education for the Handicapped Act state grant program to extend the comment periods on any proposed changes in regulations and to prohibit the promulgation of any regulation which would *have the direct or indirect effect of weakening the protections of handicapped children under existing law and regulation.*

In addition, the law: increases the responsibility of the regional resource centers to improve dissemination of information to state agencies, professionals who work with disabled children, and families of handicapped children; reduces the direct service role of deaf-blind centers because of decreasing numbers of deaf-blind children; establishes the Office of Special Education Programs as an organizational unit of the Office of Special Education and Rehabilitative Services, Department of Education; reestablishes the National Advisory Committee on the Education of Handicapped Children and Youth; requires additional evaluation activities on the costs of special educational services and the transition of secondary youths out of the school system; allows the Secretary to bypass the state educational agencies in providing special educational services to handicapped children attending private schools; and, mandates a special study on children and youth with serious emotional problems.

Other federal laws with provisions for education of the disabled include: Library Services and Construction Act of 1957 (P.L. 84-597), as amended; Higher Education Act of 1965 (P.L. 89-329), as amended; Vocational Education Act of 1963 (P.L. 88-210), as amended; Department of Education Reorganization Act of 1979 (P.L. 96-88); Career Education Incentive Act of 1977 (P.L. 93-380 and P.L. 95-207); Impact Aid to Federally Affected Areas (1951) (P.L. 81-874 and P.L. 81-815) for school districts with high percentages of military dependents; and Education Amendments of 1974 (P.L. 93-380), as amended.

Maternal and Child Health and Crippled Children's Services

The Sheppard-Towner Act, first enacted in 1921 and also known as the Maternity and Infancy Act, was the forerunner of current maternal and child health programs. In 1935, provisions of the Sheppard-Towner Act were expanded and amended under Title V of the Social Security Act establishing the first federal–state system of crippled children's services, and a centrally administered special fund for demonstration projects and personnel training. In 1963, the program was further expanded to improve prenatal care to women from low-income families who were at greater risk of mental retardation and other birth defects; grants to states were increased; and, a research program was added to increase knowledge and improve service programs.

The 1965 amendments to the Social Security Act added special project grants for the development of comprehensive maternal and child health care services, a program for multidisciplinary training of specialists to work with retarded and handicapped children, and a project grant program to improve health and related services to preschool and school-aged children in low-income neighborhoods. Early intervention with children at greater risk of developing handicapping conditions was intended to help reduce the risk and lead to more productive lives for these children.

The 1967 Amendments to the Social Security Act consolidated maternal and child health and crippled children's services under a single grant authorization with allocations to be divided 50% for formula grants, 40% for project grants, and 10% for research and training. In subsequent amendments, the 40% for special projects was combined with the state's formula grant. Since 1974, 90% of the funds have been available to the states by this formula. State plans must include provisions for activities similar to those previously authorized. Research and training programs are administered by the Maternal and Child Health Division in the Department of Health and Human Services with the remaining 10% of the authorized funds.

Thus, the Maternal and Child Health Program authorized under Title V of the Social Security Act, as amended, provides for formula grants, special project grants, and research and training. Grants-in-aid are available to the states for maternal and child health services (Section 503) and crippled children's services (Section 504). State plans must provide for: cooperation among the maternal and child health, nursing, education, welfare, and vocational rehabilitation agencies and organizations; early identification of children in need of health services and follow-up care and treatment to reduce the effects of chronic conditions; and, programs designed to prevent mental retardation and other handicapping conditions originating at birth, with emphasis on mothers and children in low-income areas.

Support to states and institutions of higher learning is available for programs or projects to reduce infant mortality, and to improve the health of mothers and children; to reduce the incidence of mental retardation and other handicapping conditions resulting from perinatal complications; to promote the health and dentition of preschool and school-aged children; and, for special projects of regional or national significance to improve maternal and child health. Funds are also available to improve medical and related services to crippled children and children suffering from conditions that lead to crippling conditions; to locate crippled children and to provide medical, surgical, corrective, and other services, including diagnosis, hospitalization, and aftercare. Crippled children are defined to include those under 21 years of age who have an organic disease, defect, or condition which may hinder achievement of normal growth and development.

Research project support is available to advance the state-of-the-art in maternal and child health and in crippled children's services. Funds are also available to train personnel for health care and related services to mothers and children, particularly mentally retarded children and children with multiple handicaps. Support may be provided for faculty, traineeships, services, clinical facilities, and short-term workshops and institutes. The majority of the support for training-related activities has been provided to university-affiliated facilities for developmentally disabled children since this part of the program was authorized in 1965. The Developmental Disabilities Assistance and Bill of Rights Act will be discussed later.

Grants to States for Medical Assistance: Medicaid

Title XIX of the Social Security Act provides the statutory authority for the Medicaid program. First enacted under the Social Security Amendments of 1965, the program was intended to improve access to and the quality of medical care for low-income Americans. While specific reference to handicapped individuals is not found in the 1965 amendments, the program is a primary source of funding for services to severely disabled individuals because many are low-income. Also, specialized benefits for institutionalized mentally ill and mentally retarded persons were included in subsequent amendments to the Act.

Handicapped persons may be eligible for medical assistance based on financial need if they are categorically or medically needy. Under the categorically needy provisions, states must provide medical assistance for individuals receiving Aid to Families with Dependent Children (AFDC), i.e., those receiving cash benefits under Title IV-A of the Social Security Act; and, to those receiving Supplemental Security Income (SSI) under Title XVI of the Social Security Act, or those who meet more restrictive Medicaid-eligible conditions set by the particular state. In addition, states may elect to cover certain groups whose incomes are higher than SSI or AFDC maximums under the medically needy provisions. Participating states have broad flexibility in providing medical assistance. The federal share for reimbursement may vary from 50 to 78% based on a formula taking into account the state's relative per capita income.

Inpatient hospital services (except in mental hospitals and tuberculosis facilities), outpatient services, laboratory and x-ray services, skilled nursing facility and home health services for individuals over 21 years of age, physician services, early periodic screening, diagnosis and treatment (EPSDT) services for individuals under 21, family planning services, and certain rural health clinic services must be provided without charge for those who are categorically needy. However, states may limit the amount, duration, and scope of such mandated services so long as care is adequate. States are also required to assure that recipients can get to and from needed services, freedom of choice for recipients among qualified providers, and access to health services on a statewide basis.

Federal matching funds may also be approved for certain optional services specified in the state's plan, including: private duty nursing; clinic services; dental services; physical therapy, occupational therapy, and treatment for speech, hearing, and language disorders; prescribed drugs, dentures, prosthetic devices, and eyeglasses; other diagnostic, screening, and rehabilitation services; inpatient hospital services, and skilled nursing facility services; intermediate care facilities, including specialized services for the mentally retarded; inpatient psychiatric services for individuals over age 65 and under age 21; and, any other type of medical or remedial care recognized under state law and approved by the Secretary of Health and Human Services.

Other Relevant Legislation

Other relevant legislation in the area of health affecting the handicapped includes the following: The *Medicare program* established under the Social Security Amendments of 1965, although primarily intended to provide medical insurance coverage for those over 65 who are eligible for Social Security benefits, also provides for coverage for certain handicapped persons including children. The *Community Mental Health Centers Act of 1963,* as amended, is an important source of support for services to mentally ill children and adults. Inpatient and outpatient services, and consultation by other local agencies coming in contact with mentally ill persons may be covered, as well as, specialized mental health services for children. Eligibility is based on residence in the geographic area covered by the center which may be public or nonprofit entities authorized to charge fees for services based on the client's ability to pay. The *Public Health Services (PHS) Act of 1944* (P.L. 78-410), as amended, is a major, long-standing source of federal support for basic health care services. The control of communicable diseases that lead to disability, prevention of lead-based paint poisoning which can cause mental retardation, screening and counseling for genetic diseases that may result in disability at birth, hemophilia treatment centers, and physical fitness are among its provisions (under Title III) which affect handicapped children. Mental health research, training, statewide planning, and service provisions are also contained in Title III. *Title IV of the PHS Act* established several national research institutes in support of biomedical research activities relating to diagnosis, treatment, and prevention of various types of disabling conditions. *Titles XV and XVI of the PHS Act* established a national program to stimulate improved health planning and resource development. Its main goals are to improve the health of American citizens; and, to increase accessibility (including overcoming geographic, architectural, and transportation barriers), acceptability, continuity, and quality of health services. Meeting the special health and related services needs of handicapped children and adults are authorized. The *Military Benefits Act Amendments of 1966* (P.L. 89-614) expanded health care benefits for dependents of active-duty members of the uniformed services. Certain services for handicapped dependents of military personnel, spouse, and children, are covered under the Civilian Health and Medical Program of the Uniformed Services (CHAMPUS) program. The Program for the Handicapped may cover health- and education-related costs for: diagnosis; inpatient, outpatient, and home treatment; training rehabilitation and special education; and, institutional care in public and private nonprofit institutions and facilities, and related transportation when necessary. This program was established to help defray the high costs in meeting the special needs of mentally retarded and physically handicapped dependents. Active service members pay for services on a sliding scale based on grade. CHAMPUS does not pay benefits when local community or state public resources are available to the handicapped dependent.

Child Welfare Services

Title IV-B of the SSA defines the term child welfare services as: public social services which supplement, or substitute for, parental care and supervision for the purpose of (1) preventing or remedying, or assisting in the solution of problems which may result in the neglect, abuse, exploitation, or delinquency of children; (2) protecting and caring for homeless, dependent, or neglected children; (3) protecting and promoting the welfare of children of working mothers; and (4) otherwise protecting and promoting the welfare of children, including the strengthening of their own homes where possible or where needed or by providing adequate care of children away from their homes in foster family homes, day-care, or other child-care facilities.

Title IV-B authorizes a program of formula grants to designated state agencies for the provision of child welfare services. States receive allotments based on the relative number of children under the age of 21, compared to the United States total in this age group. Funds may be used for (a) referral or provision of special care of mentally and physically disabled children and assistance to children discharged from institutions; (b) licensing and setting standards for private child-care agencies and institutions; and (c) foster care, day-care, homemaker services, return of runaway children, and adoptive placements of children. States are required to develop a child welfare plan for the expenditure of funds that includes provisions for coordination with other programs and agencies providing health, educational, and related services to children. Funds are also allocated for research, demonstration, and training projects in child welfare. Grants for child welfare services have been awarded under the SSA since its inception in 1935. Amendments in 1972 (P.L. 92-603) authorized a major increase in federal funding aimed at expanding foster care and preventing the removal of children from their families, thus avoiding the need for foster care. The increased funds were also to be used by the states for adoption services, including activities to increase adoptions among hard-to-place children.

The Adoption Assistance and Child Welfare Act of 1980 (P.L. 96-272) revised the allotment base for Title IV-B grants as well as the specification for qualifying for federal support. The main aim of these amendments was to minimize the need for foster care placements. P.L. 96-272 also adds a new Title IV-E to the Act, authorizing federal support for adoption subsidies.

Social Services Program: Title XX of the SSA

Title XX authorizes formula grants to assist state social service agencies to support activities aimed at achieving the following goals on behalf of certain low-income, needy persons and recipients of public assistance: (a) achieving or maintaining economic self-support to prevent, reduce, or eliminate dependency; (b) achieving or maintaining self-sufficiency, including reduction or prevention of dependency; (c) preventing or remedying neglect, abuse, or exploitation of children and adults unable to protect their own interests, or preserving, rehabilitating, or reuniting families; (d) preventing or reducing inappropriate institutional care by providing for community-based care; or (e) securing referral or admission for institutional care when other forms of care are not appropriate or providing services to individuals in institutions. Social services directed at these goals may include: child care services, protective services for children and adults, services for children and adults in foster care, services related to the management and maintenance of the home services, and appropriate combinations of services designed to meet the special needs of children, the mentally retarded, the blind, the emotionally disturbed, and the physically handicapped. Funds are also available for training workers in these areas.

The Developmental Disabilities Assistance and Bill of Rights of 1975 (P.L. 94-103)

The Developmental Disabilities Act contains provisions for specialized services, their planning, coordination, and delivery to persons who are developmentally disabled including individuals with severe, chronic or physical impairment, which originated at birth or during childhood, is expected to continue indefinitely, and substantially restricts the person's functioning in several areas of major life activity. Dyslexic children and adults who also suffer from mental retardation, cerebral palsy, epilepsy, or autism are among those eligible for services. Under the Act, grants are available to states for planning and services, and separately for protection and advocacy systems. Grants are also available to University-Affiliated Facilities (UAF's), and to public and private nonprofit agencies for special projects.

To qualify for planning and services grants, states must establish a Developmental Disabilities (DD) Planning Council. The Council together with the state agency has responsibility for developing a state plan identifying gaps in services and areas for improvement in which the state will focus its attention. Priorities may include: case management services, child development services, alternative community living arrangement services, and employment-related services (added by the 1984 amendments). Activities may be supported to improve: the delivery of services, the development of model service programs, the delivery of institutional services, coordination, outreach, and provider training.

The 1984 amendments to the Act (P.L. 98-527) emphasize increased independence, productivity, and integration of developmentally disabled persons into the community; and, added "prevention" services to the list of specialized services which may be supported. Provision was made to add employment-related services as an admissible priority area under the state grant program. State Councils are mandated to provide employment-related services in Fiscal Year 1987, if appropriations equal or exceed $50.25 million. Required representation on the state DD Council was expanded to include state agencies administering the Rehabilitation Act, Education of the Handicapped Act, and Medicaid, the Protection and Advocacy System, and each UAF or satellite, if any, in the state. The DD Councils must also submit an annual report of their activities to the Department of Health and Human Services.

Protection and advocacy system grants are authorized to pursue legal, administrative, and other appropriate remedies to protect the rights of developmentally disabled persons, and to help assure that they receive appropriate care and treatment. New means for protecting developmentally disabled persons living in residential settings were authorized in the 1984 amendments. The protection and advocacy agency must be able to function as an autonomous unit, independent of any agency providing services to the developmentally disabled including the Developmental Disability Planning Council. A report is made to the Secretary of Health and Human Services by each of the protection and advocacy agencies.

The UAF supported under the Developmental Disabilities Act provide an opportunity to blend academic training and preparation with clinical practice for a mix of disciplines concerned with the developmentally disabled. Support may be provided for interdisciplinary training, demonstration projects to develop exemplary services, and for applied research to improve service delivery. Under the 1984 amendments, service-related training may also be provided to parents of developmentally disabled persons, and to professionals, volunteers or other service providers to increase or maintain the independence, productivity, and integration into the community of the developmentally disabled.

Special project grants to public and private nonprofit agencies may be made to improve public awareness, training, community involvement, and to otherwise advance the field of practice. Under the 1984 amendments, the Congress asked the Secretary of HHS for a report including recommendations for improving services to mentally retarded and developmentally disabled persons under Title XIX Medicaid.

CONCLUSION

This review of Federal legislation, although not exhaustive, suggests that there are firm statutory bases to protect all children from harm; to provide for the education for all children; to assure early, periodic, diagnosis, and treatment for the medically needy; to provide service for crippled children; and, to provide for the needs of the developmentally disabled and mentally retarded. Though none speaks directly to the subpopulation of children who are both handicapped and maltreated, or vulnerable to maltreatment, taken in combination existing federal legislation does demonstrate significant leadership in protecting these children.

Common to almost all of the legislation discussed are the repeated references to the states, reinforcing their role and responsibilities in providing for systems of service and administration at the state and local levels. The legislative requirements which must be met to qualify for federal support are typically satisfied at the states' option. Nevertheless, most states recognize the value of the standards inherent in the requirements and do meet the challenge. Most states do qualify for the available federal grants and reimbursements. In many instances, their expenditures for the programs discussed depend much more on general revenues raised through taxes and other means within the state than on federal funds.

Provisions of the various statutes also emphasize the importance of different disciplines and professional groups in addressing themselves to the problems of children in need of specialized services. Federal discretionary grants programs for research, demonstration, and training programs are available to advance the state-of-the-art and to improve the field of practice in child protection, education, health, and in dealing with the handicapped.

The willingness of the citizenry to support the many services needed by vulnerable populations, particularly children, is made evident in the increasing volunteerism, networking within communities, and other local efforts to make programs work. Federal grants often provide the impetus for creating greater public awareness and generating local support.

Some advocates may argue that a greater federal presence is needed to protect children who are both handicapped and abused because they are even more vulnerable than either group—a situation of double jeopardy. But, they will not be well served by adding to the magnitude and diversity of federal mandates; they will be better served by careful attention to existing legislation and how it can be interpreted and implemented—to ensure the protections that children deserve; to promote prenatal, maternal, and infant care to prevent handicapping conditions and the risk of abuse or neglect; to help assure that children reach their full potential through proper education, mainstreaming, and early development; and, to assure that children grow in warm, nurturing environments.

part **III**

INTERVENING TO PROTECT HANDICAPPED CHILDREN

chapter 7

THERAPEUTIC
ISSUES

Patricia M. Sullivan
John M. Scanlan

INTRODUCTION

The vulnerability of handicapped children to maltreatment necessitates a consideration of psychotherapeutic issues, methods, and techniques with this population. This chapter presents a rationale for the implementation of psychotherapeutic methods with maltreated handicapped children through a survey of current research on the effects of maltreatment on nonhandicapped individuals. Some preliminary data on handicapped children are also presented. General perspectives and therapeutic considerations in the provision of mental health services to maltreated handicapped children are described. Specific therapeutic methods and techniques are suggested, and barriers to therapy and therapeutic progress are discussed. Finally, current and future needs in the therapeutic domain with this population are presented.

A major problem confronting mental health professionals who work with maltreated handicapped children and youth is a paucity of available treatment programs with the clinical and staff competence to serve them. Longitudinal research on the effects of maltreatment and outcome studies on the efficacy of therapeutic methods are also lacking with the handicapped population. Given these intervention and research limitations, the practitioner must often rely upon what is available for nonhandicapped children and youth in the hopes that adequate treatment will result.

Although somewhat better, state-of-the-art clinical practice and research-based therapy programs with nonhandicapped children and youth are far from ideal. In 1981, only a handful of child maltreatment intervention programs for nonhandicapped children existed (Sgroi, 1982). These treatment facilities were quickly swamped with referrals, and a trend emerged wherein the demand for services quickly out-stripped available resources. Child maltreatment intervention is, ac-cordingly, an evolving field, and intervention methodologies based on prospective longitudinal data have yet to emerge. Within this zeitgeist, one can only convey perspectives on state-of-the-art clinical practice.

It is within these contexts that this chapter presents some treatment perspectives on therapeutic issues with maltreated handicapped chil-dren and youth. These perspectives, accordingly, have a clinical practice rather than a research base and are subject to all limitations inherent therein. They are based on the psychotherapy treatment plans and progress notes of 100 handicapped children and youth between the ages of 4 and 21 who received therapy services on a weekly basis from 6 months to 1½ years at the Center for Abused Handicapped Children.

As pilgrims in the field of child maltreatment intervention, until data-based efficacious therapeutic methods are developed and emerge, the mental health practitioner must make individual value judgments on the credibility and applicability of existing information and advice. In the words of the fourteenth-century pilgrim poet, Geoffrey Chaucer, we must "taketh the fruit and let the chaff be still."

RATIONALE FOR TREATMENT: CURRENT PERSPECTIVES ON LONG-TERM EFFECTS OF CHILD MALTREATMENT

Although there is wide consensus among professionals that child victims of maltreatment are at risk for future psychological maladjust-ment, there are few well-controlled empirical studies that have inves-tigated this issue (Lamphear, 1985). This makes it difficult to draw de-finitive conclusions on the effects of maltreatment on subsequent psychosocial development and the necessity for psychotherapeutic in-tervention. Methodological limitations include an absence of opera-tional definitions of child maltreatment which confound the multiple forms of abuse and neglect in data analyses and lack of matched control groups and longitudinal follow-up studies. However, recurrent patterns do emerge in these studies that can be interpreted tentatively until more conclusive research is undertaken.

Physical Abuse and Neglect

Physically abused children exhibit more behavior-management dif-ficulties than nonabused children (Egeland & Sroufe, 1981; Kent, 1976; Kinard, 1980). These behavioral difficulties include tantrums, aggression toward peers and adults, and noncompliance. They also manifest so-cialization difficulties with parents and peers (Reidy, 1977; Wolfe & Mosk, 1983; Mash, Johnston, & Kovitz, 1983; Perry, Doran, & Wells,

1983) and poor school adjustment and performance (Martin & Beezley, 1977; Calam, 1983). Retrospective studies with juvenile offenders and violent criminals suggest an association with antecedent physical abuse as children (Olweus, 1979). Physically neglected children also exhibit behavior-management difficulties including aggression and school and academic difficulties (Reidy, 1977; Aragona & Eyberg, 1981). The documented existence of social and behavioral problems within the physically abused and neglected child population supports the need for intervention.

Special Education Placement

Maltreated children are found more frequently in special education classes than nonabused controls (Christiansen, 1980). Type of maltreatment was related to type of educational placement in this study of 138 school-age children. Sexually abused children were placed more frequently in classes for the emotionally disturbed than in programs for the educable mentally retarded or learning disabled. Victims of neglect were found more often in classes for the educable mentally retarded. Physically abused children were found in all three types of placements but not significantly more so than other types of maltreated children. The frequency of maltreated children in specialized residential institutions was also found to be significantly higher than the incidence found in normal controls with over one-half of the maltreatment being sexual abuse. Although a history of child maltreatment plausibly may seem connected to special education and/or institutional placement, the Christiansen study (1980) demonstrated a correlational rather than a causational relationship between them. Also, it is unclear if these children were in special education placements before the maltreatment occurred or placed therein as a result of it.

Sexual Abuse

There has been debate over the existence of adverse effects of childhood sexual victimization. There is a body of opinion that too much emphasis has been placed on childhood sexual victimization as a causitive agent in subsequent psychological maladjustment (Storr, 1965; Yates, 1978). Proponents of this view maintain that a preoccupation with harm regarding manifestations of childhood sexuality neglects the positive elements of the normal expression of sexual behavior during psychosexual development (Pomeroy, 1974). Indeed, these writers argue that childhood sexuality should be encouraged and developed at a level appropriate to the child's chronological age and the dangers of sexual victimization downplayed (Constantine & Martinson, 1982; Pomeroy, 1974; Yates, 1978).

There is some, albeit equivocal, research evidence from adult retrospective studies to support the contention that childhood sexual victimization is not necessarily prognostic of adult sexual dysfunction and/or psychoneuroses. Gagnon (1965) examined data on 333 women from Kinsey's sample who had been sexually abused as children and found a 4–7% incidence rate of serious psychological disturbance. This was interpreted as a small percentage of "negative outcome." However, psychological difficulties are qualitative rather than quantitative, and any incidence rate is a matter of concern for mental health practitioners and patients. A small incidence rate in one sample does not minimize the existence of adverse effects of sexual victimization. In addition to the interpretation weakness, the Gagnon study did not include a control group of nonvictimized peers. Tsai, Feldman-Summers, and Edgar (1979) compared adult victims with a control group of nonvictims on a variety of retrospective objective outcome measures including Minnesota Multiphasic Personality Inventory (MMPI) scores, sexual responsiveness and satisfaction with sexual relations, and self-rated adjustment. There were no significant differences between the victim and nonvictim control group on these measures. Method selection for subject victims included media advertisements for individuals both interested and not interested in receiving therapy. Significant differences were found for the therapy seekers within the victim group and the nontherapy-seeking victims as well as controls. However, scores of the therapy-seeking victims were not of sufficient magnitude to reach significance between the entire victim and nonvictim groups. Nevertheless, it would appear that a portion of the victimized sample did present with long-term psychosexual difficulties. A major flaw in this study, however, is the possible existence of a skewed victim sample given subject selection procedures (Finkelhor, 1984).

A study involving the status-post assessment of child victims of sexual abuse was touted in the media (*Boston Globe*, Associated Press, May 6, 1985) as indicating that some sexually abused children and youth "escape emotional scars." This newspaper account of the Gomes-Schwartz, Horowitz, and Sauzier (1985, pp. 503–508) study stated: "some young victims of sexual abuse can suffer severe emotional problems but most of them seem to recover from these encounters without long-lasting scars," and "preschool children and teenagers seem best able to cope with sexual abuse, while pre-teen school children are more likely to be hampered by emotional difficulties".

The study in question assessed emotional distress in 112 sexually abused preschool, school-age, and adolescent children by having their parents complete the Louisville Behavior Checklist (LBC) (Miller, 1981). These parent ratings were compared to the LBC normative data for the general and psychiatrically disturbed populations on the checklist. Results indicated that preschool and school-age children exhibited more behavior problems than the normative population and fewer problems than the psychiatrically disturbed normative group. No data were reported for adolescents in comparison to the normal population, but data in comparison to the psychiatrically disturbed group suggested fewer problems. The authors concluded that recent preschool and school-age victims of sexual abuse manifest more behavioral/emotional problems than children in the general population, but these problems are not so severe as those seen in psychiatrically disturbed children.

These results from the original study are in contrast to those reported by the media, an unfortunate but all too common occurrence in today's society. The Gomes-Schwartz et al. (1985) study, however, is also subject to methodological criticism. The criterion measure for determining the presence or absence of psychological disturbance, the LBC, has major flaws in scale development and lacks adequate content and predictive validity (Gordon, 1985). Only a few of the diagnostic scales were derived from factor analysis, norms for the general population consisted of a sample from the Louisville, Kentucky area only, and the psychiatric "norms" were constructed on the basis of clinical judgment and thereby possess only face validity. Thus, the Gomes-Schwartz et al. data suggest that their victimized sample from the greater Boston area exhibited more behavioral difficulties than a general population group and fewer difficulties than a clinically generated list of emotional indicators by clinicians in the Louisville, Kentucky area. Accordingly, the criterion measure employed severely limits the generalizability of results.

These studies, which have been interpreted to indicate that childhood sexual victimization is not necessarily emotionally harmful, are, thus, on close analysis, subject to both methodological and interpretive flaws. This is unfortunate because they contribute to ambiguity in the professional literature, which often leads to ambiguity of social response (Summit & Kryso, 1978) to a pressing social problem.

Any professional involved in child maltreatment who spends a portion of his/her day providing intervention services knows that some children have long-term emotional and behavioral reactions to sexual victimization. There is a wealth of clinical experience in this regard and some empirical evidence to support these clinical observations.

Retrospective studies with adults with sexual dysfunction (McGuire & Wagner, 1978), prostitutes (Janus, Scanlon, & Prince, 1984), and drug abusers (Benward & Densen-Gerber, 1975) indicate that high proportions of these individuals were sexually victimized as children. In contrast to the Gagnon (1965) retrospective survey of adult women, Finkelhor (1979) found a 66% incidence rate of self-reported emotional distress attributed to the childhood sexual victimization. Retrospective studies with adolescent runaways (Nakashima, 1982) and juvenile offenders (Jones, Gruber, & Timbers, 1981) have also indicated significant amounts of prior sexual victimization. This research, however, is subject to the limitations inherent in retrospective studies: The effects found may be a function of other pathological elements.

In a study of the long-term effects of child sexual victimization, Finkelhor (1979) found that, as a group, victimized individuals have demonstrable long-term deficits, primarily related to sexual self-esteem, compared to nonvictimized controls. Clinical case studies in the psychiatric literature indicate an increase in the epidemiology of multiple personality in childhood with child sexual abuse being etiologically related to this hysterical dissociative psychoneurotic condition (Kluft, 1984; Wilbur, 1984). This research provides empirical support for the existence of long-term (Finkelhor, 1979) and status-post (Kluft, 1984; Wilbur, 1984) adverse emotional effects of childhood sexual victimization. The contribution of this research is the association of the effects to the abusive experience itself, rather than to other pathological elements. However, further well-controlled research is needed to address these issues.

Characteristics of Sexually Abused Handicapped Children

The research summarized thus far has been with nonhandicapped children and adults, with the exception of the Christiansen (1980) study. Our own preliminary results of a status-post and longitudinal follow-up study of 67 handicapped victims of childhood sexual abuse suggest the presence of immediate and measurable adverse psychological effects. All handicapped children and youth referred for therapy at the Center for Abused Handicapped Children routinely receive a behavioral assessment which includes the completion of the Child Behavior Checklist (CBC) (Achenbach, 1983) and, if hearing impaired, the Meadow Kendall Social Emotional Assessment Inventory for Deaf and Hearing-Impaired Students (Meadow, 1983). These forms are completed by the child's parents or houseparents, if residentially placed, and the problem behaviors indicated therein are verified by the child's counselor through clinical interviews with the child and significant others in his/her environment who have the opportunity to directly observe the behavior in question. The 67 children were all victims of sexual abuse by someone 18 years or older within the previous 18 months prior to evaluation. The age range was from 4 to 19 years. The sexual abuse was verified by police investigation and clinical interviews by therapists with anatomically correct dolls. The sample included 57 hearing impaired, 7 learning disabled, and 3 mentally retarded children. These handicapping conditions were verified through audiological and/ or psychological evaluations, as appropriate.

The CBC is one of the better assessments currently available to distinguish between children who have problems and those who do not (Freeman, 1985; Kelley, 1985). It is well standardized by age and sex on normal and psychiatrically referred children. Internalizing and externalizing descriptive scales permit the identification, based on factor analyses, of significantly elevated scores in the externalizing and internalizing behavioral domains. The Meadow–Kendall provides a measure of a child's social and emotional adjustment and self-image in comparison to hearing-impaired age mates. These two checklists were selected to investigate the existence, within the handicapped population, of the self-esteem, acting-out, and anxiety-related problems that have been reported in nonhandicapped samples. Results are given in Table 7.1.

Our preliminary data analyses support the hypotheses of Gomes-Schwartz et al. (1985) that sexually abused children are often emotionally harmed by the experience, and this harm is characterized by internalized anxieties or by externalized rage. A total of 39 of the children evaluated earned elevated scores (T ≥ 70) on the externalizing scale of the CBC. Some 28 earned significantly elevated scores on the internalizing scale. All children in the sample earned an elevated score on either

TABLE 7.1. Secondary Behavior Problems[a]

Behavior	N[b]
Externalizing	39
Internalizing	28
Overly compliant behavior	28
Poor peer relationships	47
Inappropriate sexual play with peers or toys	45
Lack of trust	67
Extraordinary fears	41
Seductive behavior/promiscuity	25
Low self-esteem	45
Clinical depression	23
Sleep disturbance	23
Running away from home	6
Regressive behavior	20
Suicidal ideation	23
Suicide attempts	2
Pregnancy	2
Substance abuse	22
Abuse of others	25
School-related problems	45
Multiple secondary problems	67
No secondary problems	0

Source: Sullivan, Scanlan, Brookhouser, and Andrew, in preparation.
[a]Age range is 4–19 years.
[b]Total of 67 handicapped victims of sexual abuse.

the internalizing or externalizing scale in comparison to the normal standardization population of the CBC. Youngsters with elevated externalizing scores exhibited poor peer relationships, seductive behavior and/or promiscuity, runaway reactions, substance abuse, and/or abuse of others. Some 25 of these youngsters sexually abused younger children. The two reported pregnancies were not the result of the initial sexual victimization but of subsequent sexual acting-out behavior. Children with elevated internalizing scores generally exhibited overly compliant behavior, extraordinary fears, clinical depression, regressive behavior, and/or suicidal ideation. Two adolescents attempted suicide. All children demonstrated an impaired ability to trust others, particularly adults. School-related problems were evident in some 45 of the youngsters, with this being manifested in school phobia and/or a decline in academic performance. Low self-esteem was documented in 45 of the hearing-impaired children by means of below average scores on the self-image scale of the Meadow–Kendall. All 67 youngsters were rated as exhibiting more than one behavior problem area to be addressed in their therapy. Subsequent psychiatric evaluation of the youngsters indicated acute posttraumatic stress disorders resulting from sexual victimization for all 67 children, and psychotherapy was prescribed.

These preliminary data are taken from standard intake procedures and an in-progress therapy efficacy study, with the CBC and Meadow–Kendall as criterion measures, comparing the pre- and postsexual abuse behavior of 31 hearing-impaired children who received therapy and 38 hearing-impaired children who did not receive therapy (Sullivan, Scanlan, Brookhouser, & Andrew, in preparation). They are reported here to support the need for psychotherapeutic intervention with sexually abused handicapped children. Children who present with measurable behavioral and/or emotional conflicts need psychological assistance in resolving them.

Conclusions

Finkelhor and Browne (1985) have hypothosized four traumagenic processes as a model to explain why specific psychological problems may develop as a result of childhood sexual abuse. These include: traumatic sexualization, betrayal, powerlessness, and stigmatization. The trauma surrounding the sexual abuse varies as a function of the child victim's understanding of sex and the seriousness of the abuse. Betrayal can result when the child is victimized by a trusted authority figure who failed to protect him/her and can lead to difficulties in interpersonal relationships. Powerlessness occurs when the child is unable to exert any locus of control, either internal or external, to stop the abuse, and this can be associated with subsequent reality testing and life-functioning difficulties. Stigmatization, which may or may not occur, results from the negative reactions of significant others in the child's environment to the abusive experience. The child may be blamed for reporting the abuse, removed from the home, and/or punished by family and peers. This can result in lowered self-esteem and internal and external acting-out behaviors. Although not yet empirically validated, Finkehor and Browne's model of the sexual abuse process makes intuitive "street sense" to therapists involved in the treatment of sexually abused children. In addition, it offers content goals to the process of the therapy itself.

Available evidence suggests that nonhandicapped victims of maltreatment are often emotionally harmed by the experience, and this harm can manifest itself in different patterns. However, some children appear to emerge from the experience without emotional or psychological consequences. There is considerable debate in the literature about the existence of psychological trauma, its long-term effects, and its relationship to the abusive occurrence. Preliminary data on handicapped victims of sexual abuse suggest that the children are emotionally traumatized and require therapeutic intervention. Clearly, further research is indicated to address these issues. In the interim, therapeutic intervention is justifiable given the documentation, through psychological and psychiatric evaluations, of emotional and/or behavioral difficulties that appear to result from or coexist with the maltreatment.

PERSPECTIVES AND GENERAL CONSIDERATIONS

Certain crucial considerations are fundamental to the provision of adequate psychotherapy services to maltreated handicapped children and youth. These include the issues of involuntary patients, authoritative intervention, ancillary patients, and the site of the therapy itself. Additional considerations are accessible facilities for handicapped patients and necessary characteristics of therapists.

Authoritative Intervention

The need for authoritative intervention in some cases of child maltreatment has been addressed and described by Sgroi (1982). This need is based on the premise that the dynamics of child maltreatment, particularly sexual abuse, involve issues of power and control over the child rather than aberrant expressions of sexuality and/or physical force. Power disorders require powerful intervention for successful resolution. Authoritative intervention entails a combined authoritative and supportive approach to patients in the therapy setting with the backing of statutory authorities to ensure that the patients come to therapy and cooperate in the process.

An additional dynamic in the treatment of maltreated handicapped children that is germane to the authoritative intervention issue is denial. The dynamics of denial are multifaceted and power-related. They involve the refusal of parents and/or significant others in the child's environment to admit that the maltreatment occurred, to recognize the need for therapeutic intervention to address the emotional issues engendered by the maltreatment, to cooperate in the child's therapy program, and to support the child throughout the course of therapy. The child, in effect, is punished for having reported the maltreatment and denied access to therapy by the power such adults exert over him/her. Authoritative intervention is necessary to obviate these impediments to therapy. The cooperation of legal authorities and high-level administrators in educational settings, where applicable, is necessary in such cases to insure that the child's rights to treatment are both protected and exercized.

Clearly, these power issues do not apply to all patients. Some children are willing participants in the therapy process and receive the support and cooperation from parents and significant others to enhance therapeutic progress. Indeed, such children tend to benefit the most from therapy, and the adverse effects of the abuse seem to be moderated (Fisher, 1985).

Involuntary Clients

The need for authoritative intervention often results in involuntary patients. Child maltreatment, particularly sexual abuse, has been described as the most denied and concealed issue facing our society (Summit & Kryso, 1978). Accordingly, adult and adolescent perpetrators do not react in a positive, grateful, or cooperative manner to the news that their victims have reported the maltreatment and that therapy is forthcoming. Nor do some parents and school or institutional personnel to the revelation that maltreatment occurred to their children or charges at the hands of others in settings where they had entrusted their children or are employed. The inevitable results are involuntary and/or ancillary patients.

Involuntary patients drafted for therapy by statutory authorities present particular problems to mental health therapists. This is because college/university training programs and internship/residency sites traditionally stress that involuntary patients are poor candidates for therapy, at best (Brammar & Shostrom, 1982; Enelow, 1977). Thus, therapists are unprepared both conceptually and practically to deal with involuntary patients. Rather, they are imbued with the therapeutic orthodoxy that patients must recognize the problem, decide assistance is needed and wanted, seek out and find a help source, and present themselves for therapy. In the therapy domain of child maltreatment, many patients do not fit the description. Providing services to involuntary patients does not constitute therapeutic heresy. In reality, a heterodoxy needs to be developed within the therapeutic field of child maltreatment wherein techniques for treating involuntary patients are implemented, tested, and accepted.

Some of these techniques have already been espoused and described (Sgroi, 1982) and were discussed in the authoritative intervention section. Other techniques that we have found to be of heuristic value in dealing with involuntary patients include the standard therapeutic practices of reassurance (Kelly, 1955; Brammar & Shostrum, 1982) and resistance strategies (Brammar & Shostrum, 1982).

Reassurance techniques are fundamental to the treatment of involuntary patients because, behind the facade of angry resistance, are frightened and desperate human beings in need of help. Many were victims of maltreatment themselves. We have encountered hearing-impaired students and/or graduates of residential facilities who were socialized to a dormitory system wherein harsh physical punishment and sexual exploitation of some children by a few pedophiles on staff were common place. Some of these individuals assumed such behavior was socially acceptable and were shocked when legal sanctions were imposed upon themselves or others. Social-learning theory techniques (Bandura, 1969) are imperative with these kinds of patients for inclusion in therapy treatment plans. Through didactic techniques, the therapist presents socialization concepts that reassure the patient by the provision of an opportunity to learn them. Other reassurance techniques that we have found successful include the following:

1. The ambience of the therapy setting itself tends to be reassuring. The standard characteristics that therapists are trained to exude (i.e., acceptance, attention, warmth, structured limits, and outward signs of friendship) have a powerful reassuring effect on involuntary patients (Brammar & Shostrom, 1982).

2. Most of us resent being criticized and told that our behavior is wrong. In the initial stages of therapy, patients must have some feeling of security about the ideas or feelings they are expressing. Clients need to feel free to express themselves and to be given the reassurance that they can change themselves and that the counseling will be an effective means of help in this endeavor (Brammar & Shostrom, 1982).

3. Prediction and postdiction of outcomes (Kelly, 1955) describes for the patient consequences of the therapy that he/she may expect or may be experiencing. Examples include moodiness, guilt, remorse, and

anger expressed both inwardly and outwardly. This technique is re-assuring to the patient because of its informative nature. The patient realizes that these feelings are part of the therapeutic process, and that this behavior is predictable and makes sense to the therapist.

4. Factual reassurance is beneficial to those patients who feel their problems are unique. This technique entails assuring the patient that other individuals have suffered the same fearful bewilderment, the problem has a solution, and the cause of the difficulty is known. The sharing of diagnostic and prognostic formulations is sometimes helpful, depending upon their particular relevance to individual patients (Brammar & Shostrom, 1982).

These reassurance methods are humanistic techniques that are helpful with anxious and frightened patients who exhibit a hostile and angry facade. However, they are not useful with overly aggressive and self-confident patients who exhibit egocentric behavior. Techniques for handling resistance are more heuristic with this type of patient:

1. The therapist may note but disregard the symptoms of the re-sistance (Brammar & Shostrom, 1982). The mere presence of mild man-ifestations of resistance does not imply that they must be addressed by the therapist. Indeed, they are a normal part of the process of therapy itself. However, their presence is noted, and, if exacerbation occurs, they are addressed by one or more of the following more direct tech-niques.

2. Minor adaptations is a collective term used by Brammar and Shostrum (1982) to describe several techniques that may be imple-mented by therapists. These include lessening the emotional impact of the subject by moving to intellectual aspects of the topic, employing the judicious use of humor, where appropriate, changing the pace of the counseling session itself, and incorporating reassurance techniques within these adaptations.

3. Direct manipulation techniques are useful with patients who ex-hibit both conscious and active resistance behavior (Brammar & Shos-trum, 1982). The therapist may interpret the resistance by providing a direct explanation of what the patient is doing to resist and/or reflect the patient's feelings about the resistance. These techniques provide an opportunity for an honest and open discussion of the patients thoughts and feelings about his/her involuntary participation in the therapy. In our experience, these techniques serve as a cathartic release mechanism and, often, are sufficient in resolving the issue. The therapist and patient address the reality of the necessity for the therapy: by court order, the therapist must provide and the patient must receive thera-

peutic intervention, and the obvious recourse is to proceed with the task at hand. However, the therapist must be sensitive to his/her own countertransference to the resistive behavior of the patient, resolve it, or if unable to do so, refer the patient to another therapist. The mere existence of authoritative intervention does not give the therapist license to treat involuntary patients when countertransference, personality conflicts, and clinical competence issues impede therapeutic progress.

4. Some involuntary patients require direct confrontation of the resistance (Brammar & Shostrum, 1982). In these instances, the therapist needs to directly state: "If you continue to behave (specifics defined) in this manner, you leave me no recourse but to report this to the court with the recommendation that your lack of cooperation makes the therapy a waste of our time." The mere possibility of the wrath of the court is often miraculous in causing attitude readjustments. In using this technique, care must be taken to ensure the conceptual separation of the patient from his/her behavior. That is, it is the patient's resistive behavior, not the patient him- or herself, that may cause the therapist to make a report to the court. The patient may change this behavior, and bridges are thereby left to facilitate therapeutic progress. This technique is to be used when others fail, and the therapist needs to be cognizant of the countertransference issues described under the direct manipulation techniques.

Ancillary Clients

A maltreated handicapped child often does not come to the therapeutic setting in isolation. This is because the maltreatment itself is not the exclusive property of the child or youth. A plethora of significant others in the child's interpersonal milieu may be involved, directly or indirectly, in either the maltreatment, the therapy, or both.

One or more family members may have perpetrated the maltreatment and are subsequently mandated to obtain therapy. To ensure consistency of therapeutic methods and enhance the benefits of family therapy, which is often indicated, these family members may be referred to the same therapist or therapeutic agency as the child-victim. Therapists must expect and prepare themselves to treat other family members involved in the maltreatment.

Family members who were not perpetrators of the maltreatment require consultation services from the child's therapist. These may include: explanations of the child's therapy treatment plan, periodic reports on the child's progress, suggestions/methods for dealing with the child in the home, and reassurance about a host of questions and concerns they may have. If the child is placed in foster care, these same consultation services apply.

Another contingent of ancillary patients includes teachers, dormitory counselors, principals, school administrators, and other professionals who become aware of the child's victimization and consequently develop concerns about how to interact or deal with the child in their respective settings. Often all that is required is the reassurance that what happened to the child is tragic, but the child him- or herself is not a tragedy. This reassurance serves to debunk the myths some individuals have that a "walking on eggshells" approach is needed with children who receive psychotherapy. It also serves to depathologize the maltreatment and sets the stage for cooperative efforts, if and as needed, with the child's treatment program. Examples include consultation on how to deal with the child in respective settings as well as how to handle secondary behavior manifestations, should they occur. Such cooperative efforts enhance therapeutic progress and let the child know that significant others both approve and support his/her therapy. Given the limits of confidentiality, these individuals should not have access to any written records of the child's therapy. This is because their confidential nature cannot be guaranteed.

Courts and all appropriate legal personnel responsible for the authoritative intervention need to receive timely therapy progress reports. The court is an ancillary patient because of its power to effect change in the child's life circumstances. Therapists need to provide courts with consultation services and recommendations for consideration regarding the welfare of their patients.

Site of Therapy

Two issues are germane in this regard: the site of therapy and characteristics of the therapeutic site.

The therapy itself should take place in a setting where the child feels safe and secure in discussing the maltreatment. Thus, it should not be rendered at the site of the maltreatment. This possibility becomes an issue when several children in a school or institution were maltreated within that setting. To provide the least amount of disruption to daily routine, administrative personnel may seek to provide therapy services on site. This is counterproductive to therapeutic progress. Victims of maltreatment are likely to develop posttraumatic stress disorders. The features of this diagnosis include: recurrent memories of the event, dreams and/or nightmares reexperiencing the event, and avoidance of activities or situations that arouse recollections of the traumatic event. Clearly, the provision of therapeutic services at the site of maltreatment elicits unnecessary and excessive anxiety within the victim. Similar issues emerge in incest cases where consideration is given to holding family therapy sessions within the home where the sexual victimization occurred. We have also found this practice to also be counterproductive to therapeutic progress.

The only time therapy services should be provided at the site of the victimization is during generalization training of self-protection techniques. This typically occurs late in the therapy process. Many handicapped children, after months in therapy, are capable of exhibiting self-protection skills only in the therapy setting. Generalization training assists them in comfortably demonstrating these techniques in a variety of settings. Generalization sessions held at the site of the victimization are helpful in teaching children how to protect themselves from future victimization. They also provide opportunities for the constructive release of anger at their victimization and enhance self-esteem.

Given the high probability of authoritative intervention and the subsequent involvement of statutory authorities, the credentials of the therapy site are likely to be highly scrutinized. The credibility of therapists may be questioned during testimony regarding child maltreatment.

It is therefore imperative that therapists possess the necessary licensure and certification appropriate to their respective professions. Supervision should be provided to the therapists in the form of regular supervisory sessions. This supervision is ideally provided by a psychiatrist and clinical psychologist as most states have statutes relegating the treatment of emotional/behavioral disorders to these professions or to professionals working under their direct supervision. Tending to these issues serves as a safeguard to protect child-victims through the judicial process by providing the support of therapists with proper credentials.

Accessible Facilities for Handicapped

An additional consideration that merits individual attention is that the therapy site must be accessible to handicapped children. Common sense dictates this, but in the real world common sense is sometimes not that common. Therapeutic agencies touted as accessible to handicapped patients may not be so in reality. Accessibility entails more than ramps and restroom facilities for the physically handicapped. Rather, it encompasses all facilities, staff, and materials within the therapeutic process.

The handicapped population does not comprise a homogeneous group. Many variables may impinge on the handicapped individuals physical and environmental life space which contribute to his/her basic human uniqueness and may necessitate specialized services. These include: type and degree of handicapping condition, parental acceptance of handicap, self-acceptance of handicap, early intervention techniques, residential versus mainstreamed educational placements, placement transitions and subsequent adjustment, parental and educational expectations (or lack thereof), and handicap-specific culture issues. Professionals serving the handicapped population are well-advised to conceptualize these patients as individuals with handicaps rather than as handicapped individuals. Providing service to one or two individuals with a specific handicap does not necessarily generalize to all individuals with the same handicap. The heterogeneous nature of the population necessitates a thorough understanding of the psychologies of specific handicapping conditions and the idiosyncratic interaction of numerous handicap-specific variables as prerequisites for appropriate treatment services.

Clearly, a broad background in special education is an importance qualification for therapists. A complete delineation of ideal accessible services by handicapped condition is beyond the scope of this chapter. However, we are providing below some minimal accessibility requirements for some specific handicaps.

Speech/Language Disorders. Impaired speech and language development is often a central feature of psychiatric disorders in childhood (Cantwell, Baker, & Mattison, 1979). Most child therapists are, therefore, familiar with the distinctions between speech and expressive and/or receptive language disorders and their respective therapeutic implications. Children with cleft lip and/or palate often have speech and/or language problems and are self-conscious about their physical appearance. Children with speech/language disorders require therapists with whom they feel comfortable in communicating. Correspondingly, the therapists must be able to understand the child's communication. The main task of accessibility is to make allowances for the child's expressive and/or receptive communication problems within the therapy (Beitchman, 1985). The consultation services of a speech/language pathologist are often invaluable in this regard.

Learning Disabilities. Children with learning disabilities are truly a "mixed bag" because of the many forms in which the disorder may manifest itself. In addition to specific learning problems in one or more academic subjects, these children often exhibit associated symptoms of distractibility, impulsivity, hyperactivity, and impaired social relationships. Consultation with the child's classroom teacher and/or learning disabilities resource-room teacher is helpful in making the therapy match the unique learning modes and styles of the child. In addition, the therapist needs to be cognizant of the child's tolerance levels, to control important variables (i.e., elements in the therapy room which lead to distraction, proximity to the therapist, and rate of presentation of materials), and to emphasize both the verbal and nonverbal components of the therapeutic process (Gearheart, 1980). These children often exhibit pronounced memory difficulties. Generalization training is helpful in reifying the self-protection concepts presented in therapy and in teaching the child to use them in a variety of settings.

Mental Retardation. Mentally retarded children require therapeutic procedures that are commensurate with their overall developmental status. Many of these children have speech and language difficulties, and appropriate communication modes must be employed with the child. Generalization training is imperative with the mentally retarded because many of these children can demonstrate concepts presented in therapy only in the therapeutic setting and remain highly vulnerable to further victimization. There are some excellent curricula available for the mentally retarded which outline therapeutic goals, methods, and techniques (O'Day, 1983; Seattle Rape Relief, 1979).

Visual Impairment. Because the visually impaired child cannot experience the therapy through seeing it expressed, therapists need to provide sound stimulation, touching, and body manipulation to present concepts. Adapted play therapy toys (i.e., audible balls), audible locators, real objects (called realia), models, and modeling are important therapeutic tools (Gearhart, 1980). Therapeutic curricula are also available for the visually impaired (O'Day, 1980; Seattle Rape Relief, 1979).

Physical Handicaps. This categorization refers to a conglomerate of children with many different types of impairment including neurological, orthopedic, cardiovascular, respiratory, and metabolic disabilities. The therapy needs to incorporate the use of prostheses, adapted furniture, and adapted play-therapy materials as required by the child's handicap (Gearhart, 1980). Communication boards and other augmentive communication devices are often needed with these children. Suggested adaptations for physically handicapped children are available in existing curricula for maltreated handicapped children (O'Day, 1980; Seattle Rape Relief, 1979).

Hearing Impairment. Therapy with hearing-impaired children must be undertaken in the child's mode of communication. This may include: oral only (speech and speechreading) or total communication (the simultaneous use of speech, sign language, and fingerspelling). Children may communicate in a variety of sign language systems, including American Sign Language (ASL) or one of the signed English systems. The use of an interpreter is not recommended because rapport is rarely established with the therapist. The child attends to the interpreter rather than the therapist, and this makes the therapeutic interaction awkward. In addition to sign language communication skills, the therapist needs to have some specific coursework and internship experience in the psychology of deafness. The O'Day (1980) and Seattle Rape Relief (1979) curricula also have adaptations for the hearing impaired.

Psychosis/Autism/Emotional Disturbances. Most child therapists have extensive training and clinical experience with this type of handicapped child. We have found that these children often exhibit concomitant cognitive, learning, and/or communication difficulties. Accordingly, adaptations appropriate for mentally retarded, learning-disabled, and communicatively handicapped children are often appropriate.

Multiple Handicaps. Therapists who work with handicapped children are aware that some children present with more than one handicapping condition. The result is not simply additive, but comprehensive, effecting the child's total behavior (i.e., cognition, affect, and actions). It is often difficult, if not impossible, to ferret out the child's primary handicapping condition. We have found that these children are best served on an individual basis with adaptations for a particular handicap applied or implemented on an as-needed basis.

CHARACTERISTICS OF THERAPISTS

There are three main ingredients that make a good therapist: aptitude, training, and experience (Wolman, 1983). These characteristics are necessary attributes for success in any profession. Aptitudes are innate talents that an individual brings to the training process, and these are embellished and enhanced through experience. Aptitude cannot be acquired like training and experience.

Researchers have addressed therapist variables in psychotherapy process and outcome studies. Extensive reviews of this literature indicate vague results because therapist variables (i.e., sex, social class, race, personality traits, training, and experience) are inevitably confounded with other therapist, patient, and treatment characteristics and/ or techniques (Parloff, Waskow, & Wolfe, 1978). Lists of characteristics thought to be essential for effective therapists have been generated (American Psychological Association, 1952; Cottle, 1953) but not empirically validated. Currently, the therapist variables that are therapeutically relevant remain obscure. Until these are definitively isolated and identified through well-controlled research, we can only relate our impressions from experience. Given this state of affairs, we offer the following necessary characteristics for therapists working with maltreated handicapped children.

A cardinal characteristic of therapists is that they must enjoy working with children, particularly handicapped children, and interact with them in an accepting and nonjudgmental manner. This is not a profession for individuals with the Annie Sullivan complex (Luterman, 1979), who view the children as tragedies and poor creatures to be helped. This characteristic is an aptitude and, in our opinion, cannot be acquired through training or experience. The individual must have a gift for and enjoy working with children.

Corollary characteristics are flexibility and creativity. Working with handicapped children can be stressful and doing so in a rigid and controlled manner only exacerbates the stress. Therapists need to be flexible in their interactions with handicapped children and make changes in therapy plans to meet the child's needs and not their own. Creativity is essential because therapy materials must often be developed or implemented in innovative ways. Prior special education experience, either in the form of coursework or teaching, is often invaluable in this regard.

Therapists who work with sexually abused children must be comfortable with their own sexuality as well as with both the technical and slang language of sexuality. They also must be nonjudgmental about the sexual feelings, behaviors, and attitudes of their patients. However, in treating perpetrators, they must be willing to confront patient denial of any adverse effects of their sexual misconduct.

In our opinion, child advocacy comes within therapeutic purview. Advocacy efforts need to take place in the home, school, community, courts, and political system. Therapists must be willing to assume this role.

In the general psychotherapy literature, the effect of therapist sex on outcome is unconfirmed, and the interactive roles of therapist versus patient sex have not been adequately tested (Parloff et al., 1978). We have found that female therapists are more successful in working with maltreated handicapped children than male therapists. The reasons for this are unclear, and this therapist effect needs to be empirically investigated. The fact that male perpetrators vastly outnumber females in retrospective studies (Pettis & Hughes, 1985) may be an explanation. Accordingly, children victimized by males find it anxiety-provoking to relate to a male in a therapeutic relationship, and this is counterproductive to therapeutic progress. The majority of children in our clinical sample were victimized by males.

Work with maltreated handicapped children is difficult because of the highly charged feelings aroused by such work. In addition, emotional gratification from and visible signs of progress in patients are often minimal and occur only after long-term intervention. Therapists often have anxieties about being physically harmed by angry parents or patients. An increased susceptibility to burn-out has been documented in professionals who work with hearing-impaired children (Meadow, 1981), and it likely applies to all handicapping conditions. Therapists need to be able to separate personal from professional responsibility with patients. Belief in a "life after work" is helpful in this regard, and it also reduces the risks of burn-out. Continuing support groups for therapists as well as supervisory sessions which allow the therapists to process their feelings about their patients are also helpful (Copans, Krell, Gundy, Rogan, & Field, 1979).

Finally, we have found that handicapped adults often make excellent therapists with maltreated handicapped children. They provide invaluable role models for the children and allow handicapped individuals some input and power in providing service to a population that is traditionally controlled by nonhandicapped individuals. We have had particular success with hearing-impaired therapists.

THERAPEUTIC METHODS

This section will discuss the processes involved in developing a treatment plan, specific therapeutic methods and techniques, and typical treatment goals for maltreated handicapped children.

Treatment Plan

The development of a treatment plan for a maltreated handicapped child is a process that encompasses a series of evaluations. A comprehensive clinical interview is undertaken with the child suspected of being the victim of maltreatment, utilizing the anatomically correct dolls, to ascertain the nature and extent of the maltreatment endured and to determine the need for therapy as a result of the maltreatment. More than one interview is often needed with a given child. We have found that several sets of anatomically correct dolls are often needed with handicapped children to ensure that all possible personages and settings that may have been involved in the maltreatment are presented to the child. Many handicapped children have difficulties manipulating the dolls symbolically and, therefore, require that they be presented in as concrete a manner as possible. For example, if the maltreatment occurred in a swimming pool, then swimming clothing is required for the dolls.

Multidisciplinary team evaluations are of assistance in providing a comprehensive analysis of a maltreated handicapped child's medical, psychiatric, psychological, and neurological status to determine the nature and extent of the maltreatment endured and concomitant medical and psychological disorders. They are also of assistance in developing a treatment plan to be carried out at the Center for Abused Handicapped Children or in the child's home community. The primary multidisciplinary team consists of a psychiatrist, pediatrician, psychologist, neurologist (if indicated), and a mental health counselor. If a physical examination is required, as is often the case in sexual abuse, it is helpful if the pediatrician is not the same sex as the alleged perpetrator. This assists in making the examination less anxiety provoking for the child for obvious reasons. A collective report is written that includes a history, description of the maltreatment endured, statements of current medical, psychiatric, psychological, and neurological status, and specific components of a treatment plan as indicated from these evaluations. An identified child may require additional speciality evaluations to meet his/her total treatment needs. These may include audiological, speech/language, academic, learning disabilities, and aural rehabilitation evaluations.

Intervention planning ensues on the basis of the results of these evaluations. The pediatrician makes any needed medical treatment recommendations. The bulk of the psychotherapy treatment plan results from the findings and recommendations of the psychiatrist, psychologist, and mental health counselor. The treatment plan requires ongoing parent or school liaison contacts to ensure that relative components are carried out in these settings. In addition, the treatment plan requires continuous monitoring for efficacy, effectiveness, and relevance of goals contained therein. We provide parents or appropriate personnel a copy of a child's treatment plan as well as formalized psychotherapy progress reports that are given approximately every 3 months. The psychotherapy treatment plan includes a relevant case history and background information section, specific counseling goals and objectives, treatment methods that are used with the child to meet the goals outlined within the report, and a prognostic statement about how long the child will need to remain in counseling. The psychotherapy progress report summarizes the child's progress to date in meeting the goals and objectives outlined in the treatment plan, treatment methods that were used in meeting those counseling goals, and specific recommendations that need to be made regarding the child's counseling.

Therapeutic Methods

The nature and principles of the therapeutic methods used with maltreated handicapped children do not differ from those employed with nonhandicapped youth. The implementation of these techniques does, however, differ. In essence, it involves a basic understanding by the mental health service provider of the handicap and its impact on the communication, social, emotional, and behavioral development of the individual. Implicit in this understanding are the assumptions that handicapped individuals have the same psychological needs as other people, and that the handicap itself does not invariably result in markedly different psychological dynamics.

Intervention methods which have heuristic value in the treatment of maltreated handicapped children and youth are common in clinical practice and will be described only briefly here.

Counseling/Psychotherapy

Counseling is a form of therapeutic aid that helps handicapped children and youth understand and resolve their adjustment difficulties. It includes the giving of advice and mutual discussion. Psychotherapy, in the most commonly used sense, means the psychological treatment of mental disorders. It represents a systematic attempt to help the handicapped youth achieve maturity, autonomy, responsibility, and skill in living. Psychotherapy takes many forms (i.e., analytical, behavioral, directive, patient-centered, implosive, interactional, nondirective, insight, Gestalt, rational, and interpersonal). Thus, it is based on diverse theoretical principles and assumptions. Counseling generally employs the same theoretical principles and assumptions. It differs from psychotherapy in relation to the problem exhibited by the handicapped youth (i.e., an adjustment difficulty versus a diagnosed mental disorder).

Mental health service providers typically have preferred counseling/ psychotherapy philosophies and methods. In general, counseling/psychotherapy is a valuable intervention technique to implement with maltreated handicapped children and youth. The therapeutic techniques employed depend upon the preference and skill of the therapist and needs of the child. The counseling/psychotherapy may take place on an individual, group, or family basis. Any or all of these methods may be used with a given maltreated handicapped child and his/her family. The counseling/psychotherapy may be therapeutic and didactic. It is therapeutic in the sense that the resulting social/emotional adjustment problems, mental disorders, and/or secondary behavioral characteristics are addressed in a therapeutic manner. It may also be used to teach handicapped youth empathy for the feelings of others, problem-solving skills, and affective/emotional concepts. Group counseling/psychotherapy is an efficacious treatment model with handicapped adolescents. The ideal group contains no more than 10 youths. Larger groups make it difficult for the handicapped youth to attend to the communication interaction among all participants. Parents, grandparents, and siblings may need assistance in dealing with a given maltreated handicapped youth or may play a contributing role in the problem itself. The family member(s) receive therapy services addressing the maltreatment perpetrated against the child. Family counseling/psychotherapy addresses the dynamics of the family as a unit as well as those manifested by individual family members. Both the identified child and family members typically receive individual and group counseling as a family unit.

Behavior Modification/Therapy

Behavior modification refers to any change in the structure or function of a given behavior through the application of behavior or learning-theory techniques. Behavior therapy is the class of methods used to shape and elicit adaptive behaviors and modify or extinguish maladaptive ones. These methods are based on experimentally established paradigms in learning theory including: classical and operant conditioning, reinforcement contingencies, avoidance learning, modelling and imitation, and behavioral contracting. The principles and techniques of behaviorism are particularly applicable and useful with handicapped children and youth who exhibit social, emotional, and/or behavioral difficulties secondary to the maltreatment. They may be used in isolation or in conjunction with individual and/or group counseling/psychotherapy.

Psychosituational Family/Classroom/Dormitory Intervention (PSI)

Psychosituational Intervention (PSI) is a technique that is efficacious in treating the secondary behavioral/emotional characteristics that maltreated handicapped children may exhibit as a direct result of the maltreatment. The procedure was developed for nonhandicapped youth to be used in the classroom, dormitory, or family situation (Bardon, Bennett, Bruchez, & Sanderson, 1976). The child is not removed from the classroom, dormitory, or family for private individual meeting but is helped to change his/her behavior in the place where the problem(s) occur. To accomplish this, the mental health therapist may use the gamut of intervention techniques. PSI does not limit the choice of intervention strategies but only refers to the site of the intervention. This technique has several advantages. It fosters realistic attitudes about the intervention technique by locating it in full view of others. It allows the mental health therapist to interact with teachers, dormitory counselors, and family members who are not usually involved with psychological services. The therapist can address and work on problems soon after they occur in the classroom, dormitory, or at home. Finally, PSI allows the therapist to work within the environment that may create and maintain the behavior problem.

Psychiatric Hospitalization

Psychiatric hospitalization, either short- or long-term, is sometimes required in the treatment of a maltreated handicapped child or youth, depending upon the severity and behavioral manifestations of the mental disorder that they may exhibit. Aggressive youth may require hospitalization to provide a structured environment and external behavioral control. Some youth may make suicidal gestures or attempts and require hospitalization. Medication may be appropriate for a particular child, and hospitalization provides the correct environment to monitor its effectiveness. The ideal psychiatric hospital setting for a handicapped youth is accessible to all handicapping conditions and staffed by mental health workers with training, sensitivity, and experience in dealing with a variety of different handicapping conditions. Unfortunately, this is not always available. We have treated a profoundly deaf adolescent who was hospitalized in a psychiatric facility for 8 months without benefit of an interpreter. In the absence of ideal services, networking with the hospital staff is essential if the handicapped child or youth is to benefit from the hospitalization. The mental health service provider who refers a handicapped youth for hospitalization should accompany the youth to the hospital and ascertain that the staff are aware of his/her special needs.

Consultation Services

Consultation services are a necessary ingredient of a given maltreated handicapped child's treatment plan. These services may need to be given to family members, school personnel, or other professionals directly involved with the child's care. The rationale for this consultation was discussed in the ancillary patient section. These consultation services deal primarily with an identified child's secondary emotional/behavioral characteristics which result from the maltreatment endured and may manifest themselves in the home, school, foster home, or a variety of other settings.

Networking (Naisbitt, 1984) is particularly germane to the treatment of maltreated handicapped children and youth. It is the sharing of ideas, information, and resources through communication between individuals. The key component of networking is the communication that creates linkages between people and clusters of people. Networks foster self-help, share resources, exchange information, and serve as catalysts to effect change. Communication networks between the mental health service provider and school and community personnel are essential to the success of any intervention technique employed with a maltreated handicapped child or youth. Community networking is particularly essential because it establishes communication linkages between the handicapped child or youth and significant agencies and organizations within the community. These agencies and organizations include the police, public defender's office, social service agencies, and probation officers. The mental health service provider may need to be in contact with any or all of these agencies/organizations during the course of treatment with a maltreated handicapped child or youth.

These community agencies may have limited experience with handicapped youth and require consultation and assistance to adequately deal with them.

Continuum of Intervention

These therapeutic methods are best implemented on a continuum of intervention with a given maltreated handicapped child. This is because of the possible long-term effects of the maltreatment and the fact that children need to be exposed to therapy and information that is developmentally appropriate. A child who endures prolonged sexual abuse at 4 and 5 years of age, for example, may require some type of intervention until he/she is an adolescent or young adult. In therapy, preschool children need to be taught self-protection concepts and how to inform others, should they be mistreated. They also need to be given labels for their emotions and feelings. When these youngsters attain adolescence, the complex issues of relationships, abusive behavior in general, values about coercive behavior, and issues about how the abusive experience effects the adolescent's personal sexuality need to be addressed. Just as the child's sexuality is developmental in nature so is the therapy and required intervention (Adams, 1986).

Therapeutic Techniques

The following therapeutic techniques are presented as guidelines to mental health providers who may work with a wide range of handicapping conditions. The techniques presented are by no means exhaustive and are intended to serve as suggestions for implementation with maltreated handicapped children.

Nondirective Counseling Techniques. These techniques entail the encouragement of an atmosphere of unconditional positive regard toward the child, thereby encouraging the child to express his/her thoughts and feelings in the counseling/psychotherapy sessions. This technique also encourages the child to develop insights into his/her difficulties and to make decisions based upon those insights. Insight techniques are generally limited to those handicapped youth with the sufficient affective vocabulary and language-reasoning skills to benefit from them. However, attempts should be made to assist handicapped youth with deficits in these areas to develop them.

Directive Counseling Techniques. This counseling approach entails providing the youth with options about how to make decisions and choices in their lives. It is more directive in nature and is required for those children and youth who do not have good decision-making skills.

In addition, we have found that therapists need to be a bit more directive in their therapy with handicapped children and youth than therapeutic orthodoxy generally prescribes. Some children will not discuss the mistreatment unless asked about it. However, the therapist must take steps to ensure that he/she does not direct all aspects of the therapy sessions.

Play Therapy. This is a nondirective psychotherapeutic technique in which the child is encouraged to express his thoughts and feelings during play. It is most beneficial with handicapped children who possess speech and language difficulties, visual impairments, hearing impairments, and mental retardation. We consider art therapy to be an adjunct to play therapy and have also found this to be most heuristic in allowing children with communication disorders to express their feelings. It is also beneficial in teaching children affective vocabulary concepts by having the children draw their feelings and then having the therapist apply labels to these emotions. Art therapy is particularly beneficial with sexually abused children (Kelley, 1984).

Didactic Counseling Techniques. These counseling techniques entail teaching the child specific things that relate to his/her individual therapy goals. Examples include concepts regarding human sexuality, interpersonal relationships, and affective vocabulary. We have found that therapy with handicapped children has many didactic components. These are particularly manifested in the instruction of self-protection skills.

Reality Therapy. This is an *in vivo* approach to therapy wherein the child is directly confronted with consequences of his/her behavior. This assists the child in making reality-based decisions for action, controlling impulses, anticipating consequences for behavior, and learning to accept the consequences of behavior. It is particularly useful with handicapped adolescent perpetrators.

Transactional Analysis. This is a therapeutic approach in which the child is taught basic interaction patterns in his/her life that include transactions between parents, adults, and children in all possible permutations of these interactions. This approach is useful in teaching the child about the various interaction patterns that he/she may possibly encounter in life.

Behavioral Contracting. This is a specific approach from behavior therapy that entails negotiating a contract between the child and his parents or the school to assist in eliminating inappropriate behavior.

Psychodrama and Roleplaying. We have found these techniques to be most useful with handicapped adolescents, particularly visually-impaired, hearing-impaired, language-disordered, and learning-disabled

youngsters. We have used this technique in group counseling/psycho-
therapy wherein the youth are asked to act out meaningful situations
in the presence of peers. This helps the youngster understand himself/
herself and to act spontaneously which facilitates self-understanding.
They are particularly useful in teaching self-protection techniques. We
have also used these techniques with adolescent perpetrators and had
the youngsters portray roles of both victim and victimizer. This is useful
in building empathy skills in perpetrators.

Pet Psychotherapy. The value of pets as therapy is now well recognized
in the medical profession, and the term "pet-facilitated psychotherapy"
is accepted. Pets are recommended as therapeutic agents for a variety
of medical conditions. We have found pets to be most therapeutic with
uncommunicative, physically abused, and sexually abused children.
These children will respond to a puppy or kitten, and the therapist can
work with the child either in the therapy setting or in the child's home.
Since many children are initially afraid of a clinician, a pet can serve
to help the child feel more relaxed. The child can play spontaneously
with the animal that is not associated in his/her mind with anxiety. When
a child plays with a dog, for example, desensitization occurs as the
child learns trust. Accompanied by the dog, the child can risk relating
to the therapist. Thus, the pet becomes an ally in the child's facing of
his difficulties, and a sense of adequacy, self-sufficiency, and self-confidence develops (Levinson, 1979).

Generalization Training. Therapists need to provide for follow-up and
generalization of concepts that are presented and discussed within the
therapy setting in in vivo situations. Handicapped children characteristically have difficulties generalizing concepts taught in a specific situation, such as the therapy setting, to appropriate settings outside the
therapy setting where these concepts are applicable. Generalization
training in specific situations helps to overcome this difficulty.

TREATMENT GOALS

The following are typical goals that we include in the psychotherapy
treatment plans for children seen at the Center for Abused Handicapped
Children.

1. *To alleviate guilt engendered by the maltreatment and to assist
the child in regaining the ability to trust peers and adults.* Much work
is spent with every child involved in therapy at the Center for Abused
Handicapped Children to emphasize to them that the maltreatment
they endured was not their fault. This goal also entails providing the

child with appropriate methods of preventing and/or avoiding future abusive situations, should they occur. This helps to restore the child's ability to trust peers and adults.

2. *To help treat the depression that is often manifested by children who have been maltreated.* A primary secondary behavioral characteristic of maltreated children is depression. The symptoms include sleep disturbance, difficulties in concentrating, loss of appetite or excessive eating, ruminations, and sometimes suicidal thoughts and gestures. If the child manifests depressive symptoms, these should then be addressed in the treatment plan.

3. *To help the children learn to express anger relating to the event that happened to them in appropriate and productive ways.* Victims of maltreatment generally express anger regarding this victimization at sometime in their therapy. Therefore, the therapy needs to teach the child how to express this anger in appropriate and productive ways rather than harboring it for years and leaving it unexpressed. Sometimes this anger is expressed toward men or women in general (depending upon the sex of the perpetrator) and can potentially interfere with healthy interpersonal relationships.

4. *To teach basic information about normal human sexuality and interpersonal relationships.* A major component of a therapy treatment plan is to provide, through didactic and directive counseling techniques, basic sex education concepts and knowledge about establishing and maintaining appropriate interpersonal relationships with peers, family members, teachers, and adults. This didactic technique is undertaken at a level appropriate to the chronological age of the child. It is an integral part of the therapy program because, often, parents and caretakers consider handicapped individuals to be asexual and, accordingly, neglect this aspect of the handicapped child's development.

5. *To teach the children sexual preference and homosexual issues, as appropriate.* Many adolescents who experience sexual abuse by adults or older peers of the same sex exhibit sexual identity problems regarding their sexual preference. Didactic counseling techniques are useful to teach these adolescents the meanings of the terms heterosexuality, homosexuality, and bisexuality. We have found that these adolescents often have many misconceptions about the various sexual preferences.

6. *To teach maltreatment issues, as appropriate.* The major thrust of this goal is to teach the children, at a level appropriate to their developmental status, information about the meanings of physical, sexual abuse and incest, where appropriate. This goal assists the children in understanding what happened to them and helps alleviate the guilt

and "damaged goods" syndrome that is often associated with victimization.

7. *To teach the child self-protection techniques.* This goal entails teaching the children how to recognize and exhibit their own personal strengths and powers, how to identify potentially dangerous situations and respond assertively, how to exhibit assertive body language and the mechanics of saying "NO," and how to demonstrate effective communication skills when seeking help. Children are taught specifics about maltreatment laws and appropriate people to report such maltreatment to, including parents, school officials, police officials, and social service workers. These self-protection techniques are from the Kidability Program, developed by Girls Club of Omaha, and have been adapted for handicapped populations (Sullivan, 1985).

8. *The development of an affective vocabulary to label emotions and feelings.* Before emotions can be appropriately expressed, the child must have the language to do so. We have found that most handicapped children have a limited affective vocabulary and often have an emotional label repertoire limited to: happy, sad, mad, and bored. Therefore, each child's treatment program needs to include the teaching of various language concepts for emotions. The children are encouraged to express their emotions and are given language labels for these emotions. The "feelings box" technique is helpful wherein the children are encouraged to express emotions and collect a label signifying these emotions in their "feeling box." Degrees of emotion may also be taught by giving the children a "feeling line" wherein the children can assign a degree of intensity to a given emotion on this quantitative visual aid.

9. *The attainment of emotional independence.* This goal entails assisting the child in learning how to recognize and express his/her emotions, accept the consequences of the expression of these emotions, and thereby, to develop independence from external individuals for permission and validation for the expression of emotions. Included in this goal is teaching the children to understand their own personal strengths and powers and how to employ a decision-making model to assist them in analyzing a situation, determine appropriate emotional responses to this situation, and make an appropriate choice about the emotion to display.

10. *Assistance in the establishment of a meaningful and stable identity.* This goal entails engendering within the child a positive self-concept and feeling of self-worth. Characteristically, children who have been the victims of maltreatment have low self-concepts. Part of each therapy session with each child is spent in enhancing their self-concepts.

11. *Development of a personal value system*. This goal entails teaching the child appropriate and inappropriate social behavior, as well as the ability to make value judgments about their own behavior and the behavior of others in the world around them. Some children who are victims of maltreatment also victimize other children. When therapy begins, these youngsters typically have little or no understanding about maltreatment and why it is inappropriate. These youngsters, who became offenders as a result of being victimized themselves, need to understand the difference between an abusive and a nonabusive situation. Directive, didactic, and nondirective as well as insight-counseling techniques are used with the children to assist them in meeting this goal.

12. *The development of a capacity for lasting relationships and for both tender and genital love*. This goal entails teaching the children, at a level appropriate to their developmental status, how to make friends, maintain friendships, establish dating relationships, terminate dating relationships, choose whether or not to engage in sexual activity with another individual, and choose a marriage partner. It is generally used with adolescent children, but some of these concepts may be taught at a rudimentary level to younger children.

13. *Treatment of secondary behavioral characteristics*. Many children who have been the victims of maltreatment exhibit secondary behavioral or emotional characteristics as a direct result of the maltreatment. Indeed, these secondary behavioral or emotional characteristics are often the original reason for referral to mental health service providers. These secondary behaviors have been well documented in the literature and were discussed in the rationale for treatment section of this chapter. Examples of these behaviors include: depression, suicidal ideation, suicidal gestures, aggressive acting-out behavior, poor peer relationships, school phobia, regressive behaviors, enuresis and/or encopresis, promiscuous acting-out behaviors, inability to emphathize, negative attention-seeking behaviors, and chemical dependency. These difficulties also need to be addressed in a given child's treatment plan.

IMPEDIMENTS TO THERAPY

Thus far, we have presented a rationale for the provision of psychotherapy services to maltreated handicapped children and youth and have described necessary considerations and components of the therapy. Unfortunately, these positive factors are not sufficient to ensure that a maltreated child will receive treatment services. There are impediments to therapy that must be considered.

The primary impediment to therapeutic services that we have encountered is denial. The dynamics of denial are multifaceted and all too familiar to mental health service providers in the field of child maltreatment. If the maltreatment itself is denied by parents and/or caregivers, then therapy becomes superfluous and an unwelcome reminder that the child or someone else reported the maltreatment. Both perpetrators and nonperpetrators can participate in the denial process. With perpetrators, the self-protective defense mechanism of denial is predictable. Nonperpetrators, which may encompass a plethora of significant others in the child's environment, exhibit denial because they are unable to accept the reality that they sent their child to an unsafe place or are affiliated in some way with an institution, agency, or family unit where maltreatment occurred (Summit, 1985). This denial can be exacerbated if charges are not filed or are dropped against alleged perpetrators. The need for treatment often still exists, even if insufficient evidence was available to allow the courts to intervene. Lack of court intervention is interpreted to indicate that maltreatment never occurred, and this is not necessarily the case. Other barriers to treatment provision identified in the literature that reinforce denial are lack of evidence or jurisdiction for courts to intervene and court action that did not support treatment recommendations (Meddin and Hansen, 1985). These denial obstacles are difficult to overcome. When forthcoming, authoritative intervention is an antidote to denial. When not forthcoming because overwhelming evidence is needed for nonvoluntary service provision, children are sadly denied access to treatment services.

Media issues can reinforce denial and inadvertently play a contributing role in barring children from treatment. Cases of child maltreatment are typically widely publicized, particularly when they occur in institutions. Victims and nonvictims suffer the ignominy of publicized guilt by association, triggering the dynamics of denial. Victims as well as individuals who reported the maltreatment (Durkin, 1982) may be ostracized. We have encountered situations where nonvictimized peers shunned and teased victims for being disloyal to the school by reporting their victimization. Further, social service personnel sent to the school periodically to monitor and audit the safety of victims often meet with resistive patients because they can no longer endure peer and staff pressure. Institutional maltreatment of children is a sad fact in our society (Gil, 1982), but all individuals associated with institutions are neither involved nor to blame for the maltreatment. In a free society, the media has both a charge and a duty to report the disease. It can play a role in the cure by responsible reporting, which places the maltreatment in its appropriate context so that victims are not subjected to the emotional fall-out that inevitably follows media exposes. The media can and should play a role in dealing with social problems, but it must sensitize not sensationalize (Wilkinson, 1980).

Family and institutional insularity are additional barriers to treatment. Families typically react with alarm to reports of maltreatment within their constellation. When forced to receive therapy, any or all members may exert passive–aggressive sabotage to thwart its effects. There is a high degree of insularity within institutions. Resistance to outside intervention and change is endemic in most institutions. This is manifested in tendencies to rely on professionals within their own immediate institution for intervention services. This is counterproductive to therapeutic progress for the victim because the professional's real patient is the institution, often for economic and political reasons, rather than the victim. We have found authoritative intervention and the consultation and networking techniques discussed earlier to be effective antidotes with these issues.

Poor cooperation between agencies is another impediment to therapy. Agencies do not readily cooperate with one another, and the children they purport to serve are further victimized (Silverberg & Silverberg, 1982; Thomas, 1982). Networking, consultation, and cooperative efforts between agencies are essential, if the child is to benefit from intervention.

Unfortunately, treatment programs can only be expected to assist a small percentage of victims (Finkelhor, 1984b). This is because most children do not reveal the maltreatment, and, when it is revealed, families are unlikely to seek help (Finkelhor, 1984a). Indeed, this reality is the rationale and logic for the need for prevention programs. Due to the cyclical nature of maltreatment, prevention and treatment efforts need to be colloborative to address this pressing social problem. As prevention and awareness efforts become more widespread and successful, more children and their families should report maltreatment and seek out therapeutic services.

CONCLUSIONS/NEEDS

Mental health professionals are faced with a high incidence of maltreatment among handicapped children and youth and a subsequent need for therapeutic intervention services. These youngsters require mental health service providers with clinical competence and training in psychology of handicapping conditions.

In order to meet the need for therapeutic services, more accessible treatment programs for handicapped children and youth need to be developed. University specialty programs are also needed to provide the necessary coursework, practicum, and internship training experience to ensure the clinical competence of mental health service providers treating the handicapped population. Ideally, national and state certifications in treating handicapped patients should be developed.

Criteria for preferred psychological services to the hearing-impaired have been proposed (Turkington, 1982). We suggest similar standards for counselors and therapists providing services to handicapped patients. The following levels from most to least preferred are proposed:

Level I: Graduate level coursework and an internship with emphasis in or that includes the psychology of handicapping conditions and supervised therapy with maltreated handicapped children and youth

Level II: No specific coursework or internship in the psychology of handicaps but acquired on-the-job training and experience

Level III: No specific coursework, internship, or acquired on-the-job training and experience with handicapped patients

Consumers of mental health services for handicapped individuals have a right to be informed of the competence and skill level of the providers. As more treatment programs for maltreated handicapped children and youth appear, the necessity for standards for service providers, certification, and possibly licensure will become more apparent.

Therapists working with maltreated handicapped children and youth need to be both scientists and healers. As scientists, they need to either engage in or encourage longitudinal research on the effects of and efficacy studies on treatment methods and techniques with maltreated handicapped children and youth. Until this needed research is forthcoming, the therapist's primary role is that of a healer. In the words of Edna St. Vincent Millay, in her poem about a little child lost in hell, they must:

> Be to her, Persephone,
> All the things she might not be.
> Take her head upon your knee
> Say to her, my dear, my dear
> It is not so dreadful here.

chapter 8

MEDICAL ISSUES

Patrick E. Brookhouser

INTRODUCTION

During the decades following Kempe, Silverman, Steele, Droegemueller & Silver's (1962) seminal contribution to society's awareness of the plight of the "battered" child, health professionals have increasingly recognized their potential for detecting and preventing many forms of child abuse and neglect. Abuse and neglect of handicapped children involve a class of victims with whom physicians and other health professionals are quite likely to have direct contact in the course of providing care and treatment related to their handicapping conditions. This chapter will explore relevant aspects of the present system for delivery of health services to handicapped children and their families, as well as present specific strategies for detecting, documenting, and preventing maltreatment of these particularly vulnerable youngsters.

THE HANDICAPPED CHILD AND FAMILIAL STRESS

The birth of a child with a serious defect or disability is a painful event for parents, siblings, and others related to the family. The family's hope for a "perfect child" must give way to an acceptance of the child's limitations, need for specialized evaluative and habilitative services, and potential for chronic dependency upon the parents, even into adulthood. Normal parents may be overwhelmed by the demands of caring for a handicapped child who, in return, may provide little parental satisfaction by achieving normal communicative and developmental progress. The disabled child's presence often restricts interaction within the family, as well as with other relatives and friends. The mother, who is less likely to leave the house daily in pursuit of a career, may feel this isolation more acutely than the father. Such everyday tasks as finding an appropriate babysitter to afford a respite for the parents from their caretaking responsibilities may prove to be nearly impossible.

Medical costs associated with the child's care may pose a serious threat to the family's financial security and serve as a source of discord among other family members who feel their own basic needs are being subordinated to those of the disabled child. In some instances, institutional placement of the child for educational or vocational services is judged to be necessary, fostering separation anxiety and fear, often well-founded, for the child's safety while away from home. Parental feelings about the child may become colored by anger, denial, and guilt which characterize the normal "grieving" process experienced by parents of severely handicapped children. According to Wikler, Wasow, and Hatfield (1981), chronic sorrow rather than gradual adjustment to the child's disabilities typify the experience of parents of retarded children. In their sample, parental sorrow tended to recur with a periodicity related to the developmental stage through which the child was passing. Ten critical periods were identified as potentially stressful for families of mentally retarded children. Five of these parenting experiences are related to normal developmental milestones that serve to focus parental disappointment on the handicapped child's failure to achieve these benchmark behaviors on schedule (see Table 8.1). The other five events are unique to families with handicapped children and revolve around increased, but often unrewarding, caretaking demands, as well as placement issues (see Table 8.2).

Most studies have focused on families with children who have severe disabilities (e.g., spina bifida or mental retardation) rather than less severe but long-term handicapping conditions such as communication disorders or cerebral palsy. Holroyd and McArthur (1976) postulated that it may be easier for a family to adjust when the developmental course of the child is known (e.g., Down's Syndrome) than it is when the child's rate of progress and ultimate outcome are unclear (e.g., very low-birth weight infant). Willner and Crane's (1979) findings reinforce the impression that parents of children with marginal handicaps, such as a learning disability, have a more difficult time coming to terms with their children's handicap than do parents of children with a clearly

TABLE 8.1. Five Parenting Events Related to Normal Developmental Milestones

Stress-trigger: Parental expectations versus child's actual achievement
Walking
Talking
Beginning of school
Onset of puberty
Twenty-first birthday: The symbol of independence

TABLE 8.2. Five Other Parenting Events Unique to Families of Handicapped
Children

Diagnosis of disability (e.g., mental retardation)
Younger normal sibling matches or exceeds the developmental achievements
of the affected child
Discussion of residential or school placement
Stressful behavior by the child (e.g., seizure disorder or other health problems)
Discussion about guardianship and care

defined defect. While the parents of a retarded child may be described
as suffering from chronic sorrow, the parents of a marginally handicapped child may be said to experience chronic disappointment. These
marginally affected children often appear competent to perform effectively in the educational and social mainstream, but their specific
disabilities can lead to repeated failure and frustration, coupled with
parental disappointment.

Gliedman and Roth (1980) observe that "our society seems to lack
anything like a tradition for raising reasonably happy, reasonably self-
fulfilling handicapped children." Few parents have had the personal
experience of being handicapped, and in the absence of a cultural tradition relating to the successful rearing of a handicapped child, they
may despair of ever being free of their on-going burdens and caretaking
responsibilities. Weber and Parker (1981) identified variables felt to have
the greatest positive impact on the successful adjustment of families
with a disabled child, including:

- Early parental awareness, knowledge, and understanding of their
  child's condition
- Support from parent groups, extended family, and friends
- Having more than one child
- Economic security
- Accessibility to appropriate ongoing professional services for the child
- Personal faith and religion

HEALTH CARE SERVICES FOR HANDICAPPED CHILDREN—
A MULTILEVEL ARRAY

Before discussing medical issues involved in identification and treatment of abused handicapped children, it is necessary to explore the
typical interfaces existing between the child/family constellation and
the health care delivery system. Primary health care professionals, involved in routine modes of service delivery, play a critical role in de-

tecting the presence of a handicapping condition and referring the child and family for definitive evaluation and management. Delays in identification and referral, resulting from an insensitivity of health providers to the subtle signs and symptoms of disability, constitute a serious, although often unrecognized, form of child neglect inherent in the present health care delivery system.

"Well-child health maintenance" begins with appropriate prenatal and postnatal care, following which the developing child's well-being is safeguarded by the parents (particularly the mother) working in conjunction with a primary care physician. The primary physician (e.g., pediatrician or family practitioner) assumes responsibility for a continuum of well-child care, consisting of periodic monitoring of the child's nutritional status, growth, and development, together with preventive intervention (e.g., immunizations against childhood diseases) and early detection of serious disease (e.g., tuberculosis testing). This care model is geared to the normally developing child, and deviations from the norm, such as delays in growth, walking, or talking, are usually managed by referral for appropriate medical specialty evaluation. Parental history is often an important initial indicator of the child's disability, yet concerned parents are often told to "wait awhile and he'll grow out of it." The epithet "overly anxious mother," often heard in primary health care settings, reflects the health provider's unconscious bias toward expectation of a normal developmental outcome and is symptomatic of attitudes requiring modification before truly effective early identification programs can be implemented. As the child proceeds through normal developmental phases, well-child care may take the form of school/athletic physical examinations or care related to specific issues, such as gynecologic and dermatologic problems encountered during puberty.

A second category of children's health services includes "episodic care" for acute illness or injury, ranging in severity from minor childhood illnesses/lacerations to such severe, potentially life-threatening disorders as meningitis and major trauma to the long bones and skull. In addition to the primary physician, other medical/surgical specialists, including emergency room physicians, orthopedic surgeons, neurosurgeons, otolaryngologists, etc., may be involved in providing episodic care and treatment to the child. The goal of these services, which may include inpatient hospitalization, is resolution of the episodic disorder, without permanent sequelae, thus permitting return of the child to the primary health maintenance track.

In most instances, families of handicapped children must avail themselves of still another category of care and treatment which might be called "Comprehensive Disability–Specific Health Services." Beginning with diagnosis of the disorder, shortly after birth, for disabilities such as Down's Syndrome and cleft lip/palate, the primary care physician may refer the child and family for specialized evaluation and habilitation program planning. Typically, these services are provided in large medical centers, often at some distance from the child's home community, and many necessary services may not be covered by a standard health insurance policy.

Table 8.3 illustrates the diversity of services that may be required for a newly identified hearing-impaired child. Some of these evaluations must be repeated on an annual basis to assess the child's developmental and educational progress, as well as to prepare an individualized educational plan.

The family's burden of travel to a distant medical facility and requirement for out-of-pocket payment for services may be compounded by the necessity of interacting with multiple specialists who express divergent opinions concerning the child's disability and prognosis. The primary physician, who commonly serves as a supportive resource for the family during episodic illnesses or injuries, may feel incompetent to express an informed opinion about handicap-specific issues raised during the comprehensive evaluation of a disabled child. As a result, the family may feel alone and confused as they attempt to sort out recommended treatment plans and educational options for their child. To help remedy this shortcoming of the health care system, institutions such as Boys Town National Institute have developed multidisciplinary evaluation teams who participate in organized "feedback" sessions with the family to discuss evaluation results and provide well-integrated an-

TABLE 8.3. Boys Town National Institute for Communication Disorders in Children: Hearing-Impaired Indepth Assessment

ENT examination
Pediatric examination
Ophthalmologic examination
Comprehensive audiologic assessment
Neurologic assessment
Genetic evaluation
Vestibular assessment
Electrophysiologic assessment
Amplification needs assessment
Central auditory assessment
Communication skills assessment
Parent/infant habilitation
Mental abilities assessment
Behavior and social adjustment assessment
Academic achievement and learning skills assessment
Physical therapy assessment
Parent/teacher counseling
Individual educational plan
Consultation services, as required

swers to questions. One of the professionals on the team is designated as the child/family advocate or contact person with whom the family becomes familiar and to whom they can turn with any problems or additional questions.

Finally, the handicapped child in a residential institution will receive health services organized around a fourth model—"Residential Health Services." Because significant geographic distance often separates the child's home from the institution, the institutionalized child's parents and primary care physician necessarily assume a subordinate role in his/her health maintenance. The benefits afforded by continuity of parental observation and care are forfeited as the child's management is transferred to another group of health care providers, ranging from school nurses and contract physicians to emergency room physicians, in some instances. The focus of health services in residential institutions is typically episodic care for acute illness or injury (e.g., "sick call") rather than a comprehensive health maintenance program. This episodic care model significantly reduces the likelihood of detecting subtle changes in the child's behavior or physical complaints which could be indicators of maltreatment, particularly sexual abuse. An additional impediment to the detection of abuse in a residential institution may be posed by "Company Doc" behavior whereby a school nurse or contract physician assumes an advocacy role for the employer (i.e., the institution) rather than the young patient. This confusion of roles further reduces the probability of prompt recognition and reporting of signs and symptoms of child maltreatment, particularly if institutional personnel may be involved as perpetrators.

ABUSE AND THE DISABLED CHILD: AN OVERVIEW

Solomons (1979) stresses that low-birth weight infants and handicapped children are at special risk for child abuse because their care is particularly stressful—physically, emotionally, and financially—for the parents. Only 10% of newborns have low birth weights, but these children comprise approximately 20–25% of the physically abused population. Impaired maternal–infant bonding may occur with these children because the infant is perceived as less responsive to the mother as a result of immaturity, birth trauma, and/or separation from the mother during the infant's stay in a neonatal intensive care unit. Other studies by Gil (1970), Chotiner and Lehr (1976), and the Denver Department of Welfare (Johnson & Morse, 1968) reveal a 30–70% incidence of preexisting handicaps and developmental disabilities among victimized and exploited children. Apart from preexisting handicaps, deafness, mental retardation, blindness, and other handicapping conditions can also result from abusive treatment, putting the child in what Solomons refers to as "double jeopardy."

Estimates of the incidence of child sexual abuse range widely from 45,000 to nearly 500,000 victims per year, with 10% of all boys and 25% of all girls expected to experience some form of sexual abuse prior to age 18. Data from the *FBI Law Enforcement Bulletin* (Barry, 1984a) indicates that as many as 60,000–100,000 female children are sexually abused annually, while only 20% of these crimes are reported. A survey by the National Committee for the Prevention of Child Abuse (Crewdson, 1985) determined that a total of 123,000 reports of child sexual abuse were made in 1984, up 37% from 90,000 in 1983. Not all states include sexual abuse under the child abuse statutes but may lump statistics together with those for rape, for example. Camblin (1982) states: "It is generally acknowledged in research that handicapped children represent a disproportionate number of abuse and neglect victims, yet nearly half the states don't collect any information on 'special characteristics'." As a consequence, accurate statistics regarding the incidence of sexual maltreatment of handicapped children are generally unavailable. Based on media reports concerning abuse of handicapped children in residential institutions, however, a supposition that a handicapped child's disability makes him/her less desirable to the potential sexual abuser appears to be unfounded.

The abused handicapped child's reasons for nonreporting may include: feelings of shame and guilt, fear of threats from abusers, and fear of serious institutional and/or familial consequences for reporting (e.g., the father may be jailed or the child separated from the family and placed in a foster home). Victims may fear they will not be believed or, as in the case of children with communicative disabilities, simply do not have the requisite vocabulary or communication skills to report abuse. In many instances, hearing-impaired children are hampered by special linguistic barriers in describing what has been done to them, without an interpreter. When the child finally attempts to report being abused, he/she is often confronted with parents and institutional administrators who do not want to believe that children for whom they are responsible have been maltreated. This pattern of denial can affect an entire community or institution wishing to avoid the stigma of being a haven for child abusers. Law enforcement and judicial authorities frequently demonstrate an unwillingness to give credence to the testimony of an abused handicapped child.

FOCUS: ABUSED HEARING-IMPAIRED CHILDREN

The U.S. Department of Education (Karchmer, 1985) reports that during the 1982–1983 school year, approximately 75,000 students in the United States between the ages of 3 and 21 were categorized as "hard-of-hearing and deaf," not including "deaf–blind" students or those with hearing loss listed under the category "multihandicapped." Karchmer, from the Center for Assessment and Demographic Studies of Gallaudet College, estimates that in spring, 1983, 75,000–90,000 hearing-impaired children and youth in the United States had impairments severe enough to warrant some sort of special education. The geographic distribution of significant hearing impairment in the school age population is similar to that of the general 5- to 17-year-old population. Hearing-impaired students in special education are more likely to be of minority ethnic status than would be expected from examining the general U.S. population. Highly significant when assessing risk for abuse, 28% of the total were in residential schools, and 66% of the students attend programs where manual signing is used for instruction.

In a recently published article, "The Deaf Adolescent: Abuse and Abusers" (1985), Henry Klopping, Superintendent of the California School for the Deaf, explores important issues regarding the abuse of deaf children "in their home, community and school." He states:

> In recent months we have been exposed to a number of incidents involving abuse of deaf students attending several residential schools for the deaf. Charges of child abuse have led to three employees of one school being arrested for child molestation and at least one of these employees being convicted. A superintendent and dean of students in another school were recently arrested in front of TV reporters and newsmen and charged with felony child abuse for failure to report to police the sexual assault of one student upon another. In another case, a superintendent has been removed from his position for failure to report a child abuse incident. A superintendent of one residential school was fired because abuse had occurred in the school although he was not aware of the specific abuses. Finally, another school suspended a dean of students for some inappropriate disciplinary measures which were being interpreted as child abuse. Although we do not have the complete facts on these cases, it appears that the failure to report suspected child abuse to appropriate authorities has led to the current problem that these administrators must face.

In addition to these widely reported incidents of abuse at residential schools, Klopping asserts that "my experience at the California School for the Deaf reveals that there is a much greater incidence of child abuse occurring to deaf children outside the school environment." A final impression drawn from the California experience is that multi-handicapped deaf children appear to be at greater risk for abuse than "normal" deaf children.

Brookhouser, Sullivan, Scanlan, and Garbarino (1986) characterized a group of 55 hearing-impaired child and adolescent victims of physical and/or sexual abuse who have been cared for at the Boys Town National Institute's Center for Abused Handicapped Children (see Table 8.4). During the Center's first year of operation, care has been provided for handicapped children who have experienced abuse and neglect at home, in foster care settings, and in residential institutions. In many

TABLE 8.4. Demographic Information on Fifty-Five Hearing-Impaired Children Following Episodes of Sexual and/or Physical Abuse[a]

Category of abuse	Males	Females
Physically abused	1	1
Physically abused by family or nonrelative and sexually abused by nonrelative	7	0
Physically abused by family or nonrelative and sexually abused by family member(s)	1	2
Sexually abused by nonrelative	22	14
Sexually abused by family member(s)	1	2
Sexually abused by nonrelative and family member(s)	4	0

[a]From Brookhouser et al. (1986).

cases, several different perpetrators have exploited the vulnerability of these deaf youngsters over a period of years. In the view of many professionals, health providers bear a special responsibility for the detection and prevention of abuse/neglect of handicapped children for whom they are providing medical care on a continuing basis. With this issue in mind, a telephone survey of state schools for the deaf in the United States was undertaken to determine the nature and intensity of health services provided for residential clients, together with the spectrum of health providers involved. Questions included:

"How is health care provided?" (Physician on staff/on-call/physician group.)

"What is the medical specialty of the physician providing care?"

"How long has the physician been associated with the school as a provider?"

"Does the school require health reports from the child's private physician?"

"Do children at the school receive annual physical examinations?" If so, are they performed at school or by the family physician in the home community?"

"Do the hearing-impaired children see an ear, nose, and throat specialist on routine basis?"

"Are standardized checklists used as a part of the health record?"

Responses were obtained from 41 residential schools with a total enrollment of 9466 students of whom 2630 are day students and 6836 are residential students. The most common model for delivery of continuing episodic health care is a school infirmary staffed by a nurse. In 59% (24) of the schools, the infirmary is operated on a 24-hour basis, while in 12% (5) it is open 16 hours per day. An additional four schools staff the infirmary only during school hours, while the remaining 8 (20%) are equally divided between a nurse "on-call" system and no formal system for in-house care at the school.

In-school physician services are provided on a weekly basis in 21 (51%) of the schools, monthly in 1, on an "on-call" basis in 8 (20%), and by means of referral to outside physician providers in the remaining 11 (27%). The specialty training, particularly regarding child development issues, of physicians providing health services to handicapped children may be crucial to the success of any program aimed at detecting and preventing their abuse and/or neglect. At the residential schools for the deaf responding to the survey, family practitioners provide care in 25 (61%) institutions, while pediatricians are responsible in only 10 (24%) instances.

The frequency of required physical examinations for handicapped students should serve as a useful barometer for estimating the probability that unsuspected physical and/or sexual abuse might be detected by a health provider. The survey findings were somewhat discouraging in this regard. Only 14 (34%) of the schools require an annual physical examination by a physician for all students. An additional 5 schools provided for routine examinations at intervals ranging from 2 to 4 years. Most disturbing, however, was the finding that fully 54% (22) of the schools require a complete history and physical examination only upon initial admission to the institution. Because some of the students may enter during the elementary grades and remain through high school graduation, the inherent deficiencies of this health maintenance model, especially regarding abuse detection/prevention, are obvious.

IDENTIFYING THE ABUSED HANDICAPPED CHILD

The health professional's best strategy for identifying an abused handicapped child is to maintain a high index of suspicion during routine service encounters. Particularly in cases of sexual abuse, the communicatively impaired child will rarely complain specifically about what has happened. It is important that the examiner endeavor to win the child's confidence before expecting him/her to converse freely about such a sensitive issue as a sexual relationship with an adult caretaker. It may be necessary to help the child overcome fear of bodily harm or other consequences threatened by the perpetrator to prevent the youngster from divulging information about the abuse incident(s). If the child is communicatively impaired, his/her preferred mode of communication must be determined, and if appropriate, an unbiased interpreter (neither family member nor school personnel) should be present during questioning about the suspected abuse or neglect.

Recognizing Physical Abuse

A physician's suspicion of physical abuse is usually heightened by a discrepancy between the history given for an injury and the nature of the injury itself. In a useful article, Reece and Grodin (1985) comment on specific characteristics that might aid in recognition of nonaccidental injury in children (see Tables 8.5 and 8.6). When the description of the mechanism of injury changes during the course of the history or if there is significant disagreement between the stories of two adult caretakers, the likelihood of child maltreatment is further increased. A radiologic skeletal survey is more likely to reveal unsuspected evidence of trauma in younger patients (mean age 3.0 years) with one-half of the high-yield group being 1 year old or younger in one study (Ellerstein & Norris, 1984). This rule of thumb would be less applicable to older handicapped children with impaired communication in whom a skeletal survey may yield evidence of occult trauma not reported by adult caretakers or the child. While few radiologic findings can be described as absolutely diagnostic of abuse, Leonidas (1983) lists the following as highly suspicious:

- Occult bone lesions including unsuspected fractures
- Skeletal injuries out of proportion to history
- Multiple fractures in various stages of healing suggesting repeated trauma
- Combination of skeletal trauma with injury to other systems (craniocerebral, visceral)

In children under 2 years of age with skull fracture following alleged minor accidents, Hobbs (1984) suspects abuse when one or more of the following features is present:

- Multiple or complex fracture—two or more distinct fractures of any type or a single fracture with multiple components

TABLE 8.5. Recognition of Nonaccidental Injury Location of Cutaneous Injuries[a]

Inflicted	Accidental
Upper arms	Shins
Trunk	Hips (iliac crests)
Upper anterior legs	Lower arms
Sides of face	Prominences of spine
Ears and neck	Forehead
Genitalia	Under chin
Buttocks	

[a]Adapted from Pascoe, Hildebrandt, Tarrier & Murphy, M. (1979).

TABLE 8.6. Recognition of Nonaccidental Injury Burns[a]

Inflicted	Accidental
History	
Burns attributed to sibling	Compatible with observed
Unrelated adult seeks medical	injury
care	
Differing accounts of injury	
Treatment delay over 24 hours	
Prior "accidents" or absence	
of parental concern	
Lesion incompatible with	
history	
Location	
Buttocks, perineum, genitalia	Usually front of body
Ankles, wrists	Random and injury-specific
Palms, soles	
Pattern	
Sharply demarcated edges	Associated irregular splash
Stocking glove distribution	burns
Full thickness	Partial thickness
Symmetrical	Asymmetrical
Burn older than history	
indicates	
Burn neglected/infected	
Numerous lesions of varying	
age	
Pattern of burn consonant	
with implement used	
Large area with uniform dry	
burn (forced contact)	

[a]From Reece and Grodin (1985).

- Depressed fracture
- Maximum fracture width greater than 3.0 mm
- Growing fracture—an enlarged linear fracture
- Involvement of more than a single cranial bone
- Nonparietal fracture
- Associated intracranial injury

Reece and Grodin emphasize that subdural hematomas are nearly always traumatic in origin, being most common below 24 months of age (peak incidence about 6 months). The infant at highest risk is male (twice as common as females) and of low birth weight or premature. Signs and symptoms may be nonspecific: irritability, lethargy, and disinclination to feed. Alternately, there may be more classic signs of elevated intracranial pressure such as vomiting, seizures, stupor, and coma.

Kirks (1983) compared the utility of various state-of-the-art imaging techniques in diagnosing unsuspected visceral injuries. In addition to injuries of the skull and long bones, conventional radiography is important for the diagnosis of pulmonary parenchymal injury, gastric dilatation, and pneumoperitoneum (air within the abdominoperitoneal cavity). An upper gastrointestinal series is quite useful if intramural duodenal hematoma is suspected, while a diagnostic ultrasound examination can be helpful in the diagnosis of retroperitoneal hematoma, acute traumatic pancreatitis, and pancreatic pseudocyst. Radioisotope scanning of the liver and spleen is a widely available technique for assessing patients with a history of abdominal trauma. With the growing sophistication and availability of computerized tomography and magnetic resonance-imaging technology, these modalities will play an increasing role in the evaluation of patients with suspected injury to the abdominal contents (i.e., liver, spleen, pancreas, kidneys, and mesentery).

Recognizing Sexual Maltreatment

To identify those children in need of further evaluation for possible sexual abuse, the physician and paramedical personnel in the office/clinic should employ a checklist of physical and behavioral high-risk indicators. The following checklist, derived from the clinical experience of the author and Barry (1984b), has been reported previously (Brookhouser *et al.;* 1986):

INDICATORS OF CHILD SEXUAL ABUSE

Physical Appearance of Child

1. Has torn, stained, or bloody underclothing
2. Has traumatized, painful and/or pruritic cervix, vulva, penis, perineum, or anus
3. Has bruises or lesions overlying hard or soft palate and/or tonsillar pillars, including a chancre
4. Has semen about mouth, genitals, or on clothing
5. Has venereal disease, including condylomata accuminata
6. Is pregnant

Behavior of Child

1. Manifests new fears: of the dark, of being alone, of going to school or of staying home
2. Is unwilling to participate in physical activities or associate with a particular adult or older youth
3. Engages in acting-out behavior (delinquency, running away, etc.)
4. Demonstrates deteriorating or unusual school behavior, including: failing grades, absenteeism, truancy, and discipline problems
5. Appears withdrawn or engages in fantasy or infantile, regressive behavior, including bed-wetting or encopresis (fecal soiling)
6. Shows evidence of depression or low self-esteem, including: crying episodes, change in sleeping or eating habits, poor personal hygiene or dirty/torn clothing, and/or engages in suicidal gestures or attempts
7. Manifests sexually related behavior, including: seductive behavior, precocious sex play, explicit knowledge of sexual acts, or compulsive masturbation
8. Actually states he/she has been sexually assaulted by a parent, caretaker, older child, or other perpetrator

Characteristics of the Abusive Caretaker

1. Is extremely protective of the child (e.g. refuses to allow the child to be alone in the examining room or to have a physical examination of his/her genitalia)
2. Engages in seductive, sexually explicit, or extremely authoritarian behavior with the child in the presence of the physician or office staff
3. Encourages the child to engage in prostitution or sexual acts in the presence of caretaker
4. Has a history of having been sexually abused as a child
5. Is socially isolated, with few adult friends and limited involvement in activities with other adults
6. Is experiencing marital difficulties
7. Abuses alcohol or other drugs
8. May have a history of previous convictions for child sexual abuse
9. Is a surrogate caretaker (e.g., foster parent or dorm counselor)

A number of the aforementioned behavioral indicators are not pathognomonic for abuse but must be assessed in combination with other physical and circumstantial evidence in reaching a judgment regarding the need for abuse reporting and/or additional evaluation. If further evaluation is indicated, a management protocol modified from Jones' work (1982) should be followed so that no essential evidence is overlooked.

EVALUATION PROTOCOL FOR THE SEXUALLY ABUSED CHILD

1. Focused interview, apart from parents or other caretakers, utilizing unbiased interpreter and anatomically correct dolls, if appropriate:
   - What was done to the child?
   - Which sexual acts was the child forced to perform?
   - Did penetration occur? Which orifice(s)?
   - Were foreign objects used?
   - Did ejaculation occur?
   - Were any other injuries inflicted on the child?
2. Forensic medical examination, to be performed by a physician:
   - General appearance, emotional status, condition of clothing, injuries observed
   - Material evidence, such as fingernail scrapings and/or blood or hair of the abuser to be gathered
   - Examinations for sperm and semen (skin, vagina, rectum, and mouth)
     - Wood's lamp—semen, if present, will fluoresce dark green
     - Wet mount, for sperm
     - Prostatic acid phosphatase sample sent to lab
     - Serum blood group antigens
     - Precipitin test for human semen
   - Pelvic and digital rectal examination
   - Anoscopy, if anal tears, fissures, or blood are present
   - Cultures for gonococci (vagina, rectum, mouth) before antibiotics
   - VDRL
   - Pregnancy test
   - Photographic recording of any visible injury
3. Forensic dental examination, including photography, of any human bite marks.
4. Medication: (a) gonorrhea prophylaxis; (b) tetanus prophylaxis.

5. Protection of child—inpatient admission may be necessary as immediate precaution to prevent further abuse.

6. Notification of appropriate public agency and the police.

7. Examination of other family members if indicated (incest) or other sexual contacts for venereal disease control.

8. Arrange for follow-up: (a) Medical; (b) psychologic; (c) cultures gonococci; (d) VDRL; (e) social; and (f) legal.

Physicians often find no physical abnormalities when they evaluate suspected child sexual abuse victims. To determine the frequency of sexually transmitted disease among victims of sexual abuse, White, Loda, Ingram, and Pearson (1983) reviewed 409 cases of suspected sexual abuse. Sexually transmitted disease was identified in 54 (13%) of the 409 children: 46 cases of gonorrhea, 6 cases of syphilis, 4 cases of trichomoniasis, and 3 cases of condyloma acuminata. They concluded that sexually transmitted disease was more likely to be transmitted by an extended family member or a nonrelative than by a father/stepfather. The epidemiology of sexually transmitted disease in prepubertal children has not been intensively studied, but the work of Branch and Paxton (1965) suggests that gonorrhea in children, ages 1–10 years, was spread by sexual contact in 98% of the cases. Until recently, many health professionals regarded vaginal and urethral infections in children as nonsexually transmitted, broadly categorizing them as nonspecific vaginitis or urethritis. Gonorrhea infections of the pharynx and rectum are almost always asymptomatic. In studying female children with vaginal gonorrhea, White et al. (1983) reported that 41% of anal cultures and 21% of oral cultures were also positive in this group. A laboratory search to identify the presence of sexually transmitted disease in a prepubertal child may provide corroborating objective evidence of sexual abuse.

PHYSICIAN REPORTING OF ABUSE

Morris, Johnson, and Clasen (1985) noted that 16,314 cases of suspected abuse or neglect were reported to the Central Registry for Child Abuse in Ohio in 1981, but only 202 (1.2%) reports were made by private physicians. Because of differing socioeconomic characteristics of their patient population, medical personnel in emergency rooms and public clinics appear more likely to encounter blatant examples of child maltreatment than physicians in private practice. Therefore, faced with a case that might arouse suspicion of abuse, the practicing physician's lack of action may be influenced by a fear of losing patients or an institutional client, inability to make a positive diagnosis, and concern about the negative consequences of falsely accusing parents or residential care personnel of abusing a child. The physician must resist the natural tendency to accept the caretakers' explanation of the mechanism of injury before seeking an independent history of the incident from the child. In view of the high percentage of practicing physicians supervising the continuing care of handicapped children in residential institutions, it is mandatory that these physicians acquaint themselves with high-risk indicators for child abuse and neglect. Physician documentation of continuing medical education credits in this important area should be made a condition for continued employment by the residential facility. In addition, medical specialists involved in caring for specific subpopulations of handicapped youngsters (e.g., ophthalmologists—blind children; otolaryngologists—deaf children) should be apprised of the need to maintain a high index of suspicion regarding possible abuse and neglect of the young patients they serve.

CONCLUSIONS AND RECOMMENDATIONS

1. All parties involved in the care of handicapped children must confront the unpleasant reality that these youngsters are at special risk for physical and/or sexual abuse but may be unable to report it.

2. Prevention and detection of abuse must occupy a central role in the handicapped child's health maintenance plan.

   a. Beginning at the time of diagnosis, parent counseling must include a frank discussion of the familial stress and parental frustration that often complicate the rearing of a handicapped child. The counselor should specifically identify those parenting events most likely to be associated with disappointment and sorrow, which are normal emotional responses in many instances.

   b. Parents must be acquainted with community support mechanisms and preventive intervention aimed at minimizing family isolation from relatives, friends, and professionals. A specific action plan should be developed for use by the parents for the purpose of defusing a crisis situation in the home.

   c. Implement a series of regularly scheduled "well-child" physical examinations (annually or more often), including specific efforts directed toward determining whether or not the child has suffered any maltreatment.

      i. Utilizing the child's preferred mode of communication (unbiased sign language interpreter, if necessary), ask questions about any maltreatment. Have anatomically correct dolls available for child's use in describing any sexual abuse incidents.

     ii. Include noninvasive elements of a forensic medical examination in standard well-child physical with these children.

   d. For children in residential institutions, establish a regular communication link between institution's health care personnel and the child's primary care physician at home.

3. Establish a "critical incident" reporting mechanism for episodic illness or injury suffered by any handicapped child in a residential institution. External reports should, at a minimum, go to parents, the child's primary care physician, and the state agency with oversight responsibility for the institution.

4. Establish a blue ribbon Medical Audit/Quality Assurance Panel in each state with responsibility for monitoring the health and safety of children in residential institutions (public and private) throughout the state. The panel should be appointed by and report to the state's governor.

   a. Membership might include, among others, the president of the state medical society, the president of the state chapter of the American Academy of Pediatrics, and the chairman of the department of pediatrics from each of the state's medical schools.

   b. The panel should have access to and establish a mechanism for review of all health maintenance examination results and all critical incident reports for each child in each institution.

   c. A schedule of unannounced site visits to each institution should be implemented including, in some cases, physical examination of any children suspected of being abused or neglected.

chapter 9

SPECIAL LEGAL PROBLEMS IN PROTECTION OF HANDICAPPED CHILDREN FROM PARENTAL MALTREATMENT

Gary B. Melton

THE PARENS PATRIAE POWER AND DUTY

In order to understand the special legal problems in protecting handicapped children, it is useful to first examine the general approaches the law takes to protect children and to enhance the welfare of handicapped children. The authority for state intervention to protect dependent persons—both children and mentally disabled adults—is termed the *parens patriae* power. Meaning the sovereign as parent, the parens patriae power is based on *state* interests rather than the interests of the child. It developed from the desire of the sovereign to protect the estates of dependent persons—specifically, the taxes to be derived from them. Hence, in its origins in English common law, there was no illusion that the state was primarily interested in protection of the welfare of dependent persons, a point that we can recall usefully in the contemporary climate of child advocacy.

With the coming of industrialization, a broader concept of the parens patriae power developed. For the state, particularly a democratic state, to preserve itself in a technological society, an educated, healthy citizenry is needed (see *Prince v. Massachusetts*, 1944, p. 168). To protect state interests in such a context, the juvenile court, child labor laws, and compulsory education—and, with them, adolescence—were "invented" around the turn of the century (see Bakan, 1971; Kett, 1977; Platt, 1977). This intertwining of the state and the developing child welfare system led to a somewhat confused, but greatly and perhaps illogically expanded, parens patriae doctrine (cf. *In re Gault*, 1967, pp.

16–17). Now ostensibly concerned with the best interests of children, the state proclaimed the congruity of its interests with those of children. With this new sense of unity of interests, the parens patriae *power* was transformed into a *duty* to protect children. The moral arguments for the protection of children became mixed (and confused) with political arguments for the investment of state resources in children's healthy socialization. This change from political power to moral duty is best illustrated by legal and quasi-legal manifestos (see, e.g., United Nations, 1959) for children's *rights* to a wide array of special entitlements to goods and services believed to be related to their nurturance.[1]

FAMILY PRIVACY AND PARENTAL DUTY

It is important to remember, however, that the state's protection of children is ultimately grounded in its own interests. This principle helps to clarify some of the situations in which would-be child savers find themselves frustrated by lack of support from the legal system. As a general rule, the law assumes that the state's interest in the socialization of children can be best accomplished by solicitude for parents. In oft-quoted dicta, the Supreme Court has proclaimed that "it is cardinal with us that the custody, care and nurture of the child reside first in the parents, whose primary function and freedom include preparation for obligations the state can neither supply nor hinder" (*Prince v. Massachusetts,* 1944, p. 166). Indeed, the philosophical basis for the historic view of children as the chattel of their fathers was a conviction that men would not sire and rear children were it not for their economic value (Hobbes, 1651/1839–1845). Thus, in the early common law, the not-so-benign neglect of children was based on preservation of state interests as much as respect for property rights per se.

In a liberal democracy, a laissez-faire approach to families also has other, more principled, bases. The family stands as a buffer between the individual and the state. The privacy of the family helps to ensure diversity of values and beliefs by "exclud[ing] any general power of the state to standardize its children" (*Pierce v. Society of Sisters,* 1925, p. 535; see also *Wisconsin v. Yoder,* 1972). It also establishes zones of personal matters in which individuals may claim "*the right to be let alone*"" (*Olmstead v. United States,* 1928, dissenting opinion of Justice

---

[1] Children's rights are not necessarily conceptualized in terms of special entitlements. A second school of child advocates emphasizes the competence rather than the vulnerability of children and, accordingly, their rights to self-determination (see, e.g., Holt, 1974; Melton, 1983).

Brandeis, p. 478, emphasis in original; see also *Ginsberg v. New York*, 1968; *Roe v. Wade*, 1973; *Whalen v. Roe*, 1977).

This right to family privacy—in this context, parental autonomy—is not absolute, however, To use other well-worn language from *Prince*, parents are not "free . . . to make martyrs of their children" (*Prince v. Massachusetts*, 1944, p. 170). Just as there is a mixture of right and duty in regard to the parens patriae power itself, so is there such a mixture in regard to parental autonomy. Even in *Meyer v. Nebraska* (1923), the first of the series of Supreme Court cases sometimes mislabeled "children's rights" cases, the Court acknowledged that the "right of [parental] control" is accompanied by "the natural duty of the parent to give his children education suitable to their station of life" (p. 400). In another case in the series (*Pierce v. Society of Sisters*, 1925), the Court concluded, "The child is not the mere creature of the state; those who nurture him and direct his destiny have the right, *coupled with the high duty*, to recognize and prepare him for additional obligations" (p. 535, emphasis added).

The duty to care for one's children is heightened when the child is handicapped. For example, it is well established in common law that parents retain a duty to support disabled children past the age of majority (see, e.g., *Castle v. Castle*, 1984; *Davis v. Davis*, 1954; *Stern v. Stern*, 1984). This duty may even arise when the child becomes disabled after reaching adulthood (*Sininger v. Sininger*, 1984).

Nonetheless, through significant expansion of social welfare programs for handicapped children in the past 15 years, the state has formally recognized that parents cannot do it all (see Hobbs, 1975). The most notable example of such recognition was the enactment of the Education for All Handicapped Children Act (EAHCA) of 1975 (see also Rehabilitation Act of 1973, especially section 504). Although the EAHCA does not necessarily require school systems to provide handicapped children with the services needed to meet their potential (*Board of Education v. Rowley*, 1982), it does mandate that every handicapped child receives a "free appropriate public education," including whatever "related services" (e.g., psychological services; therapeutic recreation, speech therapy) are necessary to permit the child to make use of the education (*Irving Independent School District v. Tatro*, 1984). Handicapped children from low-income families are also eligible for direct cash assistance under the Supplemental Security Income (SSI) program (Supplemental Security Income, 1985; Social Security Amendments of 1972; see also *Hinckley ex rel. Martin v. Secretary of Health and Human Services*, 1984; *Powell ex rel. Powell v. Schweiker*, 1981). Subsidies are available for prospective adoptive parents who are willing to take responsibility for a handicapped child (Adoption Assistance and Child Welfare Amendments of 1980).

TRENDS IN THE LAW ON CHILD MALTREATMENT

Some basis for legal intervention in families in which children were abused or neglected came with the juvenile court's invention and its broad jurisdiction to assist "wayward" children. However, a clear investment in child protective services is a relatively recent phenomenon. Indeed, policy on child maltreatment has been remarkably "trendy," in the sense that professional and public beliefs and attitudes have been prone to wide swings. After the battered child syndrome was "discovered" by Kempe and his colleagues in the early 1960s (Kempe, Silverman, Steele, Droegemueller, & Silver, 1962), every state enacted a compulsory reporting law within a 4-year period (Wadlington, Whitebread, & Davis, 1983). Currently, state legislatures (Bulkley, 1985) and the Congress (e.g., Missing Children's Assistance Act of 1984; Subcommittee on Juvenile Justice, 1984) are hurrying to enact new legislation on sexual abuse after its "discovery" (Weisberg, 1984), in part through made-for-television movies (for a comprehensive review of the law on sexual abuse, see Lloyd, Melton, & Rogers, in preparation). In short, child protection policy has been the product of a potent, if not necessarily coherent, social movement (cf. Melton, in press).

No consistent orientation exists among child advocates about either the nature of child maltreatment (Melton, Petrila, Poythress, & Slobogin, in press, section 12.03; Rosenberg & Reppucci, 1983) or the appropriate threshold for, and nature of, state intervention (Melton et al., in press, section 12.01[b]; compare, e.g., Garbarino, Gaboury, Long, Grandjean, & Asp [1982] with Goldstein, Freud, & Solnit [1973, 1979], Melton [in press], and Wald [1975, 1982]). The fact that the Juvenile Justice Standards Relating to Abuse and Neglect (IJA/ABA, 1977) have never been adopted by the American Bar Association is illustrative of this controversy.

The one point on which there has been near consensus among scholarly commentators is the desirability of tightening and clarifying the statutory bases of intervention. Commentators generally have advocated a requirement of finding specific and severe harm to the child before intervention. For example, the Juvenile Justice Standards (IJA/ABA, 1977) would permit the state to assume jurisdiction over children only when they suffer a "substantial risk" or actual occurrence of "disfigurement, impairment of bodily functioning, or other serious physical injury" as a result of parental behavior. Similarly, intervention on the ground of emotional abuse or neglect would require a finding that "a child is suffering serious emotional damage, evidence by severe anxiety, depression, or withdrawal, or untoward aggressive behavior toward self or others, and the child's parents are not willing to provide treatment for him/her" (IJA/ABA, 1977, Std. 2.1[C]). The focus on evidence of harm is consistent with parens patriae doctrine in that state interests can be asserted validly only if there is a significant harm to the child that is likely to interfere with his or her healthy socialization.[2] Parents may engage in unwise, even nasty behavior toward their children, but without harm or substantial risk of harm, it is difficult to argue a compelling state interest justifying intrusion upon family privacy.

Two assumptions underlie the recommendation to narrow and more clearly operationalize the statutory grounds for state intervention. First, statutory definitions of abuse, neglect, and parental fitness have often been so broad and vague as to invite arbitrary and unreliable application (Giovannoni & Becerra, 1979; Melton et al., in press, section 12.02), sometimes to the point of violation of constitutional guarantees of due process (see, e.g., Algaser v. District Court of Polk County, 1975). Second, the state-of-the-art of treatment (see Rosenberg & Hunt, 1984, for review) and the realities of state resources and bureaucratic behavior (Bush & Gordon, 1978; Mnookin, 1973) are such that state intervention may be even more harmful than leaving children in a possibly unsafe home, as dramatized by Goldstein et al.'s (1973, 1979) advocacy of substitution of the term least detrimental alternative for best interests of the child. Therefore, state intervention should be reserved for those instances in which there is a clear, present or imminent, and substantial danger.

Most commentators on family law acknowledge the wisdom of rejecting vague grounds for intervention (e.g., "excessive" corporal punishment; "inadequate" care; lack of "proper supervision"). Nonetheless, the current legislative trend appears to be toward expanding jurisdiction for state intervention to protect children from maltreatment. The conventional wisdom among child advocates, legislators, and the general public seems to be that there is a need for procedural and evidentiary reforms to make civil and criminal prosecution of sex abusers easier (see Bulkley, 1985; Skoler, 1984), and for broad definitions of abuse focusing on psychological harm (see Brassard, Germain, & Hart, in press; Garbarino, Guttman, & Wilson, in press). I doubt both the utility and the constitutionality of such legislation (Lloyd et al. in prep.; Melton, 1984; 1985; Melton & Thompson, in press; see also Rosenberg, 1984; Routh, 1984; Weithorn, 1984). Nonetheless, in the current political climate, measures purported to protect especially vulnerable children, like those who are handicapped, would be likely to achieve public support.

[2] Applying the same logic, demonstrable harm to the child may be insufficient to warrant state intervention. It is arguable that the state interests are infringed only if there is lasting harm. Short-term discomfort for the child may be of no significance to the state if the child still is likely to grow into a healthy, productive adult.

PREVENTION OF HANDICAPS

As I have already implied, the purpose of abuse/neglect jurisdiction is and must be ultimately future-oriented, even though the best basis for prediction is past behavior. The family court has a central goal of protecting children from harm. Although jurisdiction should be taken only when events have occurred that demonstrate the serious risk to a child, the purpose of state intervention is *preventive*.[3] Viewed in such a light, a corollary question is whether child protective services can be used to prevent handicapping conditions.

Formidable practical, ethical, and legal barriers stand in the way of such an approach, at least as applied to *primary* prevention.[4] Perhaps the most basic problem is that use of child protective jurisdiction individualizes and "psychiatrizes" what are really social issues. Such a transformation both unfairly may blame the victim (Ryan, 1971) and be ineffective (Melton & Thompson, in press). Consider the following hypothetical case. Suppose that a bacteria-infested well is located in a densely populated area. Instead of covering the well or purifying the water (or requiring the landlord to do so), the state chooses to reduce illness resulting from the well by taking jurisdiction over families in which children drink from the well or are thought to be at risk of drinking contaminated water. Although the state's strategy may deter some parents from negligent behavior and protect some children otherwise in danger, it clearly is the less desirable option, in terms both of a utilitarian calculus and respect for family privacy. (For a comprehensive review of the law and efficacy of various public health strategies, see Bonnie [in press].)

Substantial problems also arise from attempts to identify children at risk for development of preventable handicapping conditions. Even if it were possible to develop a highly valid screening mechanism,[5] there will usually be many false positives in identification of children at risk

---

[3] Civil child protective jurisdiction is thus fundamentally different from criminal inquiries into child maltreatment. The latter is necessarily backward-looking. It would be unjust to punish a parent for mere propensities to mistreat children, but family courts may be justified in preventing probable harm to children, even if no abusive act has yet occurred.

[4] In *primary* prevention, intervention takes place before any untoward event occurs. *Secondary* prevention focuses on groups at risk who have shown some indication of problems. *Tertiary* prevention is a misnomer of sorts, aimed at rehabilitation of affected persons. (See Caplan [1964] for application of prevention concepts to mental health.)

[5] Some screening profiles have shown an uncanny hit rate in differentiating known abusers from parents of matched social class who have not been determined to be abusers (see, e.g., Milner, 1980). However, it is important to emphasize that existing studies have been postdictive, not predictive.

of handicapping conditions which occur relatively rarely, a statistical truth which most people, including most clinical professionals (Monahan, 1981; Shapiro, 1977), fail to comprehend (Kahneman & Tversky, 1973).[6] When the children identified really would have been false positives, the very identification of them as vulnerable may be a self-fulfilling prophecy (cf. Hobbs, 1975) with stigmatizing effects (cf. Mercer, 1973). Moreover, the use of group probability data as the basis for determination of families to subject to coercive preventive interventions is likely to offend the community's sense of fundamental fairness (see Monahan & Walker, 1985). When parents have yet to harm their children, it seems unjust to single them out for state intervention on the basis of a profile. Without clear link to behavior, such state action would probably violate both the due process and equal protection clauses of the Fourteenth Amendment.[7]

A somewhat different set of issues is posed when a parent has engaged in behavior that is often injurious to children, but the child is not yet known to have been harmed. The most dramatic example is when the behavior of a pregnant woman places the fetus at substantial risk (see Morris & Sonderegger, 1984). Hundreds of studies indicate increased risk of low birth weight, congenital anomalies, or behavioral abnormalities as a result of mothers' smoking (Abel, 1982b), drinking alcohol (Abel, 1981, 1982a), exposure to lead, mercury, or PCBs (Fein, Schwartz, Jacobson, & Jacobson, 1983), or ingestion of narcotics (Rementeria, 1977). Indeed, when chromosomal aberrations are believed to result from toxic exposure, risk to the fetus may result from parental behavior even prior to conception.

State interests in such circumstance squarely collide with the woman's[8] privacy and sometimes her freedom of movement and economic interests (e.g., when her job involves contact with teratogenic chemicals). Indeed, as one commentator put it, the conflict between

[6] Consider the following hypothetical case. Assume the following: (a) John Jones matches an abuser profile. (b) There are 150 million adults in the country. (c) Of these, 5% are abusers (a hypothetical figure). (d) The abuser profile has been developed with appropriate statistical methods. (e) Of abusers, 90% fit the profile. (f) Of other adults, 90% do not match the profile (a much higher hit rate than most extant profiles can claim).

Given such assumptions, the probability that a person with Mr. Jones's characteristics is an abuser is only one in three!

[7] Despite protests to the contrary, child protective jurisdiction does not have a retributive aura. Note, for example, the consensual sense of injustice of finding "neglect" if parents' poverty puts their children at risk of harm (see, e.g., IJA/ABA, 1977).

[8] The obvious threat is to women's privacy because of the significance for fetal development of the conduct of pregnant women. However, the same argument is applicable to fertile males when toxic exposure may result in chromosomal damage.

the goals of equality of economic opportunity and protection of the fetus raise the spectre of "firing the woman to protect the fetus" (Williams, 1981; see Andrade, 1981; Furnish, 1980; *Hayes v. Shelby Memorial Hospital*, 1984; see also *Oil, Chemical and Atomic Workers International Union v. American Cyanamid Co.*, 1984 [chemical company's policy requiring female employees of childbearing years to be sterilized does not constitute a "hazard" of "employment" under the Occupational Safety and Health Act]). Besides intruding upon the woman's privacy and autonomy, state intervention on behalf of the fetus might require direct assault on her bodily integrity through *in utero* fetal therapy (*Raleigh Fitkin-Paul Morgan Memorial Hospital v. Anderson*, 1964; Robertson, 1983) or mandatory prenatal screening (*Grodin v. Grodin*, 1980; Robertson, 1983).

The possible application of child protective jurisdiction to expectant mothers also raises the highly charged issue of whether the fetus that has been "abused" is a "child" (cf. *Roe v. Wade*, 1973). For example, a mother in California who was addicted to heroin was charged with felony endangerment of a child after she delivered twin boys who were addicted. The appellate court that considered the case dismissed the charges because a fetus could not be presumed to be a child, absent express legislative instruction (*Reyes v. Superior Court*, 1977; accord, *Wynn v. Carey*, 1979). Applying *Reyes*, another California appellate court held that a juvenile court had exceeded its authority by using neglect jurisdiction to detain a mentally disordered but uncommittable pregnant woman to protect the fetus (*In re Steven S.*, 1981).

On the other hand, in a case similar to *Reyes*, a Michigan appellate court upheld the state's assuming protective jurisdiction over the newborn infant of a heroin addict (*In re Baby X*, 1980). The court reasoned that "since a child has a legal right to begin life with a sound mind and body, we believe it is within his best interest to examine all prenatal conduct [of the mother] bearing on this right" in order to establish neglect (p. 739, citation omitted). In the 1980 survey of Michigan family law, Lombard (1981) noted the far-reaching implications of *Baby X*:

> Assertion of juvenile court jurisdiction . . . raises slippery slope problems. Since a host of activities by pregnant women are suspected of causing harm to the fetus, *e.g.*, smoking, consumption of alcoholic beverages, etc., a result such as the court reached in *Baby X* opens the door wide for increased state intervention in family affairs. Perhaps *Baby X* can be limited to its facts; a juvenile court might be more willing to assume jurisdiction over the child of a heroin addict given the illegality of the mother's conduct and the obviousness of the harm to the child. In the case of moderate alcohol consumption or smoking, the maternal conduct is not illegal nor are the harmful effects immediately apparent. Yet the *Baby X* precedent is there, and while one might hope that all pregnant women would think first and foremost of their unborn child's well-being, whether or not the

state should enforce maternal conduct in this manner implicates other issues which the *Baby X* court did not touch upon. (pp. 822–823).

In fact, legal commentators thus far have approved of states' intervention on behalf of the fetus, at least after the fetus has achieved viability (King, 1979; Levine, 1974; Robertson, 1983). The emphasis on the point of viability is consistent with the "trimester" approach the Supreme Court has taken in analysis of state interests in abortion cases (*City of Akron v. Akron Center for Reproductive Health*, 1983; *Roe v. Wade*, 1973). There is no fundamental right to ingest drugs or alcohol (see, e.g., *Felix v. Milliken*, 1978), and measures carefully and narrowly drawn to restrain pregnant women from so endangering the fetus are likely to pass scrutiny for rationality under the equal protection clause.

Nonetheless, state regulation of pregnant women's behavior—for example, forbidding sale of liquor to pregnant women; invoking protective jurisdiction for neglect of prenatal medical care—would raise a terrible spectre of intrusion upon privacy and discrimination against women. In a recent California case, for example, a woman convicted of child endangerment—among other things, she subjected her children to a macrobiotic diet—was forbidden from becoming pregnant as a condition of probation. The appellate court overruled this order as overbroad (*People v. Pointer*, 1984). However, the appellate court did suggest that it would be appropriate to order Pointer to submit to pregnancy tests and, if she became pregnant, follow a nutritious diet. Consistent with the view of commentators (King, 1979; Robertson, 1983), the *Pointer* court seemed to imply that the state may not interfere with women's right to make decisions about procreation, but it may regulate their behavior during pregnancy in order to promote state interests in the health of children.

Use of child protective jurisdiction during pregnancy would be so intrusive that it may be unwise policy, even if constitutional. The irony, though, is that prenatal intervention to prevent toxic effects would be more likely to prevent harm to children than intervention in childhood after a finding of postnatal abuse or neglect. In the current political climate of support for restrictions upon liberty in order to protect public health (see Bonnie, in press), the possibility that child protective jurisdiction will be used to prevent prenatal harm (and thus handicapping conditions) to children bears close attention.

EVIDENTIARY PROBLEMS

Obviously, most protective cases involving handicapped children do not involve prenatal abuse or neglect. We now turn to the special problems which may be encountered in adjudicating such cases.

Competency to Testify

The tradition in Anglo–American common law has been that children and psychotic or mentally retarded adults are presumed incompetent to testify (see Melton [1981] for a review of the relevant law and developmental literature). Courts may be especially reticent to hear the testimony of a child handicapped by mental retardation or a communication disorder. In general, witnesses must be able to differentiate truth from falsehood, comprehend the duty to tell the truth and the consequences of breach of an oath, form a just impression of the facts (perceive an event accurately), recall the event accurately, and maintain independence from the suggestions of others. In most American jurisdictions, children must be found competent through an interview in court by the judge or attorneys (a "voir dire") before being permitted to testify (but see Federal Rule of Evidence 601).

I have argued that the relevant tasks are insufficiently developmental to warrant special procedures to determine whether children's testimony is admitted (Melton, 1981, 1985). Regardless, the real question of competency is the competency of the fact finder to make proper inferences from children's testimony, not the competency of the child to testify. As long as the fact finder is not misled by what children have to say (especially misled toward criminal conviction or civil invocation of protective jurisdiction), justice will be served by the admission of the testimony, especially given the time that would be consumed in any event by the voir dire.

Although I would eliminate the necessity of qualifying child witnesses, I must also express my discomfort with the trend toward admission of children's hearsay statements in abuse proceedings, in part, on the ground that their poor communication skills make them "unavailable" to testify (e.g., *State v. Pendleton*, 1984; see Skoler, 1984, for commentary). It is indeed a strange contortion of the principles of evidence and the defendant's rights to confrontation and due process to permit admission of hearsay testimony about the out-of-court statements of children whose in-court statements are judged to be too unreliable to permit them to testify.

Proof of Harm

Beyond issues of what evidence may be admitted, the state may face special problems of proof in alleging abuse or neglect of a handicapped child. In jurisdictions which require a showing of harm as an element of abuse or neglect, prosecutors may encounter difficulty in establishing the cause of a child's disabilities. For example, is a child's retarded development the product of genetic heritage or prenatal insult, or is it the result of maltreatment? If it is acknowledged that a child had significant handicaps even before abuse allegedly occurred, how is the court to know whether parental behavior seriously exacerbated these problems? These questions may be particularly troublesome when the causes of a syndrome—for example, failure to thrive, hyperactivity— are usually multiple, controversial, or unknown.

As a practical matter, however, the problem of proof may not be so great as it would seem. I suspect that judges are inclined to view hand- icapped children as especially vulnerable to harm. If so, the state's the- ory of causation may seem especially plausible. Even if harm cannot be established directly, the *risk* of harm from parental maltreatment may be especially easy to prove when a child is handicapped.

DISPOSITIONAL ISSUES

The heart of protective cases is often at the dispositional, not the adjudicative, phase. Will the child be removed from the home? What rehabilitative services will be provided to the family? Will the parents' rights be terminated?

Dispositional Planning

Consistent with the tendency to view child maltreatment as the product of a parent's pathology, the dispositional inquiry often focuses almost exclusively on the "fitness" and mental health of the parent. This perspective results in ignorance of the social and economic sup- ports that are necessary for parents' care of their children (Cochran & Brassard, 1979; Garbarino & Crouter, 1978; Garbarino & Sherman, 1980; Melton et al., in press; Pelton, 1981; Rosenberg & Reppucci, 1983). The dismally poor rate of success of treatment programs for abusive parents is doubtless related in part to this myopia (Rosenberg & Hunt, 1984).

The focus on parental pathology also overlooks the fact that children differ in the nature of the care they need. Children do have effects on parents (Bell & Harper, 1977). One of the positive outcomes of the new focus on abused handicapped children may be to turn the attention of judges, social workers, and mental health professionals to the fact that successful dispositional planning requires examination of the characteristics of the child as well as the parents and their social context. As I have stated elsewhere:

> Ecological theorists . . . recognize that cause–effect relationships are rarely unidirectional, although differentials in power may make effects in one direction stronger than the other. For example, it is obvious that, in most families most of the time, parents have more effect on children than the converse. Parents generally have greater control over reinforcements and greater physical strength, cognitive skills, social experience, and behavioral

repertoire. However, it is also clear that the presence of children changes the life of adults, and that the care of some children is much more demanding and stressful than the care of others. Although there are probably other reasons as well, it is likely that part of the explanation for the disproportionately high rate of abuse of infants is their great need for care. Consistent with this hypothesis, premature and handicapped infants, who tend to require the most care of all, are at especially high risk for abuse. Similarly, older abused children may often unwittingly have learned behavior that really "gets to" their parents. We do not mean to suggest, of course, that children should be viewed as responsible for parental abuse. At the same time, however, it is important to recognize that a parent with poor childrearing skills, high stress, and a limited system of social supports might be able to cope adequately with an "easy" child but not with one who requires special care. Evaluators for disposition and planners of interventions may find that work to increase the social competence of the abused child may be an important ingredient in reducing the probability of child maltreatment (Melton et al., in press).

At disposition, the best interests of the child is usually an important criterion, although not necessarily the only criterion. The indeterminancy of this standard has been justly criticized for the arbitrariness and unreliability it invites (Mnookin, 1975). Nonetheless, the best-interests standard does provide the opportunity to individualize dispositional plans. Courts and social service agencies should take a child's special needs (in interaction with parental and systemic strengths and weaknesses) into account in developing such plans.

Termination of Parental Rights

Special needs of children are likely to be given most attention if the state seeks to terminate parental rights. The difficulty of caring for a particular child may figure into an assessment of the parent's ability to reach a level of competence sufficient to permit the safe return of the child to the natural home. For example, in affirming the termination of a father's rights to his multiply handicapped 5-year-old son, the Washington Supreme Court concluded that "the severe developmental disabilities of this child present problems in parenting beyond the capabilities of most normal parents, let alone one with the emotional problems exhibited by Dan Esgate" (In re Dependency of Joseph Esgate, 1983). As Esgate suggests, when the child is handicapped, the state may bear less of a burden as a practical matter when it seeks to prove parents unfit as a basis for termination of parental rights. For example, the model statute of the National Council of Juvenile and Family Court Judges requires a finding that "the conduct or condition of the parent is such as to render him/her unable to properly care for the child and that such conduct or condition is unlikely to change in the foreseeable future" (reprinted in Wadlington et al., 1983, p. 882). Parental fitness rests on determination of competence to care for the particular child, not children generally.

A child's handicap may also work at times to make termination of parental rights more difficult than it would be otherwise. The principal positive effect of termination is to render a child free for adoption. Therefore, if the child's handicap raises a question as to whether adoptive parents willing and able to provide proper care can be found, the desirability of termination may also be questioned. A good example is provided by the case of Michael G., a developmentally disabled boy aged 7 at the time of termination proceedings (*In re Michael G.*, 1983). Michael was not toilet trained, his language skills were limited, and he was said to be emotionally disturbed. Michael's parents were themselves developmentally disabled and employed in a sheltered workshop. The trial court's undisputed finding was that Mr. and Mrs. G "are not able to appreciate Michael's special needs or to provide a home in which he can fully develop" (p. 747). Nonetheless, the appellate court reversed the termination of parental rights. The appellate court noted that Mr. and Mrs. G loved Michael, were interested in him, and bonded to him. Their visits were not detrimental to Michael, and he was doing well in foster care. The fact on which the case turned was the slim likelihood of finding an appropriate adoptive home. Given that context, the court held that it would not be in Michael's best interests to terminate his natural parents' relationship with him.

ISSUES IN TERMINATION OF RIGHTS OF HANDICAPPED PARENTS

Thus far in this chapter, special issues in the legal system's response to maltreatment of children, who are or may become handicapped, were examined. It is probably useful to note that there are also special legal issues in consideration of the rights of handicapped parents.

In the first half of this century, states commonly placed restrictions on marriage and procreation by mentally retarded persons and, less frequently, other groups believed to be genetically inferior (e.g., mentally ill persons, criminals, epileptics). Compulsory sterilization of mentally retarded adults was common. The Supreme Court upheld this practice in *Buck v. Bell* (1927). In one of the less noble opinions of his career, Justice Holmes proclaimed that "three generations of imbeciles are enough" (*Buck v. Bell*, 1927, p. 207). Gradually, however, eugenics fell into disfavor, and some of the arbitrary use of the eugenic statutes to sterilize the poor or minority groups became exposed. Substantial legal barriers to sterilization of mentally retarded persons now exist in many jurisdictions (Melton & Scott, 1984).

Although eugenics may be in disrepute, distrust of handicapped adults' capacity to care for children is not. As a result, many states have statutory presumptions in favor of termination of the parental rights of mentally ill and mentally retarded parents, once protective jurisdiction is taken. Generally, challenges to these statutes on grounds of violation of due process and equal protection have been unsuccessful. In fact, virtually every issue of the *Mental and Physical Disability Law Reporter* contains several decisions of appellate courts affirming the termination of the rights of parents on the ground of unfitness because of mental illness or mental retardation.

In holding that statutes do not violate due process when mental illness or mental retardation is the basis for termination, courts generally have relied on the fact that a finding of abuse or neglect and sometimes unfitness is also necessary in states with such a presumption. However, courts sometimes have upheld statutes requiring little evidence of relationship of the parent's disability to the child's well-being. For example, the Rhode Island Supreme Court construed its state's termination statute properly to require no finding of harm when unfitness was based on mental illness (*In re Crystal A.*, 1984). Citing analogous holdings in several other states, the Arkansas Supreme Court oddly defended the lack of any statutory criteria for "mental illness" and "emotional illness" because of the broad (some would say arbitrary and unpredictable) discretion it gave trial courts in terminating parental rights: "Since the particular disabilities of parents are diverse, it would be impossible to catalogue each disability, and the statute must be broad enough to encompass proscribed behavior" (*Thompson v. Arkansas Social Services*, 1984, p. 882).

Equal protection arguments have also typically failed (see Wakefield, 1983, for summaries of several such cases). In rejecting arguments that special provisions for termination of the rights of handicapped parents violate equal protection, courts have commonly asserted that legislatures reasonably have found a relationship between mental illness or mental retardation and parental incapacity (see, e.g., *In re Montgomery*, 1984). However, the rationality of such legislation is in fact questionable. A detailed review of the relevant literature is beyond the scope of this chapter (for such reviews, see Grunebaum, Weiss, Cohler, Hartman & Gallant, 1982; Jacob, Favorini, Meisel, & Anderson, 1978; Kauffman, Grunebaum, Cohler, & Gamer, 1979; Melton et al., in press, section 12.05; Melton & Scott, 1984; Reed & Reed, 1965; Thurman, 1985; Vaillant, 1983). Suffice it to say that most children of severely mentally disordered parents develop normally. The higher developmental risk that is observed tends to disappear when appropriate controls for social class and heritability are added.

These findings are certainly counter to the intuition of courts and legislatures and, I suspect, most mental health and social service professionals. I present them as a closing caveat. Handicapped people are not always so "special" as our stereotypes present them. Equality before the law is an important, although not absolute, principle of the American legal system. I submit that it is a wise and just starting point. As problems of handicapped abused children are considered, let us take care not to advocate special legal strictures regarding them without close scrutiny of the desirability of such reforms. The problems that confront maltreated handicapped children, their families, and providers of services to them may really be the problems that pervade the child protective system.

chapter 10

ABUSED HANDICAPPED CHILDREN IN THE CRIMINAL JUSTICE SYSTEM

William Modzeleski

INTRODUCTION

Over the past few years, we have heard a great deal about the abuse and neglect of children. A child in Maine is burned to death in an oven while his parents stand by and chant. A young girl from Indiana is continuously molested for 5 years by her grandfather from the time she was 7. A 2-month-old child is starved to death in Maryland. A mother in Wisconsin is accused of sexually molesting her 2-year-old son. A wealthy Arizona businessman is accused of sexually abusing his teenage daughter and causing her to seek psychiatric care. A child in Florida was found to have gonorrhea of the throat after a stay in a nursery. A priest from Louisiana is given a 20-year sentence for sexually abusing dozens of boys from various churches where he was stationed. A Washington State man is given a 10-year sentence for killing his 3-month-old stepdaughter: She had two fractured legs, a skull fracture, several broken ribs, a ruptured liver, a bruised spleen, bite marks on both feet, and numerous bruises. A 13-year-old girl is killed by her father when she resisted his advances. These are not fictitious headlines manufactured to sell cheap novels, they are events that actually happened during the past year in various parts of our country.

While it appears that society in general is just becoming acutely aware of children being abused by parents, relatives, or other caretakers, the fact is that the abuse and neglect of children, hereafter called child maltreatment, has been part of society's response to the care and handling of children for literally thousands of years. Dr. Allan Carlson, Executive Vice President of the Rockford Institute, stated that "without much exaggeration the history of childhood might fairly be summed up with the phrase: The slaughter of the innocent. Until recent centuries, abominable child care practices, the sexual exploitation of children, child abuse, and infanticide were closer to being the norm than the exception" (Carlson, 1984).

History is literally scarred with vivid examples of punishment, infanticide, abandonment, and exploitation; all very real forms of child maltreatment or abuse. Over 5000 years ago in the schools of Sumer, boys were punished (whipped) upon the slightest provocation. "Spare the rod and spoil the child," was a dictum backed by the Bible and supported in many countries by law. Samuel X. Radbill pointed out that throughout history it was taken for granted that parents and guardians had every right to treat their children as they saw fit.

As stated previously, common beatings by parents, guardians, and teachers were not the only forms of abuse suffered by children. In ancient times, Romans, Greeks, and Egyptians did not consider the child human until certain ceremonies were performed. If the child was unwanted for a variety of reasons—illegitimacy, poor health, deformity, economic stresses, or proximity to another sibling—it was killed. Many of those who survived early days of childhood were later abandoned by their parents or caretakers. In most ancient societies, this abandonment led to either death or slavery.

Finally, throughout history we find that children consistently have been the subjects of various forms of exploitation. In ancient Greece and Rome children were prostitutes and favored sexual companions, and during the Industrial Revolution, children as young as 5 were forced to work up to 16 hours a day in mills, factories, and mines, often after being brutally beaten and whipped by tyrannical overseers.

These various forms of child maltreatment were often supported by laws and/or religious beliefs and practices. The old Roman law provided that fathers had absolute power over their children, including the right to decide on matters of life or death and slavery or freedom. The state enforced these rights, and no persons or agencies were permitted to intercede on behalf of a child. The common law of England stipulated that fathers had *supreme control* over their legitimate minor children and were entitled to their custody. Fathers had moral, but not legal, obligations to support and protect their children. In the United States, the Mosaic law, which was adopted by the Massachusetts Court in 1646, imposed the death penalty upon unruly children; Connecticut followed suit in 1651. Public whipping, however, was usually substituted for execution.

Laws protecting children from some abuses such as infanticide were recorded as early as ancient Egypt (infanticide was common but not legal) and were continued on through the Middle Ages when the doctrine of parens patriae (the state has right to assume parental authority when parents have failed to fulfill their responsibility) was established.

Real efforts at reform, however, did not begin until the latter part of the nineteenth century—almost 100 years after our country was created!

In the mid-1800s, the concept of parens patriae began to gain legal recognition, and in the 1870s, several chapters of the Society for the Prevention of Cruelty to Children (SPCC) were established to protect children, who, until then, were still considered chattel of their parents. It is interesting to note that the SPCC was formed after the Society for the Prevention of Cruelty to Animals (SPCA) and as a result of a successful attempt on the part of the SPCA to remove a maltreated child from a home.

For the most part, matters dealing with child maltreatment were considered social and medical problems to be dealt with by a variety of social service agencies, hospitals, and civil or family courts. The criminal justice response has, historically and until very recent times, been confined only to the very serious cases of maltreatment that led to severe injury or death.

The criminal justice system felt that issues relating to child maltreatment were best dealt with by social service agencies. The President's Commission on Law Enforcement and Administration of Justice (1967) viewed child abuse as a family problem and as a social issue and as such to be handled by social service agencies. The Commission felt that law enforcement was being handicapped because it was spending too much time on problems that bore no relationship to the criminal process. They felt this criminal process should be defined narrowly so that issues such as child abuse and drunkenness would be excluded. This attitude of noncriminal justice interference was exhibited by the Law Enforcement Assistance Administration (LEAA). The LEAA, which was formed in 1968, operated from 1968 to 1980. During this period of time, it spent approximately $8 billion funding thousands of demonstration, training, and technical assistance projects in the criminal justice area. It did not fund a child maltreatment-related project until 1975, a full 7 years after it was formed. The first child maltreatment project was a $60,000 grant awarded to Boston University to prepare a Prescriptive Package that would synthesize the best programs, methods, and procedures being used by communities across the country to reduce the incidence of child abuse. The final product, "Child Abuse Intervention," was published in 1976 (Schuchter, 1976). It concluded that criminal justice processing is required in only the various serious cases of child abuse such as the death of a child. Law enforcement was instructed to take the "Least disruptive intervention necessary to protect the life and safety of the child" (Schuchter, 1976).

From 1975, when LEAA funded its first child abuse program, to 1979, when it funded its last, it supported a total of only 11 projects directly related to child maltreatment and approximately 12 that had child abuse prevention as one of several objectives. A majority of the projects directly related to child maltreatment was funded under LEAA's Victim Witness Program and Family Violence Demonstration Program. The nature of as well as the extent of programming began to change in 1980. By comparison to the 12-year period that LEAA was in existence when only 11 child maltreatment projects totaling $1.72 million were funded, the 5-year period from 1980 to 1985 yielded 25 projects totaling $9.5 million. During this latter period, the Office of Justice Programs, the predecessor to LEAA, not only spent a considerable amount more funds in the area, but it also began to change the focus of the programming. The focus of many of these projects was on examining the links between abuse and delinquency, intervention on part of the criminal justice system in child maltreatment cases, the maltreated child as a victim of crime, and the missing and exploited child.

These programming changes were prompted and supported by various changes in the public attitudes and perceptions about child maltreatment and subsequent legislative changes. The focus of these changes was a recognition that child maltreatment was not only social or medical, or a problem to be dealt with by doctors, mental health personnel, and social work personnel, but also a crime to be dealt with by the criminal justice community.

These changing perceptions, attitudes, and laws were caused by a long series of events, a few examples of which included: The President's Task Force on Victims of Crime; The Attorney General's Task Force on Family Violence; the showing on national television of the films "Something About Amelia" and "Adam"; the Manhattan Beach/McMartin Case; and the Third Annual Conference on Child Sexual Victimization.

The Final Report of the President's Task Force on Victims of Crime, which was issued in December 1982, not only championed the rights of victims but also made several strong recommendations concerning the serious nature of child molestation. Judiciary recommendation No. 10 stated: "Judges should recognize the profound impact that sexual molestation of children has on victims and their families and treat it as a crime that should result in punishment, with treatment available when appropriate." There was a similar recommendation for prosecutors. The significance of these recommendations and others related to children as victims should not be underestimated, for the Chairperson of the Task Force on Victims of Crime, Lois H. Herrington, later became the Department of Justice's Assistant Attorney General for Justice Programs. In this capacity she was able to set a policy direction for the Department of Justice that essentially complied with the recommendations of the Task Force. In addition to overall policy direction, Mrs. Herrington steered the resources of those bureaus under her supervision to those areas outlined in the Task Force report. Having these bureaus adopt as their priorities such victim issues as child molestation or improvement of the rights of child victims eventually led to many state and local governments following suit.

During 1984, several more events transpired that helped to change our attitude regarding child maltreatment. In May 1984, the National Children's Hospital held its Third National Conference on Child Sexual Victimization. The Conference itself was not so notable as that which took place at the Conference—the disclosure by U.S. Senator Paula Hawkins that she had been sexually molested as a child. The public announcement not only helped to propel the issue of child abuse into the public sphere but also helped to dispel the myth that these crimes only happen to the poor and disadvantaged. The public announcement also helped add political credence and acceptability to the issue of child maltreatment. Child victims now could look to Senator Hawkins as a supporter who was one of them; someone who knew issues not only substantively but also personally.

Senator Hawkins serves in a key leadership role in the Senate. In her position as Chair, Senate Subcommittee on Children, Family, Drugs, and Alcoholism, she is able to hold numerous hearings on the issue of child maltreatment and to sponsor major legislation in the area. Much of the legislation she sponsored involved the legal aspects of child abuse and the criminal nature of abuse, especially child sexual abuse. The Children's Justice Act (S.140), a bill introduced by Senator Hawkins in the 1985 Legislative Session, is designed to encourage states to enact child protection reforms that can improve legal and administrative proceedings in the investigation and prosecution of child sexual abuse cases. If passed, it would become part of the Child Abuse Prevention and Treatment Act, thereby adding a criminal justice focus to a piece of legislation that traditionally has had a social service orientation and focus.

As previously mentioned, during 1984, two films were shown on national television that did more than any other film, series of films, or programming to heighten public awareness of the problem of child maltreatment. These films, "Something about Amelia" and "Adam," were viewed by millions of people throughout the United States. "Something about Amelia" made people acutely aware of the fact that child abuse—in this case child sexual abuse—could be found anywhere, and that even though involvement by the criminal justice system is not always accepted by the family, there is an appropriate role for it. "Adam" concerned the abduction of a child from a shopping center. Although not dealing directly with child abuse, it indirectly probably did more

for the cause of child abuse than any other film and/or event that preceded it. "Adam" can be called the beginning of the Child Safety
Movement—one that recognizes the vulnerability and high victimization
rates of children to all types of offenses, including child maltreatment.
While the missing children's issue has been at the forefront of the child
safety movement, child maltreatment has become part of the broader
issues of child safety, and its proponents have been very successful in
rationalizing a need for criminal justice involvement in all aspects of
child safety and in obtaining criminal justice participation in a wide
variety of child safety efforts.

In September 1983, a trash collector named James Rud was arrested
for sexual abuse of children in Jordan, Minnesota. Eventually, 25 other
adults, ranging from a housewife to a law enforcement officer, were
implicated and arrested. This case was followed by a case in Manhattan
Beach, California, where, in April 1984, 249 counts of child molestation
were brought against 7 persons who owned and operated the McMartin
Preschool. Among those accused of sexually abusing children at the
day-care center were the owner of the school, Virginia McMartin, a 78-
year-old grandmother, confined to a wheel chair, her daughter, and
her grandson.

Although all charges of sexual abuse, except those against one person
in the Jordan, Minnesota case, were eventually dropped, and a majority
of charges against those in the Manhattan Beach case were also
dropped, neither case proved conclusively that these events do not
happen. (This case is still in the preliminary hearing stage, and charges
were dropped when children refused to testify against the alleged perpetrators.) On the contrary, these two cases received an enormous
amount of publicity and helped to heighten public awareness of the
very serious nature of the alleged abuse. Even absent any conviction
in court, there were many who believed that these events, in part or
in total, did occur; and because of the bizarre and serious nature of
the allegations—which ranged from the sexual abuse of children, killing
of animals, use of children in pornography, transportation of children
to different sites in order to sexually exploit them, and use of children
in many different rituals—required immediate action on part of the
criminal justice system.

In September 1984, the Attorney General's Task Force on Family Violence issued its final report. The underlying premises of this report were:

• That family violence (to include child abuse) was to be considered a
  crime
• That the legal response to family violence must be guided primarily
  by the nature of the abusive act and not the relationship between
  the victim and the abuser

- That family violence is learned behavior
- That family violence is cyclical in nature
- That special procedures need to be developed to ensure that children are not doubly victimized by the nature of the abusive act

The report was explicit in the fact that it expected the legal system to treat assaults in the family as seriously as it would treat the same assault if it occurred between strangers. The message extended by the report is straightforward.

Law enforcement officers ordinarily do not arrest two strangers who have shoved each other, and neither do they ordinarily arrest two family members engaged in similar behavior. But when an officer enters a home and finds a mother or child who is the victim of an assault, the officer is dealing with a crime—a crime with its own distinctive characteristics but first and foremost a crime. When a prosecutor considers a criminal complaint arising out of an arrest for child, spouse, or elder abuse, incest, or molestation, the first consideration is the nature of the violation of law that has occurred. When an offender has been convicted, the judge, as in all cases, may consider all sorts of extenuating circumstances in reaching a sentence. A judge should prescribe a sentence that takes the special nature of the victim's needs into account. But the fact that the offender is related to the victim may not in and of itself be a reason for being lenient.

The rationale provided for taking what may be considered a much stronger position on child maltreatment was simple justice. The report stated that the American legal system should not countenance one person physically harming another. It goes on to explain that by recognizing and regarding that acts such as child maltreatment are crimes we can eventually help prevent some of them through a deterrent effect.

As with the President's Task Force on Victims, the person asked to implement the recommendations of the Family Violence Task Force was Lois H. Herrington. Using the authority of her office, Mrs. Herrington was able to convince every bureau within her jurisdiction to adopt the recommendations of the Task Force as priorities for research, training, and demonstration programming. During 1985, each of these bureaus allocated millions of dollars on various projects and activities related to child maltreatment. In addition to funds, a countless number of speeches and appearances were made by various Department of Justice officials promoting the Task Force report and supporting the criminal nature of family violence. Department officials were very successful in marketing the report and its findings. Several states and counties used the report as the basis for statewide and local commissions examining family violence issues, and several of these adopted state laws and regulations that were consistent with the recommendations in the Task Force report. In 1985, every state except one met in legislative session, and a majority of them considered legislation related to maltreatment and the criminal justice system.

Collectively, these five events helped propel us into an era when the criminal justice community is no longer viewed as a bit or stand-in player called upon in rare circumstances only when other service providers feel they need additional assistance but rather as a key player that is called on immediately for assistance.

And what is the role for the criminal justice system in child maltreatment cases?

In discussing the role of the criminal justice system, it is important not to stress the differences but the broad-based similarities between its role and responsibilities and those of the other systems that deal with the maltreated child, such as the social service system. We must recognize that while the role and method of operation of the criminal justice system and other systems may of necessity differ, their major objective should be the same: the safety and well-being of the child. The roles of these systems should not be competitive; but rather complementary.

Any discussion of the role of the criminal justice system has to be prefaced with the caveat that we know very little about it, and we know even less about the maltreatment of certain categories of children such as the handicapped. From a smattering of research on the topic of criminal justice intervention in child maltreatment cases, we know that certain criminal justice proceedings can be, but do not have to be, more traumatic for a child than the actual victimization.

The role of the criminal justice system should not be to add to an already traumatic experience. In cases where there is a report of suspected child maltreatment, it should intervene to protect the child; and in those cases where there is sufficient evidence (probable cause) that a crime has been committed, it should proceed with its investigation. Law enforcement must proceed with child abuse cases as it would stranger-to-stranger cases, that is, by basing their investigation and subsequent action not on the relationship of the victim to the offender but on the nature of the crime.

PROTECTION OF VICTIMS

The protection of the child victim is one of the most important roles the law enforcement community can play. When called upon to investigate a case of child maltreatment, they have to make a decision whether the child has been maltreated and whether the child will continue to be maltreated if left in the home. The law enforcement officer must weigh the drawbacks of removing the child from the home compared to the possible harm that will obtain if the child remains in the home. The law enforcement officer should be concerned primarily with the protection and safety of the child rather than the restoration or maintenance of the family.

INTERVENTION

Often in child maltreatment cases, it is necessary for law enforcement officers to intervene and make decisions about proceeding with criminal justice processing. Intervention on behalf of law enforcement is not always, nor should it always be, synonymous with arrest and prosecution. Child abuse has to be divided into two distinct categories: physical and sexual abuse. We should presume that all cases of sexual abuse/molestation fall under the purview of the criminal justice system. Sexual abuse does not happen by accident; it is intentional. Many perpetrators state that they never intended to do any harm; however, this should not be considered as a rationale for neither arresting nor prosecuting. Sexual abuse is a crime that, by its very nature, requires knowledge of the act. This form of abuse often leads to serious, long-term psychological damage. We cannot condone this behavior as criminal and proceed accordingly. We must remember that we have an obligation to protect the child. While parents and other caretakers have the same responsibility, they sometimes fail; we cannot disappoint our children twice. In general, physical abuse of a child may not always be a crime. In many locations, the term child abuse is a social service term and not a legal one. In these locations, a person could be found by protective services to be abusing or maltreating his/her child; however, the abuse or maltreatment may not constitute a crime, dependent on the legal definition in that particular state. In many states, law enforcement officers use general criminal statutes, such as assault, rape, and sodomy, to prosecute suspected child abusers. These statutes often carry a higher degree or burden of proof than child abuse statutes used by protective services to determine whether a child has been abused.

When investigating child maltreatment cases, law enforcement officers are confronted with many different kinds of cases. There are some that are very clear cut, that is, long-term, deliberate abuse that results in serious injury or death; few would argue *against* law enforcement intervention in these cases. There are other cases that are accidental and result in minor injuries, such as cuts, abrasions, and bruises; few would argue the need for law enforcement intervention. These two extremes, one requiring law enforcement intervention and the other not requiring it address only a portion of the child maltreatment cases investigated by law enforcement officials; a great number fall in categories outside those given above: nonserious injury/nonaccidental or deliberate or serious injury/nondeliberate, accidental or nondeliberate.

There is not an overall consensus, even among the criminal justice community, on the role of law enforcement in these latter two areas. In those cases where there was a deliberate intent to cause harm but the injury was relatively minor, law enforcement has traditionally either not been involved with the case (i.e., they never received the report), or upon investigation, find that the injury was relatively minor and turned the case over to social services, provided that the child did not appear to be in further danger of immediate injury or abuse. Today, many law enforcement agencies are handling these cases the same way; however, many understand the complexities of these cases and potential for further abuse or harm and are developing a coordinated investigative approach by reviewing all child maltreatment cases with representatives of other disciplines, such as the social services system, mental health and health communities, involved in child maltreatment. Together they can formulate a systematic approach with defined protocols that minimize the trauma suffered by the child victim and maximize the opportunity to change the abusive patterns of the offender. Protocols should clearly define what types of abuse will be prosecuted and under what circumstances. Criteria for prosecution should be based on such characteristics as: severity of and length of abuse and not on the relationship of abuser to victim.

The multidisciplinary approach is not meant to abrogate any one agency's role in the processing of child maltreatment cases. The recognition of the complexity and seriousness of these types of cases and the most effective and efficient utilization of community resources needed to bring these cases to successful resolution should be established.

Multidisciplinary teams are especially useful in the areas of child sexual abuse, maltreatment of the very young, and the abuse of the handicapped. Each of these categories presents special problems to all those investigating allegations of maltreatment. Frequently, these children suffer additional harm and trauma at the hands of those agencies that provide the help. Misguided practices, such as repeated interviews and working at cross- or differing purposes, can be avoided by establishing multidisciplinary teams that operate under protocols that clearly define the responsibility of each agency or organization while avoiding unnecessary duplication of effort.

Intervention on the part of law enforcement, whether individually or as part of a multidisciplinary team, regardless of how efficient the established process may be or how caring the intervenors are, is not the panacea to the problem. Law enforcement agencies can intervene and protect the child and place sanctions on the abuser, thereby sending a clear message that the behavior is inappropriate and will not be condoned. They cannot, however, put an end to this travesty or provide the solution to the problem. In order to deal effectively with all forms of child maltreatment, it will be necessary to learn how to prevent its occurrence. Even the Attorney General's Task Force on Family Violence, which many professionals have called projustice system intervention, has acknowledged that the best strategy for dealing with family violence is its prevention: "today's abused children will become tomorrows abusers, runaways, and delinquents."

While prevention may be the best strategy to deal with child maltreatment, it is by no means the only one. If we are to succeed in preventing and reducing the rates of maltreatment, we are going to have to recognize child maltreatment as a complex sociolegal problem and to develop and initiate a variety of comprehensive and coordinated programs that acknowledge the special needs of child victims. Funding, or the lack thereof, should not be an excuse for failure to initiate new programs. Existing child maltreatment programs and processes need to be critically examined. Those that fail to achieve predetermined goals should be abandoned, regardless of how well entrenched they are in the community, and should be replaced with programs and processes that:

- *Acknowledge the fragile nature and rights of children*—programs and policies cannot revictimize the child
- *Do more to focus on the offender*—perpetrators have to be dealt with; they cannot be ignored
- *Fully utilize existing community resources*—private/public partnerships need to be created. This is a problem that affects society as a whole, and society (both the public and private sectors) is going to have to deal with it.

We are also going to have to learn more about the problem of child maltreatment, especially as it relates to criminal justice community involvement in the problem and its effects on particular categories of youth, such as the handicapped.

What little we know about the involvement of the criminal justice system in child maltreatment cases is only exceeded by what little we know about abuse of any particular category of the child population, such as the handicapped. However, we do know enough about handicapped children, maltreatment in general, and the criminal justice system to make some rational judgments about what we need to do to effectively deal with handicapped children who have been identified as being maltreated.

By recognizing that normal children have difficulties when involved with the criminal justice system, it can be safely assumed that handicapped children, regardless of this handicap, will probably experience even greater difficulties. Handicapped children present us with a variety of complex problems that must be overcome if we are to successfully utilize the criminal justice system in intervening in and satisfactorily resolving abusive situations. The first problem a handicapped child may experience, especially if his/her handicap relates to a speech disorder, is effectively communicating that he/she has been abused. Relating an abusive experience to a law enforcement official for such an individual may take considerably longer than for a normal child and unless the law enforcement official has a good understanding of the specific handicap, he could easily dismiss the case as unfounded. This problem can be easily corrected by providing such children with knowledgeable professionals who can serve as interpreters thereby clarifying the situation for the law enforcement officials.

There are several other hurdles to overcome; if the handicapped child is fortunate enough to effectively communicate his/her story, the next hurdle is that of credibility—getting other persons in the criminal justice system to believe that the abuse actually happened. Many children experience some difficulties or problems convincing others that they have been abused and/or of the specific circumstances surrounding that abuse. They face even greater difficulties in cases of child sexual abuse where there is often little or no corroborating evidence. The only proof of abuse in these cases is the assertions of the child. Many who work within the criminal justice system are hesitant to proceed with only a "child's word" in a court of law. The testimony of a child is not as convincing as that of an adult, especially when the adult may be a respected member of the community.

Many of the myths concerning children (they lie, have poor memories, and are easily led into telling what we want them to say) have colored our perception of children and have altered the way we deal with them. We want to be assured, more than we would if the victim were an adult, of the circumstances and nature of a crime before we willingly undertake a case. When children are involved, especially handicapped children, we can expect the criminal justice system to ask for more evidence than what is normally required by law before the case proceeds.

Assuming a handicapped child overcomes the first two hurdles, he/she still is going to face several other barriers to getting his/her case fairly adjudicated. Competency can be, for many handicapped children, the one hurdle they cannot overcome. States establish their own criteria to determine who is and who is not competent to testify in court. While a majority of the states have adopted Rule 601 of the Federal Rules of Evidence or a commensurate rule that "every person is competent to be a witness," the remainder use various rules that measure the testimonial capacity of a child on the basis of a combination of factors:

- Present understanding of the difference between truth and falsity and an appreciation of the obligation or responsibility to speak the truth
- Mental capacity at the time of the occurrence in question in order to observe or receive accurate impressions of the occurrence
- Memory sufficient to retain an independent recollection of the observations
- Capacity to communicate the truth or translate into words the memory of such observation and the capacity to understand simple questions about the occurrence

Thus, one can see from the foregoing criteria that in those states that do not use the "presumption of competency" rule to qualify a person to testify, children, especially handicapped children, can have a very difficult time qualifying as a witness. Not being qualified to testify in a case of child abuse, again especially child sexual abuse, is tantamount to allowing the alleged abuser go free, because without a witness it is difficult to have a trial. This is especially so in cases of sexual maltreatment where usually no physical evidence exists.

If a handicapped child is able to be qualified as a witness, that is he/she is found competent to testify in court, one final hurdle remains: the trial. It can be a very traumatic and trying experience for any child, regardless of whether or not the child is handicapped. At the trial, the child will have to face the accused publicly and relate, in vivid detail, the events of maltreatment. The child will be questioned by a defense attorney who may attempt, through complex and/or lengthy questioning, to confuse the child and render his/her testimony worthless. Depending upon the handicap, these children could experience even greater difficulties in responding to some of the questions posed by the defense counsel.

There is a wide variety of means by which we can help the child who is called upon to testify in court. We can use videotaped statements, closed circuit television, anatomically correct dolls, and comfortable courtroom settings. We can exclude the public from some parts of the hearing, and can request the media not to print the child's name. We can also explore the possibility of having the judge rephrase those questions that appear to be purposely vague or misleading. The prosecutor can block off view of the defendant when the child is testifying. In addition, child advocates can assist the child throughout the court process. Many of these reforms do not require new legislation. The National Institute of Justice pointed out in a recent publication, "*When the Victim Is a Child,*" that "virtually every cause of stress on a child witness can be ameliorated to some extent within practices that fall squarely within the trial court's discretion." The keys to the development and implementation of any practice, procedure, or formal reform that further protects children and reduces the stress they are placed under when they testify are better understanding and recognition of: what children are and are not; what they are and are not capable of doing; what we should and should not do to help them. We must recognize that *all* children who come into contact with the justice system are already handicapped. They are handicapped by the fact that as children they have to face a system that was designed for adults—one that does not always take the needs of a child into consideration. Handicapped children are doubly handicapped by their mere participation in an imperfect system.

Child maltreatment is not going to disappear in this or the next several decades. There are some people, such as Dr. Robert ten Bensel, a professor at the University of Minnesota, who believe that we will have child maltreatment to contend with for at least the next 100 years, even though it has been recognized as a major social, justice, and medical problem. Child maltreatment must be met head on; we cannot shrink from our responsibilities. If we do not address maltreatment today and if we do not begin to develop and implement strategies to prevent maltreatment effectively, it will grown geometrically, and we will have to contend with it not only for the next 100 years but for hundreds after that. We must recognize that child maltreatment has devastating effects not only on individual children but on society as a whole. Child maltreatment reduces our overall quality of life and can lead to other socially unacceptable actions, such as further abuse and delinquency. Child maltreatment is not a problem for any one system or discipline to address. It is an insidious and complex problem; a problem that pervades every segment of our society. If we are to effectively reduce the rates of child maltreatment in this country, the various systems involved in dealing with maltreatment are going to have to work together toward a common goal. We can no longer afford to be dispassionate in our approach to the problem. While our objectives may differ, our goal—the protection of the child—should be uniform. We need to have a single sense of purpose. No war has ever been won with generals representing different services quarreling over their goal or mission.

Perhaps more important than getting professionals to work together is educating the public about the insidious nature of child maltreatment and its cost in terms not only of physical and mental suffering but economic as well. It is only when full support from the public is achieved that we will be able to overcome abuse.

chapter 11

MASS MEDIA ISSUES

Robert B. McCall
Thomas C. Gregory

INTRODUCTION

Few issues in child development have received more media coverage during the last decade than child abuse. Newspapers, magazines, radio, and television have treated the problem of child abuse in its many forms as a high profile and, frequently, sensational story. Ordinarily, in most contexts, front page and prime time coverage can be a public relation director's dream. However, those who are working toward prevention of a highly complex and emotionally intense problem, such as the abuse of handicapped children, may find the dream a nightmare. It is possible for even a carefully crafted media campaign on this sensitive issue to lead to misunderstanding, misinformation, and hasty misguided action. The specific task of this chapter, then, is to provide workers in the field of the abused handicapped child with information about the media— its rationale, operating procedures, and effects—so that they can work with the media more efficiently and effectively.

WHY THE MEDIA?

Media exposure can contribute to solving social problems in several ways.

Creating Awareness

It would be hard to imagine a successful campaign to prevent the abuse of handicapped children that did not make the general public aware of the problem, that did not build a public constituency for solving the problem that would push legislators and agency officials to appropriate funds and change policies, and that did not create or maintain a public intolerance of the abuse of handicapped children by parents and public officials. Specifically, while no sequential data are available, public awareness of abuse in general has risen dramatically during the last few years, partly as a result of media attention. In 1981, for example, 91% of the adult American public thought child abuse was a serious problem (Louis Harris survey, September 1981, reported in Gelles, 1982). In short, the media create public awareness (McCombs & Shaw, 1972) that is unlikely to occur without its involvement.

But will a few sensational, well-publicized cases of the abuse of handicapped children suffice? Probably not. The flow of news is very rapid, and yesterday's headline is often eclipsed in minds of readers by today's front-page story. Unless a pertinent news event breaks periodically, the issue is soon forgotten. From a news standpoint, the abuse of handicapped children does not occur very often, and when it does, it must compete with other news items for priority in the news presentation. Therefore, it is unlikely that sufficient public awareness will be created without a deliberate attempt to promote the issue of the abuse of handicapped children as a news topic—that is, to conduct a concerted media campaign to create awareness of the problem.

Agenda Setting

In addition to creating public awareness, the media can set public agendas (McCombs & Shaw, 1972). That is, they influence how much importance people attribute to one issue versus another. If the media feature a given story, the public is likely to attach relatively more importance to that issue than it might if it were not featured so prominently. This results in people talking about the topic more, thinking about it, according it more importance than other topics, and presumably increasing the likelihood of action. It is often said that the media do not tell people *what* to think so much as they tell them what to think *about*.

Of course, the media can overdo it, and the public can say that they have "had enough of the hostage situation," "the recanted rape testimony," or "child abuse." This means that once the campaign gets going, if it goes well, promoters have a limited amount of time in which to get the job done before the media and the public decide enough is enough.

Changing Attitudes

Generally speaking, media portrayals can create attitudes where none previously existed and strengthen attitudes already present, but they are less effective at reversing attitudes (McQuail, 1969).

Applied to the abuse of handicapped children, this potential has an unusual set of implications. It is reasonable to suppose that the public already holds a negative attitude toward the abuse of children. Indeed, large segments of the public found sex abuse, for example, so repugnant that they did not want to confront the issue at all; great controversy swirled around the presentation of television programs on the subject. Ironically, then, public attitudes against abuse had to be *softened* before the media could present information about the topic.

Campaigns that want to go beyond simply heightening public awareness of this terrible problem and marshal support for constructive remediation and prevention must carry this irony another step. For example, many people believe that an individual who would sexually abuse a child must be psychotic, and the appropriate consequence is to confine such a person and throw away the key. Again, these negative attitudes must be softened enough to provide information about abusers that portray them as people with problems and worthy of being helped. An attempt is being made in this regard by publicizing the slogan, "There are two victims in any case of child abuse—the child and the parent."

Fortunately, much of this early work in public attitude change already has been done in the context of child abuse in general (especially by the National Committee for the Prevention of Child Abuse and the Advertising Council) and may not need to be repeated in the specific context of the abused handicapped. Nevertheless, abusing a handicapped child is likely to be perceived as a particularly heinous act that should be treated in a correspondingly severe manner, which may require changing attitudes and understanding about abusers before remediation and prevention can effectively occur.

On the other hand, the abuse of handicapped children may have come to public attention too late. The media are already featuring stories about how day-care providers and others who work with children are so sensitized to the issue of abuse that they are afraid to touch children even in an affectionate way, lest they be accused of sexual abuse. Attitudes may have already changed, with the resulting backlash effect.

Imparting Information

Perhaps the most acknowledged goal of the media, besides entertainment, is to impart information. News, by definition, is information, and the media are the most influential textbooks and teachers of the public after formal schooling is completed (Schramm & Wade, 1967). Moreover, legislators and policymakers derive as much or more information through the media than through reports from their own agencies (Caplan, Morrison, & Stambaugh, 1975; Weiss, 1974). For example, it is widely believed that the television program, "Something about Amelia," influenced Congress and legislation on sexual abuse. At the same time, the evidence suggests that the public learns and remembers very little about what is presented in the media.

Acknowledging the existence of a large and confusing literature on the ability to recall news, especially from radio and television, and that such research is difficult to execute, a few conclusions emerge (Berry, 1983; Woodall, Davis, & Sahin, 1983). First, while adults can learn and remember substantial amounts from television and radio presentations when exposed and tested under optimal conditions, free or even cued recall minutes or a few hours after an actual broadcast "is strikingly poor" (Berry, 1983). For example, viewers can recall only 1 or 2, and rarely more than 3, of the 14 or 15 items presented on a television news program, and from 20 to 50% cannot recall *any* item (Katz, Adoni, & Parness, 1977; Neuman 1976). One-half the viewers of the television weather segment cannot recall the forecast for tomorrow when asked only 15–90 minutes after the broadcast (Hyatt, Riley, & Sederstrom, 1978).

Why the disparity between what people are *able* to learn and remember and what they *actually* learn and remember? This competence–performance distinction is old hat to psychologists, who generally search for motivational factors to explain the discrepancy. For example, one factor involved in naturalistic media presentations is lack of complete attention to the program (Woodall *et al.*, 1983). Just because the television is on and people are in the same room with it does not mean they are attentive to the presentation. Not surprisingly, then, factors that help recruit attention (e.g., importance of the topic to the viewer, newsworthiness, interest value, and vivid pictures, especially of emotionally negative events) aid attention and consequently, recall (Berry, 1983; Katz *et al.*, 1977; Miller & Barrington, 1981; Wilson, 1974; Woodall *et al.*, 1983).

It is also likely that the presentation of information on television, while calculated to recruit attention, is not presented in a format that maximizes learning and recall. For example, most factual information on television news is presented auditorily, and the pictures may not correspond to the auditory message. Instead, the who, what, and where of an event (but not its how, why, and consequences) are usually depicted visually, and viewers seem to recall those aspects that are reinforced with pictures more than the causes and consequences of the event (Findall & Hoijer, 1976).

Although some studies have sought to determine what kinds of information are learned and remembered, what presentation formats are most effective (few studies document what people learn from newspapers), and what kinds of viewers are likely to remember what kinds of information, the results thus far are not terribly clear. Indications are that complex interactions and contingencies exist between several factors (e.g., viewers whose personal experiences or interests dispose them toward a given topic that is presented in a form that attracts attention and relates the issue to those viewers' particular needs and experiences). Thus, no one denies the media's ability to inform, but that potential seems substantially greater than what is often actually achieved. The implications are that one should not try to present too much information, and that it should coalesce around a single point or attitude directed at a specific type of person.

Promoting Action

Public service campaigns have the avowed goal of altering people's behaviors—urging them to contribute money or to take certain actions (e.g., convincing women of the importance of performing self-examinations of their breasts to detect lumps that may indicate cancer). Obviously, advertisers feel that the media have the potential to change people's behavior, by persuading them to purchase a given product. Anecdotes tell about the numbers of people who obtain medical checkups shortly after a major public figure undergoes treatment for a particular disease (e.g., the President's operation for cancer, a President's wife who undergoes breast surgery). There was a 500% increase in library card applications reportedly following the airing of an episode of "Happy Days" in which the leading character, the Fonz, took out a library card. And many newspapers document the dramatic rise in calls to hot lines and other services after programs on abuse are broadcast.

Again, however, the data are not so persuasive as the potential suggests. This seems especially true for public health campaigns, which the early literature indicated had very little effect on people's behavior. More recent research, however, demonstrates that the effects can be substantial if the program embodies strategies and production techniques known to promote attention and behavior change, if the desired behavior is explicitly portrayed or modeled, and if the evaluation research is broad-based and competently done (Atkin, 1979). For example, in one of the most comprehensive and thoroughly evaluated multimedia health campaigns, researchers found that information provided in the media alone led to reductions in blood pressure and other coronary risk factors in an entire medium-sized town. The effects were often greater if the media presentations were accompanied by the support and direct reinforcement of other people (Meyer, Nash, McAlister, Maccoby, & Farquhar, 1980).

In another study (Winett, Leckliter, Chinn, & Stahl, 1984), a single presentation of a 20-minute television program dramatizing simple energy-conservation techniques resulted in general home energy savings of approximately 10–20% over several months; this was achieved with minimal interpersonal support. In a third study (Ball-Rokeach, Rokeach, & Grube, 1984), a single television program featuring Ed Asner and Sandy Hill (former anchor of "Good Morning America"), which was viewed by a very large percentage of people in a few towns, was able to alter the political values and social attitudes toward the issues of equality, freedom, and the environment. Moreover, it generated substantially more monetary contributions to subsequent appeals, which were not mentioned in the program, by proenvironment, antiracism, and antisexism groups.

But, as mentioned, the results have not always been so impressive or clear (Atkin, 1979). One reason is that media effects are different from the kinds of behavioral change that psychologists, for example, usually expect. A research or clinical psychologist typically attempts to get a substantial percentage of the treatment group to change in a specific and obvious way. In contrast, only a very small percentage of the individuals who receive the media's message may change. For instance, the presentation of seven 30-minute television programs in Finland designed to encourage people to stop smoking produced the desired result in only 1% of the smokers (McAlister, Puska, Koskela, Pallonene, & Maccoby, 1980). While that might seem like a dismal failure to research psychologists, the absolute number of individuals who stopped smoking was enormous and the cost per person who stopped was less than $1.00. No other behavioral treatment program can cure so many, for so little, in so short a time. One must, however, think of the sample size and research effort required to demonstrate such effectiveness when only 20%, for example, of the population watch the program, and only 1% of those will modify their behavior.

Not only is evaluation research on media health promotion campaigns difficult to conduct, but not all campaigns are equally effective. Factors that seem to be associated with greater impact (Atkin, 1979) include using sources of information that are credible, trustworthy, competent, dynamic, attractive, and similar to the members of the audience. Messages that are perceived to be rewarding and worthy of attention, relevant to the needs of the receiver, entertaining, and attention-getting are more effective. Concentrated bursts of messages are more effective than distributed exposure, and more messages are superior to fewer messages at least up to a point, after which oversaturation will produce negative effects.

Logical, factual appeals work better for more intelligent audiences, while emotional appeals may be more influential in motivating those people who are already convinced or indifferent, regardless of intellect.

Two-sided, balanced messages, especially regarding a highly involving problem, are superior to one-sided appeals when the audience is highly educated, initially opposed to the theme, and likely to be exposed to the opposite point of view. Informative messages may be presented best in print, while television does a better job of arousing emotions and threatening a viewer (which works predominantly in cases in which a simple concrete remedy is advocated, when receivers have low anxiety about the issue, and when a highly credible source delivers the message). Effectiveness is also improved if the audience is interested in or favorably disposed toward the message or needs the information (Ettema, Brown, & Luepker, 1983; Miller & Barrington, 1981). Finally, the media are much better at communicating information and thoughts than at changing attitudes. However attitude changes are more readily accomplished than modifying behavior.

In short, effectiveness in changing people's behavior depends on complex interactions between the nature of the message and a host of presentation characteristics. This is another argument for presenting one informational message at a time and for designing the presentation format to fit that particular message and the nature of the intended audience. As a result, short messages—public service announcements, 90-second news features—may be more cost-effective than investing in 30- or 60-minute documentaries on television.

In summary, a well-planned and well-executed media campaign on the abuse of handicapped children will, at the minimum, create some public awareness of the problem, increase understanding, and influence how much importance people attribute to the issue. Moreover, a campaign that utilizes electronic as well as print media and embodies production techniques known to promote attention and behavior change can strengthen or create attitudes and promote behavioral change and action.

Studies show that printed materials may communicate information more effectively. However, they seem to have far less impact (often none) on attitudes and behavioral change (Atkin, 1979; Winett et al., 1984), although the effectiveness of newspaper and magazine articles has not been investigated so thoroughly as television programs. The implication is that a multimedia campaign should use print media to communicate basic information while relying on television to change attitudes and promote certain behaviors.

HOW THE MEDIA WORK

It seems clear that the media must be a crucial part of any campaign to create public awareness, public concern, and public action with respect to a given issue. Since the media are independent agencies, they control what and how information is presented. Therefore, any campaign on behalf of abused handicapped children must be cognizant of the values and the procedures of the media in order to work effectively and to achieve the desired result.

Mass Media versus Targeted Communications

Media procedures, goals, and effectiveness depend in large part on the particular medium involved; there is a major distinction between mass media and targeted communications, for example.

The Mass Media. Newspapers, magazines, radio, and television send a message to a vast, undifferentiated audience in a very short span of time. They are splashy and prestigious because of this large audience, and are ideal for communicating messages that everyone, or nearly everyone, should hear. In addition, they can also be used to reach a relatively few people who are not easily identified in any other way, such as, abuse victims.

While the mass media can be very cost-efficient in reaching large numbers of people at minimum cost per contact, this advantage is gained at the expense to the professional of giving up control. The communicator—writer, editor, reporter, producer—typically exercises independent, final control over the content and format of the communication. The source of the information—the professional—has relatively little control over what is said, what aspect of the information is emphasized, and how it is presented. Not only may the message be inaccurate, misleading, or even counterproductive, but not everyone in the mass media audience should receive the same information. For example, information on prognosis that one communicates to social service workers and others who provide treatment for abusers and victims might be different from the information one would prefer to tell abuse victims who have not come forth. The mass media, then, are a shotgun approach that spray the same message indiscriminately at the general public.

Targeted Communications. "Targeted communications" are directed toward specialized audiences. Such materials include speciality magazines (e.g., the magazine *Exceptional Parent* aimed at the parents of handicapped children) as well as booklets, brochures, posters, leaflets, films, and other materials designed and distributed to specific segments of the population. Boys Town has produced several of these materials with regard to adolescent abuse.

One advantage of targeted materials is that the source of the information (i.e., the professional) controls its content and format, thereby avoiding the "middle-man" and presumably minimizing errors of accuracy, emphases, and judgment. Further, it may be more efficient to distribute information directly to "opinion leaders"—people who control or influence the actions of others—than to present the same information in the mass media. While far fewer people will be exposed to a targeted message, a greater percentage of the people who can implement the message may be reached by targeted than by mass communications.

These advantages are achieved at a price: dollars and cents. It costs money to produce and distribute brochures and films, for example, and few agencies have such funds available. Furthermore, some specific groups of individuals (e.g., abuse victims) are not readily identifiable and cannot be located to receive targeted communications.

Ultimately, a comprehensive campaign will use both methods of communication. For example, targeted materials might be sent to legislators to ensure that every legislator is exposed to certain information (e.g., the frequency of abuse, why handicapped children are at special risk, factors under their control). At the same time, it is helpful to create a public constituency for legislative action, which can be promoted through the mass media. Three out of four Americans, for example, want the government to take major responsibility for dealing with child abuse (Louis Harris survey, September 1981, reported in Gelles, 1982).

Since most individuals likely to read this chapter are unlikely to mount targeted communications campaigns, the emphasis here will be on the mass media. Readers interested in targeted communications are referred to Gregory and Stocking (1981) and McCall, Lonnborg, Gregory, Murray, and Leavitt (1982).

Understanding the Mass Media

The first step in working with the media is to understand the criteria the media use to select information to be communicated.

News. For the most part, the mass media are oriented toward news. Something is newsworthy if it is *recently discovered* (Gans, 1980; Weiss, 1984). Journalists sometimes express this criterion in the phrase "yesterday's news is today's fish wrapper." Further, news is also *new information*—something that was not widely known before, that contradicts prevailing thought, or that is unexpected or unusual. The fact that handicapped children are abused is probably not widely realized and may be newsworthy.

However, not everything that is recent and new constitutes news. The information must be *of interest or of relevance to the general public*, either because it is pertinent to social issues or policy or because it relates to the lives and experiences of the general public in an interesting or useful way.

On the one hand, the abuse of handicapped children is surprising—

it relates to the public's perception of human decency and it may pro-
voke issues of social policy (and controversy is another news criterion).
On the other hand, the general topic of the abuse has been a news
item for some time and may have passed the saturation point. Further,
because of its human drama, it is prone to being sensationalized by
the media. Therefore, the "news" may be what is different about the
abuse of the handicapped children from the abuse of nonhandicapped
children.

Independence. The press, both print and electronic, is guaranteed
freedom by the Constitution, and it is guarded fervently by journalists.
As a result, the media are very concerned about being used by members
of the public for political or social purposes. At the same time, they
want to help society. As a consequence, while a topic may be newsworthy, one normally does not contact the press directly—although it
can be done. Instead, two general routes are preferred. First, an agency
can plan an event which heightens public interest, for example, to an-
nounce the initiation of a new service, which can be covered by the
media. Second, one can provide the media with background information for feature stories. For example, when a public figure is treated
for a particular disease, that news event is taken as an "excuse"—or,
as it is called in the trade, a "news peg"—for producing feature material
about the nature of the illness or treatment that otherwise would not
be newsworthy. Similarly, if a case of abuse is discovered in an institution for the handicapped, that news event can become a "news peg"
for information about the extent of the abuse of handicapped children
either locally or nationally, why such abuse is unique, the nature of
policies and laws that might prevent such abuse from occurring, the
consequences of abuse to victims and perpetrators, and so forth.

Often, news organizations take the initiative and will contact specialists to acquire information for such feature stories. It is also legitimate for specialists to come forth at the time of a news event to offer
information, although it may be more appropriate for an intermediary
(e.g., a member of the board of trustees, a university public information
officer) to make the initial contact. Of course, this means that one may
need to wait for a "news peg" to occur before media contact is made.

Entertainment. In addition to providing news, another function of the
mass media is to entertain. While the public considers newspapers to
be sources of news, television, for example, is perceived as entertainment, including those programs whose major purpose is communicating news and information (Hofstetter & Buss, 1981; LaFollette, 1982;
Kreighbaum, 1959). While the entertainment characteristic of television
is often seen by professionals as a liability—something that interferes
with or distorts the information—docudramas, fictional stories revolving
around an issue of public concern, and standard entertainment pro-

grams are sometimes able to communicate useful information to and influence attitudes of very large audiences. This has been especially true with respect to abuse, where fictional programs on sexual abuse (e.g., "Something about Amelia") have been successful at recruiting enormous audiences and, despite particular criticisms, have portrayed common examples of abuse in more detail and with greater emotional impact than have standard news presentations. Further, the broadcasting of such programs constitutes a news event in itself which can function as the "news peg" that permits local professionals to relate the topic to circumstances in their particular towns.

The entertainment industry frequently uses professionals as consultants to advise them on program content and the accurate portrayal of special characters (e.g., abuse victims, the handicapped). For example, in the Los Angeles area clinicians and other professionals, who are known to writers and producers and are available on the short notice that television production often requires, are called upon as consultants. The National Council for Families and Television, headed by Nicholas Van Dyck (20 Nassau Street, Suite 2000, Princeton, New Jersey 08542), brings the expertise of professionals from across the country to the television entertainment industry through periodic retreats and the publication of a journal, *Television and Families*. The journal includes articles on a variety of topics pertaining to children and families that the television industry might use as background material. The preparation of an article for this periodical might be an appropriate entré to the television industry for this field.

Time. An overriding procedural constraint on journalists is time. Most local television and newspaper reporters must work at astounding speed, often producing one or more stories per day. For example, it is not uncommon for the local television news to schedule a feature segment on abuse, call up a professional seeking an interview, arrive with camera crew without much knowledge about the topic, throw out a few questions while the cameras are rolling, shoot some "action footage," leave in 30–60 minutes, and put a finished product on the air 2 or 3 hours later. Specialty writers at major publications or larger television stations often have more time and magazine writers and documentary producers have even more. But time is almost always a concern, and professionals must respect it and accept the limits it imposes.

Length. Newspaper and television news consists of relatively short presentations. The length of a typical newspaper story is approximately 300–500 words; a radio or television news segment is apt to run from 30 seconds to not more than 2 or 3 minutes. Indeed, the transcript of the half-hour network news is not much more than one complete newspaper column. Consequently, what is presented in the mass media is a summary of information, and much detail is omitted.

Typically, a news story will present mostly the *what* and little about the *why* and the *how* of an event (Burrows, 1980). This sometimes is distressing to professionals who are most interested in the causes and consequences of behaviors. In addition, when scientists, for example, criticize the accuracy of news reports of their research, a substantial number of the "errors" they identify represent omissions of information, much of which simply may be associated with the brevity of the report (McCall, 1986). Therefore, professionals who work with the media must recognize that only brief accounts will be presented and much detail omitted.

Control. While most journalists work cooperatively with their sources of information, in the last analysis the journalist has total control over the nature of the communication. Professionals are the subjects in the journalist's data collection, not the authors of the article. For many professionals who are accustomed to writing their own scholarly articles, which are rarely edited in any major way, this role reversal requires a difficult adjustment. It usually means that reporters do not call back to check the facts before they publish the article (Dunwoody, 1982; Tankard & Ryan, 1974), and sometimes the finished article or television piece does not reflect the same themes that the professional originally had in mind. For example, in a television news episode, a professional may appear for only 5–10 seconds, and the statement televised in that time may or may not be the main point that the professional made to the reporter.

More often, the inability to control the communication product sometimes translates into a distrust of the journalist by the professional (McCall, 1986). This is especially true of academics and scientists, who are often criticized by journalists for being uncooperative, obfuscatory, arrogant, and distrustful (McCall, 1986). For their part, journalists are sometimes less comfortable and more defensive in the presence of academics than other sources (McCall, 1986). This tension helps neither party and will probably be best resolved when both sides come to understand the values of the other and accept the division of labor inherent in the communications enterprise.

Accuracy. Generally speaking, news sources believe that journalists make a good many errors in presenting their information to the public. However, it is likely that sources overestimate the inaccuracies of press reports of their work. For example, approximately 60% of scientists from several disciplines, social and behavioral scientists, and the general public feel that journalistic reports of their fields are "generally accurate" or better, but approximately 95% say that a specific, actual report of their work is "generally accurate" or better. Moreover, the errors are most likely to be those of omission (e.g., information about method, results, colleagues, and qualifications) than outright misrepresentations of fact. This suggests that a portion of the "error rate" may be a lack of acceptance by the scientist of the brevity of journalistic reports. In summary, however, while errors do occur, the accuracy of journalistic reports is substantially higher than professionals generally believe. (For a review of this literature, see McCall [1986].)

HOW TO WORK WITH THE MEDIA

Most professionals will not design a media campaign, but are likely to be information sources for journalists and guests on interview and talk shows. The principal method by which journalists collect information is the personal or telephone interview. Unfortunately, the journalistic interview is comparable to requesting the professional to present one-draft dictation without notes or preparation to several thousand or perhaps over a million people of diverse backgrounds who have almost no knowledge of the subject matter. Professionals are rarely trained to communicate with each other; they are certainly not experienced at communicating with the public. Very few are able to dictate, and those who do dictate are rarely happy with their first drafts. The journalistic interview is simply a task most professionals are ill-prepared to do, and terror, rather than arrogance, would be an appropriate emotional response.

Professionals, therefore, should prepare for media interviews. Such preparation might reduce the number and intensity of professional complaints about the media and improve the communication product. Below are a few guidelines on how to do a media interview. A more complete discussion can be found in McCall (1983, 1985, 1986).

Preparation

When you are contacted initially by a reporter, for example, you should acquire some basic information. Typically the reporter will provide his or her name, the newspaper or station involved, and a sentence or two about the nature of the story he or she is working on. You might also inquire about the main point of the story, what types of information you are to provide (do *not* ask what questions will be asked of you), who else the reporter expects to interview, and the reporter's deadline.

Decisions. You then need to decide whether you are the most appropriate individual for the intended story. Many professionals, for all their protestations to the contrary, are flattered when the media call and are quite willing to talk about topics that are not their areas of specialty. If the newspaper or station is a national one, they want national experts, and you need to decide if you are among the few leading authorities in the country on that topic. If the newspaper or station is local, then you may be one of the leading local authorities even if the topic is not your primary specialty.

Outlines. Often the reporter will want to interview you immediately on the telephone. If, however, some time is available (e.g., the deadline is not imminent) and the topic is somewhat complex, it may be wise for you to request that the reporter call you back in ½ to 1 hour to give you time to "gather some pertinent information." During this time, obtain the information you need and outline answers to questions you might anticipate after having heard the kinds of information the reporter desires. For example, if the reporter is interested in the type of parent who would abuse their handicapped child, you might jot down several characteristics of a "typical" abuser or two or three of the most common types of abusers.

Such preparation is important for at least two reasons. First, you give yourself more time to organize your thoughts and identify information pertinent to the issue. Second, you are less likely to omit important pieces of information during the interview because you have an outline of what you want to say. Ordinarily, for example, when you are asked the characteristics of an abuser, you might mention the first thing that comes to mind. That may or may not be the most common or most important trait. Furthermore, before you are finished naming the other characteristics, the reporter may ask you a different question, steering the conversation into another area. The result is that only one or two of the five characteristics, for example, are mentioned and when you read the article, you become upset because information has been omitted. With an outline, however, you are more likely to tell the reporter that there are five characteristics—the first is, the second is, and so forth through the fifth.

Press Releases. If you have initiated an event (e.g., a guest speaker is appearing at a public meeting, a new service is being provided) or you are frequently contacted by the media, you might prepare a written statement announcing the event, presenting your views, and including some brief biographical information. Some organizations (e.g., corporations, universities) have public information offices staffed with experienced journalists who are capable of writing a professional-sounding news release (a statement in the form of a brief newspaper article). Most professionals, however, are *not* able to do so without help. Nevertheless, you can write a brief statement of the facts, your opinions, and your background, which can be given to a reporter and contributes to the accuracy of the presentation of that material (Berry, 1967; Tichenor, Olien, Harrison, & Donohue, 1970).

When you are preparing a release, bear in mind the news criteria and the preferences of journalists. Answers should be concise and readily respond to the four W's of the topic—Who is involved in the abuse of handicapped children and what is the extent of the problem nationally and in your locality; What is abuse; When has it occurred; Why does it happen? Have simple, concrete examples and cases ready to illustrate general points, and be sensitive to controversy (e.g., new policies) and how the issue relates to the layperson (e.g., what they can do, how they can respond, what needs to be done in society).

The Interview

Attitude. Approach the task with an attitude of cooperation and respect for the journalist.

Brevity. Try to answer questions directly and as briefly as possible. If you provide long answers, you invite the journalist to select material from what you say, and what the journalist selects may not be the same points as you would select. Long-winded answers also invite the journalist to paraphrase your statements rather than to use a direct quote.

Style. Be conversational and illustrate your points with short concrete examples that relate to people's experience.

On-the-Record. Assume that everything you say to a journalist will be quoted or used. While most (but not all) reporters will honor a request to speak "off-the-record" or "on background," that request must be made *before* you say anything (Stocking & Dunwoody, 1982). However, speaking "off-the-record" establishes a bad habit of saying things you do not want the reporter to use (McCall, 1986). To keep your mind on the task, always assume you are "on-the-record."

Limits. Be honest and straightforward, and identify those statements that are mainstream clinical practice, your personal judgment, the results of research, or rank speculation. Do not guess or estimate, and stay within your competence. You need not be afraid to say you do not know something (unless that fact alone would be newsworthy). But if you plead ignorance, it should then be explained why you do not know, what you do know about the topic, and who the reporter should contact to obtain a more complete answer.

Broadcast Interviews and Talk Shows

Live broadcast interviews, which sometimes involve call-ins or questions from the audience, require some additional skills because your performance is not translated or recast by the journalist.

Practice. Because your live performance is crucial, it definitely helps to practice being interviewed so that you become accustomed to answering briefly, colloquially, clearly, and with a simple concrete example. Remember, if the program is performed live or will not be edited, you will get only one chance to answer a question.

Ground Rules. While it is not appropriate for you to ask what questions you will be asked while on the air, it does help for you to discuss with the interviewer before the program what topics will be covered. At that time, you can also indicate the topics you feel comfortable discussing and perhaps some issues you cannot consider. While most interviewers have an assigned theme, they also appreciate tactful guidance, because they may not know much about your topic or what pertinent information you can provide.

Personal Questions. If the program involves audience participation, be prepared to deal with naive questions and questions about the behavior of specific individuals. Usually it is not appropriate for you to diagnosis or prescribe specific courses of actions for individuals over the air, but a general discussion of the problem can ensue. Further, it is acceptable to give alternatives. For example, suppose you are asked, "How should I discipline my child without using physical punishment?" You might respond with several general alternatives: "Other methods of discipline include sitting the child in a corner, withdrawing privileges. . . ." Also, you can avoid making personal diagnoses by suggesting the questioner visit a professional who could provide more help in person than you could over the air.

Bridging. Sometimes it is necessary to avoid answering a question directly. This can be done by providing a very short general answer and then changing the subject or by rephrasing the question in a way more compatible with what you feel comfortable saying. However, this takes some practice. For example: Q: "Should a child report his/her own abuse to the police?" A: "A child who feels abused should talk with someone he/she can trust—a teacher, clergyman, doctor. This can be very difficult for the child, because.

Controversy. Most interviewers are not "out to get you." But if you advocate social change or extreme positions, it is the interviewer's job to challenge you. Although it rarely happens (except on programs that routinely thrive on it), if you are "attacked" by the interviewer, a member of the audience, or another guest, remain calm, show less emotion than the questioner, listen and focus your answer on the question (or an inappropriate premise) and not on the questioner, and try to display some understanding of the other point of view, but insist on your own. Smile.

EPILOGUE

The media are a necessary component in any social policy campaign, but professionals often feel uncomfortable with the media. With a greater understanding of how the media work and some practice and experience with them, professionals can improve the accuracy and effectiveness of their communications which will benefit themselves, their cause, journalism, and the general public.

part **IV**

IN CONCLUSION

chapter 12

THE COMMUNITY BASIS FOR PROTECTING HANDICAPPED CHILDREN

Karen J. Authier

INTRODUCTION

The life of the handicapped child is touched by many individuals and institutions: family, friends, neighbors, child care staff, health care professionals, special educators, various human service professionals, and sometimes foster parents or institutional staff. For some children that touch is sensitive, caring, helpful; for others it is insensitive, uncaring, and even cruel. Sometimes family, professionals, and others work together to protect and help maximize the child's potential; at other times they work at cross purposes, turn their backs on potential dangers, and fail to protect the child from abuse or neglect. The child's community is indeed more than the sum total of its parts, and the lives and futures of vulnerable handicapped children may depend on the ability of the formal and informal networks of communities to cooperate and to coordinate efforts in their behalf.

If we recognize that various systems such as family, education, and health care are involved in serving and protecting handicapped children, the next important step then is to incorporate and integrate the specific responses of each system into a coordinated plan for community response. In her comments on the child welfare system, Hoekstra (1984, p. 291) uses a "doll hospital" metaphor to point out the problems that occur in that system when there is lack of coordination or fragmentation of services. In a "doll hospital" child welfare system, the child/doll is sent off to various craftsmen for repair with no attention or sensitivity to the whole child or the systems within which the child functions. She poses the question: "When institutions constructed to help such families suffer from dysfunctional fragmentation in themselves, can these families have the confidence necessary to work with them?" (Hoekstra, 1984, p. 290).

This chapter presents a rationale for and discusses implementation of model community approaches to bring together the concern, knowledge, resources, and efforts of the systems that already may be separately addressing the problems of child abuse and neglect and the handicapping conditions of children. While some communities may need to develop new services to deal specifically with abuse of handicapped children, in most cases modification or expansion of existing efforts will be preferable to avoid unnecessary fragmentation of community resources. While formal service systems may be most easily identified, recognized, and examined, this chapter also will stress the importance of the informal networks that make important contributions to a family's ability to cope successfully with the challenges of the child-rearing role. This chapter recognizes three essential components to a community focus on child abuse and neglect: prevention, identification, and intervention. While controversy exists regarding effectiveness or desirability of programs or policies in each of those areas, the research and clinical literature has begun to identify approaches that hold promise. With attention to those components, it is possible to move communities toward the goal of providing safe environments for handicapped children by integrating knowledge and skills of child abuse and neglect specialists with knowledge and skills of specialists who study or work with handicapped children.

Plans for integration of community efforts not only must take into account the functions of prevention, identification, and intervention, but those plans also must reflect awareness of the levels of community systems that impinge on the individual handicapped child. Bronfenbrenner (1979) and Garbarino (1982) have developed an ecological approach to conceptualizing individual development and behavior. According to the ecological model presented earlier in this volume (Dunst et al., Chapter 2), the child affects and is affected by the face-to-face contacts with family, caregivers, and peers (microsystem); the broader organization of relationships that form bridges between the child's face-to-face contacts (mesosystem); the level of once-removed connecting relationships affecting, but not directly involving, the child, for example, parent education classes attended by the parents, staff meetings at the day-care center the child attends (exosystem); and the societal "blueprints" that shape the direction of society as a whole (e.g., commitment to deinstitutionalization, forces that draw mothers into the work force) (macrosystem). At each of those levels, there are attitudes, beliefs, actions, and plans that effect the relative risk or degree of safety for the handicapped child. As Bronfenbrener has admonished: "We have to become family-centered, community-centered, neighborhood-centered, because there is no way of facilitating the development of the child except through the systems in which he has to grow. It's like saying, 'I'm going to be a plant-centered corn grower.' You've got to look at the earth, the water, and the fertilizer, the whole bit" (quoted in Senn, 1977, pp. 150–151).

Improving and strengthening general community efforts for child abuse prevention, identification, and intervention would benefit handicapped children who are abused or at risk for abuse. However, awareness of the special needs and problems of handicapped children and their families allows us to tailor prevention, identification, and intervention efforts to those needs and problems. There is great diversity of type and extent of impairment among the total population of handicapped children. Types of handicapping conditions include mental retardation, emotional or behavioral disorders, cerebral palsy, speech defect, learning disability, autism, epilepsy, and visual, accoustical, or other physical impairment. Degree of impairment may range from minimal to severe and may involve a single condition or multiple handicaps. Since there is a wide variance in degree and type of handicapping conditions, approaches must take those differences into account. For instance, family adjustment and community services for deaf, mentally retarded, and blind children are not the same. Therefore, while some issues and principles may generalize, there is a need to identify specific concerns, skills, and techniques in relationship to various handicapping conditions.

For each function (prevention, identification, or intervention) and at each community system level (microsystem, mesosystem, exosystem, and macrosystem) there is a need for communication, coordination, and planned creativity. Joint efforts can be maintained through activities such as policy formulation; lobbying efforts; media campaigns; program development; training of professionals, paraprofessionals, and volunteers, as well as provision of direct services to families and children.

PREVENTION

Unfortunately, prevention of child abuse, as well as other social problems, is often regarded as something of an afterthought or even a luxury—something achieved if there is enough money left after the fires are extinguished and the wounds bandaged. However, inattention to prevention in order to attend to immediate crises has been compared to "parking of an ambulance at the bottom of a steep mountain rather than the construction of a fence along the borders of the road" (Bourne, 1979, p. 10).

There are three types of prevention: primary, which directs efforts toward the general population; secondary, which targets an at-risk population; and tertiary, which aims at prevention of recurrence. The latter type will be discussed later in the chapter under intervention.

High-Risk Infants

The concept of prevention as it relates to abuse of handicapped children can apply both to prevention of handicapping conditions and to prevention of abuse of handicapped children. For instance, there is reason to believe that premature infants are at higher risk for handicapping conditions and for abuse than are healthy, full-term babies (Caputo & Mandell, 1970; De Hirsch, Jansky, & Langford, 1966; Fisch, Graven, & Engel, 1968; Fitzhardinge, 1975). Several studies have found that specialized intervention with low-income mothers and their premature infants resulted in improved mental abilities in the infant, improved mother–infant interaction, and mothers' more positive assessment of their infants' temperaments (Field, 1979; Ross, 1984).

Some high-risk newborns are ready for discharge after intensive intervention requiring lengthy hospitalization but require continued sophisticated, skillful caregiving in the home. By recognizing the extraordinary demands on parents of high-risk newborns, infant mental health specialists are joining hospital child protection and pediatric teams in working with cases in which high-risk infants are being discharged to high-risk parents (Horner, Theut, & Murdoch, 1984).

Societal Attitudes

At the macrosystem level, a primary prevention goal might be to modify societal attitudes that discount the value of handicapped citizens in society (Gliedman & Roth, 1980). That goal would be based on the premise of a relationship between an undervaluing of handicapped individuals and an increased risk for abuse of handicapped children. Parents or other family members who view their handicapped child as a negative reflection on individual or family self-image may lash out in anger at the child over the stigmatizing imperfections.

Education for Parenthood

Prospective parents think of their children-to-be in terms of perfection. If handicapping conditions challenge those expectations, parents must grieve the loss of their dreams and adjust to the realities and demands of the role of parenting a handicapped child (Schilling & Schinke, 1984; Roos, 1983; Menolascino, 1977). It would be unrealistic and unnecessary to equip all prospective parents with the knowledge and skills necessary to parent handicapped children since we do not even prepare our youth to become parents of nonhandicapped children. However, education for parenthood curricula should have a component on special-needs children which includes information about known preventable causes of handicapping conditions, value clarification approaches to examination of attitudes about handicapping conditions, factual material to counter common myths about handicapped individuals, opportunities to hear from and discuss the experience of parenting with parents of special needs children, and experiential training in the care of handicapped children. Good models exist for such programs that combine the elements listed above (Anastasiow, Everett, O'Shaunnessey, Eggleston, & Eklund, 1978).

Formal and Informal Support Systems

While there may be more intensive involvement of various professionals with families of handicapped children, there is some indication that these families are more isolated from informal support systems than those with nonhandicapped children (Blacher, 1984a; Friedrich & Boriskin, 1978; McAllister, Butler, & Lei, 1973). Also, the involvement of professionals, while necessary and helpful in many ways, may be problematic in other ways (Gliedman & Roth, 1980). Professionals with expertise in handicapping conditions from the fields of health or education may focus so exclusively on the medical, cognitive, or developmental needs of the child that family needs are overlooked. Professional intervention that does not focus on the total family system risks further burdening that system, contributing to parental feelings of inadequacy and encouraging focus on the needs of the handicapped child to the exclusion of the needs of other members. Lack of a coordinated team approach by professionals working with the family often adds to the stress and confusion. For example, a nurse, a physical therapist, and a teacher working with the family may outline three separate schedules of exercises to be carried out in the home. If the parent, usually the mother (Kaplan & Hall-McCorquodale, 1985), adheres to the schedules she may have no time for household chores of laundry, cooking, and cleaning, let alone working outside the home or nurturing other children. Yet if she fails to carry out those responsibilities, she may feel guilty for not meeting professional expectations.

The professionals' understanding of or interaction with the family unit often does not extend beyond the mother–child dyad. Fathers often are forgotten, characters relegated to positions of interested observers. Such limited focus actually may encourage family dysfunction by encouraging overinvestment of the mother in the child, by allowing for disengagement of other family members, or by provoking resentment toward the handicapped child. Within that system of family–professional relationships, there may be elements that contribute to the risk for abuse.

Training of professionals working with handicapped children should not be like that of Bronfenbrenner's "plant-centered corn-grower." They should be educated to be sensitive to and understand the child as part of a set of reciprocal family relationships. With that perspective, the goal of the parent–child–professional relationship would be not only to enhance the child's development in specific areas such as language, behavior, or motor development, but to enhance the family–child "fit" (Grossman, 1975). Such a "fit" occurs only when parents find a level of satisfaction with their roles as parents. Professionals, then, must be encouraged to think of their role not only in terms of specific goals for the child, but also in terms of increasing the level of a sense of parental competency and satisfaction (Horner et al., 1984).

The task of achieving a sense of competency as a parent is difficult for all parents; but often more formidable for those with handicapped children (Gath, 1977; Holroyd & Guthrie, 1979; Roos, 1983). Roos (1983) catalogs and describes various approaches to teaching parental competency with specific application for parents of mentally retarded children.

Community efforts for prevention of child abuse must include an inventory of education programs aimed specifically at parents of handicapped children. While some parents of handicapped children may feel comfortable in general education programs, those that target the unique problems and stresses of parents of handicapped children are essential components to community efforts to protect handicapped children (Roos, 1983; Schilling & Schinke, 1984).

Sexual Abuse Prevention

In contrast to physical abuse and neglect prevention programs, which generally are targeted at adults, prevention programs for child sexual abuse tend to be targeted toward children. Handicapped children may be particularly vulnerable to sexual approaches by adults or older peers for a variety of reasons including the heightened probability of institutional living, communication or physical limitations, or lack of general information and understanding about sexuality. The handicapped adolescent may be in a special position of risk. Normal developmental phenomena bring about increased interest in sexuality, yet discriminatory societal attitudes toward sexuality for handicapped persons may prevent handicapped youth from being provided with adequate information regarding their own sexuality (Craft & Craft, 1983; DeLacruz &

LaVeck, 1973). That heightened interest combined with lack of understanding and knowledge leaves many handicapped youth vulnerable
to exploitive sexual relationships.

Despite their at risk position, the offering of programs designed to
teach self-protection to handicapped children may lag behind self-protection programs aimed at nonhandicapped children, who often are
reached through their schools, church groups, or youth-serving organizations. Sexual abuse prevention programs provide an excellent
opportunity for child abuse prevention specialists to join forces with
specialists in various handicapping conditions to develop programs with
messages and techniques specifically adapted to various populations,
such as the hearing impaired, the blind, and the mentally retarded.

IDENTIFICATION

Identification of cases of suspected abuse is a necessary step in linking a child to protection through the act of reporting. While many
professionals who work with handicapped children are generally aware
of a need to report instances of child abuse and neglect, there is frequently ignorance or misinformation about the signs, reporting requirements and procedures, civil liability, and response by authorities
to a report. Ignorance and misinformation contributes to professionals'
reluctance to report (Gallo, 1983; Helfer, 1975).

Another complicating factor in identification may be a handicapped
child's difficulty with communication. The attempt to communicate
about an abusive experience may be misunderstood, disregarded, or
discredited because of the handicapping condition. Also contributing
to the reluctance to report are normal individual denial systems that
may prevent professionals from connecting a knowledge base regarding
signs of abuse with families for whom they are providing services.

It is important that community efforts to increase identification and
reporting not overlook the handicapped child. Emphasis should be
placed on ongoing training for professionals and paraprofessionals who
provide services for handicapped children to enable them to identify
instances of abuse more accurately and to provide them with information about the reporting process.

Out-of-Home Placements

Identification of maltreatment of children in out-of-home placements
is an area of special importance to handicapped children. The deinstitutionalization movement documented many horrors in the treatment
of handicapped children and adults and has resulted in a commitment

to keep handicapped individuals in the community. However, the results are not always better for each individual child. Handicapped children remain at increased risk for out-of-home placements (MacEachron & Krauss, 1983). Some of those out-of-home placements are in long-term foster homes, which provide nurture and security for the child. However, many children continue to be caught in the revolving door of multiple foster placements or are placed in abusive foster homes. Sadly, community nursing home placement has been the answer to deinstitutionalization for other children. While nursing homes may meet basic custodial and medical needs for severely handicapped children and may place a child closer to family, there are risks of overmedication and emotional neglect as may be found in any institutional setting.

Identification of abused children in out-of-home placements is difficult, and reporting problems may be compounded if the agency designated to receive the report is also the agency that places the child and recruits, supervises, or licenses the placement. Some community-based foster or group homes are administratively connected to agencies providing comprehensive care and education for the child. In such cases, as with any cases of institutional abuse, there are disincentives to identifying abuse that occurs within the system, and investigation is often hampered by a strong motive for self-protection.

Investigation of Reports

Identification and reporting are the beginning steps to linking a child to a response system. However, for the handicapped child the response of agencies designated to receive and respond to reports may be flawed by ignorance and lack of skills of agency staff in working with handicapping conditions. If the investigation is made difficult by the child's handicapping condition, the initial move to protect the child by reporting may come to a standstill. In most cases a child's ability to communicate details of the abuse is critical to identification and investigation of abuse. Since impaired communication is a common characteristic of handicapped children, the investigation phase may be frustrating for both the child and the agency. It would be unrealistic to expect each and every police officer and protective service worker to become highly skilled in communicating with handicapped children. However, it is realistic and essential to expect states to develop plans for consultation and technical assistance to ensure that handicapped children are afforded the same protection as nonhandicapped children. Again the need is apparent for a cross-over of skills between child abuse specialists and specialists in handicapping conditions of children.

INTERVENTION

If an investigation determines that a handicapped child has been abused, then what? In many communities there are no predictable answers to that question. Agencies and professionals responsible for intervention may be ill-equipped to provide services to handicapped children. In the courts, competency to testify as a witness is an issue for children in general, but handicapping conditions may make it even more difficult to qualify children as witnesses. It is important that community efforts on behalf of abused handicapped children include goals of working with county attorneys and guardians ad litum to help them advocate for abused handicapped children in the legal system.

Treatment

Community treatment resources should also be examined for inequities in services for handicapped children. Although abused children experience emotional distress, therapeutic intervention generally is directed to the needs of parents rather than to the needs of children (Garbarino, 1980). Handicapped children should not be viewed as incapable of benefiting from psychotherapy, and any effort to expand opportunities for treatment resources for children should take into account the special needs of handicapped children. Although mental health professionals historically assumed that the mentally retarded could not benefit from psychotherapy and often accepted symptomatic behavior in the mentally retarded as connected to the retardation, those views along with other myths regarding mental health and mental retardation have been challenged (Menolascino, 1983, Rubin, 1983). Rubin has developed helpful guidelines for modification of counseling and psychotherapeutic techniques for use with the mentally retarded (Rubin, 1983).

While there may be problems associated with provision of mental health services for abused handicapped children, it is hoped that communities will consider those problems as challenges rather than insurmountable obstacles. The child welfare profession is moving out of a long-standing romance with foster home placement as the invariable solution in the best interests of the child. There is growing recognition that some foster home placements are as abusive or even more abusive than the home from which the child was removed. The first placement is often just the beginning of a series of unsuccessful placements with eventual institutionalization or return to an unchanged home at the end of the line (Garbarino, 1980).

In the child welfare system, handicapped children appear to be even more at risk for multiple placements, for longer stays in foster care, and for residential placement than nonhandicapped children (Mac-Eachron & Krauss, 1983). Foster parents frequently lack specialized training in caring for and communicating with handicapped children placed in their care. In some communities, placement options have been improved by development of specialized foster homes with training, consultation, and supervision provided jointly by specialists in child welfare, mental health, and various handicapping conditions.

Professionals who report abuse of handicapped children may do so with the expectation that the child will be removed from the home. Although removal may be neither necessary nor desirable (Bryce & Lloyd, 1981), professionals working with the child may figuratively throw up their hands in despair and vow never to bother to make a report again when they learn that the protective service agency responds with plans of in-home intervention. Such misunderstanding can be lessened by communication among community professionals who make and receive reports.

Community Councils and Teams

Community councils and teams provide a sound approach to development of ongoing working relationships among professionals to minimize the potential for crossed communication and misinformation (Schmitt, 1978; Jenkins, MacDicken, & Ormsby, 1979). Community councils provide an opportunity for gathering professionals and concerned lay persons to discuss, plan, and mobilize community resources to address the problem of maltreatment of children. Inclusion of professionals and advocates who have special knowledge and concern about handicapped children in the membership of community child abuse councils encourages communication and joint efforts.

The child abuse team is another type of structure designed to facilitate communication and cooperation in relation to specific cases. Child abuse teams are multidisciplinary groups that meet regularly to coordinate planning for intervention with families reported as abusive or neglectful (Schmitt, 1978). Membership typically includes representatives from health care, protective services, law enforcement, education, and the court. When a report has been filed on a handicapped child, it is important that representatives of agencies working with the family in respect to the handicapping condition be included in team meetings. Community councils and teams are useful models for shared action and concern in the effort to protect children. They can become more effective in addressing the needs of handicapped children if individuals with a special interest in handicapped children participate on a regular basis.

Informal Networks

Formal structures are not the only or even the most important community resources available to families. A recent study of families with mentally retarded children found that positive family functioning correlated with family engagement with social support systems while negative functioning correlated with social isolation (Mink, Nihira, & Meyers, 1983). Informal networks are important to any community effort to assist abusive and potentially abusive families (Gaudin & Pollane, 1983). Support networks or parent–to–parent programs may exist in communities for parents of handicapped children (Freidrich & Boriskin, 1978; Roos, 1983) or for physically or sexually abusive parents (Giaretto, 1976; The Parents Anonymous Chairperson—Sponsor Manual, 1982). However, it is unclear whether abusive parents would feel welcome in a support group for nonabusive parents or whether self-help groups for abusive parents are helpful resources for parents of children with special needs (Gourash, 1978). There are several models in the literature for identifying natural helping networks or for developing artifical helping networks that can be applied to intervention with abusive or neglectful families with handicapped children (Froland, Pancoast, Chapman, & Kimboko, 1981; Garbarino & Stocking, 1980; Powell, 1980).

SUGGESTIONS FOR DEVELOPING A MODEL COMMUNITY APPROACH

There have been several suggestions in this chapter for incorporating an emphasis on abused handicapped children into established community child abuse and neglect programs. The following is a listing of specific questions to use in assessing and assisting your own community in providing a safe environment for handicapped children:

- Do community child abuse councils and teams have representatives or participation from groups of professionals and advocates for the handicapped (e.g., Developmental Disability Councils, local Associations for Retarded Citizens)?

- Do community child abuse councils have representation from residential facilities serving handicapped children, and do council members take an interest in the operation of those facilities, including nursing homes if appropriate?

- Do child abuse/neglect teams invite specialists with expertise on specific handicapping conditions when planning for cases involving handicapped children?

- Are sexual abuse prevention programs available to handicapped children and youth?
- Do hospital programs for high-risk neonates provide multidisciplinary discharge planning with a focus on decreasing potential for abuse and neglect?
- Are there in-home programs with staff trained to help parents cope with the stresses of caring for a medically high-risk or handicapped child (e.g., Head Start, public health nursing, other home-based programs)?
- Does the community have active public awareness and educational programs to promote positive and caring attitudes toward handicapped individuals (e.g., media campaigns, puppet programs in the schools)?
- Do education for parenthood curricula in the schools include units on handicapped children?
- Are staff in education, medical, and remediation programs for handicapped children sensitive to the needs of the total family?
- Are there parent education resources for parents of handicapped children?
- Are professionals and paraprofessionals in facilities serving handicapped children knowledgable about signs and symptoms of child maltreatment and about reporting procedures?
- Do agencies serving handicapped children have protocols for reporting child abuse and neglect?
- Are there policies preventing reports of abuse or neglect in out-of-home placements from being investigated by staff of agencies operating, recruiting, or placing children in those facilities?
- Do police, child protective service units, and county attorneys have the capacity to communicate with children whose handicaps include communicative difficulties (e.g., interpreter for hearing-impaired children)?
- Are there specialized foster placements for abused handicapped children?
- Are mental health resources available for abused handicapped children?
- Are there parent–to–parent support programs that will meet the needs of parents of handicapped children?
- Do parent crisis line volunteers receive training regarding parenting of handicapped children?
- Are there respite care programs available for parents of handicapped children?

It is hoped that these questions will help provide direction for broadening community efforts related to abused children and handicapped children.

SUMMARY

Since the 1960s we have seen growing awareness in communities regarding the societal problem of child abuse. During that same period communities also have made great strides in providing improved access to services, especially educational services, for handicapped children; in combating practices that discriminate against the handicapped; and in moving handicapped children out of institutions. Out of those separate advocacy movements, separate forces or factors have developed in communities: those advocating for and providing services for children abused or at-risk for abuse and those advocating for or providing services for handicapped children. Case-by-case communication may take place among service providers as abused handicapped children are identified. It is time to recognize the importance of moving beyond case-by-case interaction; to capture the attention, concern, and creativity of both groups; and to combine efforts to prevent, identify, and intervene in cases of abuse of handicapped children. It is time for those with a history of advocating for the handicapped in their communities and those with a history of advocating for abused children to join forces and work to cross-pollinate so that the experts on handicapped children develop expertise on child abuse and neglect and experts on child abuse develop expertise about handicapped children. Out of this crossover experience, there is potential for a hybrid alliance committed to the needs of abused handicapped children and their families.

BIBLIOGRAPHY

Abel, E. L. *Fetal Alcohol Syndrome: Vol. I. An Annotated and Compre-hensive Bibliography.* Boca Raton, FL: CRC Press, 1981.

Abel, E. L. *Alcohol and Reproduction: A Bibliography.* Westport, CT: Greenwood Press, 1982. (a)

Abel, E. L. *Smoking and Reproduction: A Comprehensive Bibliography.* Westport, Conn.: Greenwood Press, 1982. (b)

Achenbach, T. M. *Child Behavior Checklist.* Queen City Printers, Inc., 1983. Burlington, Vermont.

Achenbach, T. M., and Edelbrock, C. S. *Behavioral Problems and Com-petencies Reported by Parents of Normal and Disturbed Children Aged Four through Sixteen.* Chicago, IL: Society for Research in Child Development, 1981.

Adams, C. "Considering children's developmental stages in prevention education." In *The Educator's Guide to Preventing Child Sexual Abuse,* edited by M. Nelson and K. Clark, pp. 103–107. Santa Cruz, CA: Network Publications, 1986.

Adapted from Thomas, M. "Child abuse and neglect, part 1: Historical overview, legal matrix and social perspectives." *North Carolina Law Review,* 50 (1972): February.

Adler, A. *Social Interest: A Challenge to Mankind.* London: Faber & Faber, 1938.

Adolescent Abuse and Neglect: Intervention Strategies. U.S. Depart-ment of Health and Human Services. Washington, D.C. DHHS No. (OHDS) 80-30266, 1980.

Adolescent Maltreatment: Issues and Program Models. U.S. Department of Health and Human Services, Washington, D.C. DHHS No. (OHDS) 84-30339, 1980.

Adoption Assistance and Child Welfare Amendments of 1980, 42 U.S.C., pp. 670–676, 1982.

Alberta Association of Child Care Workers. Training course for resi-dential child care workers. Edmonton, Alta, 1985.

Alexander, Jeffrey. "Child abuse and the developmentally disabled: An overview." In *Child Abuse and Developmental Disabilities: Essays.* U.S. Dept. of Health and Human Services, 1980.

Algaser v. District Court of Polk County, 406 F. Supp. 10 (S.D. Iowa 1975), *aff'd,* 545 F.2d 1137 (8th Cir. 1976).

245

Allen, K.; Benning, P.; and Drummond, T. "Integration of normal and handicapped children in a behavior modification preschool: A case study." In *Behavioral Analysis and Education,* edited by G. Semb. Lawrence, KS: University of Kansas Press, 1972.

Aloia, G.; Beaver, R.; and Pettus, W. "Increasing initial interactions among integrated EMR students and their nonretarded peers in a game-playing situation." *American Journal of Mental Deficiency* 82 (1978): 573–579.

American Association for the Protection of Children. Highlights of Official Child Abuse and Neglect Reporting, 1984. Denver, CO: American Association for the Protection of Children, 1986.

American Humane Association. *Guidelines for Schools to Help Protect Neglected and Abused Children,* 1971.

American Psychological Association Committee on Counselor Training. "Recommended standards for training counseling psychologists at the doctorate level." *American Psychologist* 7 (1952):174–181.

Anastasiow, N.J.; Everett, M.; O'Shaunnessy, T.E.; Eggleston, P.J.; and Eklund, S.J. "Improving teenage attitudes toward children, child handicaps, and hospital settings: A child development curriculum for potential parents." *American Journal of Orthopsychiatry* 48 (4) (1978):663–672.

Andrade, B. "The toxic workplace: Title VII protection for the potentially pregnant person." *Harvard Women's Law Journal* 4 (1981):71–103.

Apollini, T.; Cooke, S.; and Cooke, T. "Establishing a normal peer as a behavioral model for developmentally disabled toddlers." *Perceptual and Motor Skills* 44 (1977):231–241.

Aragona, J.A.; and Eyberg, S.M. "Neglected children: Mother's report of child behavior problems and observed verbal behavior." *Child Development* 52 (1981):596–602.

Atkin, C. K. "Research evidence on mass mediated health communication campaigns." In *Communication Yearbook,* Vol 3, edited by D. Nimmo, pp. 655–668. New Brunswick, NJ: Transaction Books, 1979.

Attneave, C. "Social networks as the unit of intervention." In *Family Therapy: Therapy and Practice,* edited by P. Guerin, pp. 220–231. NY: Gardner Press, 1976.

Attorney General's Task Force on Family Violence, *Proceedings of Kansas City Hearing.* Kansas City, MO., January 11 and 12, 1984.

Attorney General's Task Force on Violent Crime, *Proceedings of Washington, D.C. Hearing.* Washington, D.C., April 16 and 17, 1981.

Ayoub, C.; Jacewitz, M.M.; Gold, R.G.; and Milner, J.S. "Assessment of a program's effectiveness in selecting individuals 'at risk' for problems in parenting." *Journal of Clinical Psychology* 39 (1983): 334–339.

Bakan, D. *Slaughter of the Innocents.* San Francisco, CA: Jossey-Bass, 1971. (a)

Bakan, D. "Adolescence in America: From idea to social fact." In *Twelve to Sixteen: Early Adolescence*, edited by J. Kagan and R. Coles, pp. 73–89. NY: Norton, 1971. (b)

Ball-Rokeach, S. J.; Rokeach, M.; and Grube, J. W. "The great American values test." *Psychology Today* November 1984: 34–41.

Ballew, J. "Role of natural helpers in preventing child abuse and neglect." *Social Work* 30 (1985):37–41.

Banagale, R., and McIntire, M. "Child abuse and neglect: A study of cases reported to Douglas County Child Protective Services from 1967–1973." *Nebraska Medical Journal* (September 1975): p. 353; (October 1975): pp. 393–396; (November 1975): pp. 439–441.

Bandura, A. *Principles of Behavior Modification.* NY: Holt, Rinehart and Winston, 1969.

Bank, S., and Kahn, M. *The Sibling Bond.* NY: Basic Books, 1982.

Barber, T.S. "Pitfalls in research: Nine investigator and experimenter effects." In *Handbook of Research on Teaching,* edited by R. M. W. Travers, 2d ed. Chicago, IL: Rand McNally, 1972.

Bardon, J.I.; Bennett, V.C.; Bruchez, P.K.; and Sanderson, R.A. "Psychosituational classroom intervention: Rationale and description." *Journal of School Psychology* 14(2) (1976):97–104.

Barry, R.J. "Incest, the last taboo. part I." *F.B.I. Law Enforcement Bulletin* 53 (1984):1, 2.(a)

Barry, R.J. "Incest, the last taboo. Conclusion." *F.B.I. Law Enforcement Bulletin* 53 (1984):2, 19. (b)

Barsh, E.T.; Moore, J.A.; and Hamerlynck, L.A. "The foster extended family: A support network for foster handicapped children." *Child Welfare* 62 (1983):325–337.

Beckman, P. "Influence of selected child characteristics on stress in families of handicapped infants." *American Journal of Mental Deficiency* 88 (1983):150–156.

Beckman-Bell, P. "Characteristics of Handicapped Infants: A Study of the Relationship between Child Characteristics and Stress as Reported by Mothers." Unpublished Ph.D. dissertation, University of North Carolina, Chapel Hill, 1980.

Beitchman, J.H. "Therapeutic considerations with the language impaired child." *Canadian Journal of Psychiatry* 30 (1985):609–613.

Bell, R. Q., and Harper, L. V. *Child Effects on Adults.* Lincoln, NE: University of Nebraska Press, 1977.

Belsky, J. "Child maltreatment: An ecological integration." *American Psychologist* 35 (1980):320–335.

Bennett, C. W. "A four-and-a-half year old as a teacher of her hearing impaired sister: A case study." *Journal of Communication Disorders* 6 (1973):67–75.

Benward, J., and Densen-Gerber, J. "Incest as a causative factor in antisocial behavior: An exploratory study." Paper presented at the American Academy of Forensic Sciences, 1975.

Bernstein, B.; Snider, D.; and Meezan, W. *Foster-Care Needs and Alternatives to Placement.* Albany, NY: New York State Board of Welfare, 1975.

Berry, C. "Learning from television news: A critique of the research." *Journal of Broadcasting* 27 (1983):359–370.

Berry, F. C., Jr. "A study of accuracy in local news stories of three dailies." *Journalism Quarterly* 44 (1967):482–490.

Besharov, D. "Child abuse and neglect statistics." *Child Abuse and Neglect Reports* (June 1976): pp. 1–2.

Bettelheim, B. "Individual and mass behavior in extreme situations." *Journal of Abnormal and Social Psychology* 38(1943):417–452.

Bijou, S.W. "The role of community schools in providing mental health services for retarded individuals. In *Mental Health and Mental Retardation: Bridging the Gap,* edited by F.J. Menolascino and Brian M. McCann. Baltimore, MD: University Park Press, 1983.

Blacher, J. "A dynamic perspective on the impact of a severely handicapped child on the family. In *Severely Handicapped Young Children and Their Families,* edited by J. Blacher. NY: Academic Press, 1984. (a)

Blacher, J. (ed.) *Severely Handicapped Young Children and Their Families.* NY: Academic Press, 1984. (b)

Bloom, M., and Fischer, J. *Evaluating Practice: Guidelines for the Accountable Professional.* Englewood Cliffs, NJ: Prentice-Hall, 1982.

Blumenthal, K., and Weinberg, A. *Establishing Parent Involvement in Foster Care Agencies.* NY: Child Welfare League of America, 1984.

Board of Education v. Rowley, 458 U.S. 176 (1982).

Bonnie, R. J. 1986 "Uses of the law to discourage unhealthy personal choices: A critical appraisal." In *Nebraska Symposium on Motivation: Vol. 33. The Law as a Behavioral Instrument,* edited by G. B. Melton. Lincoln, NE: University of Nebraska Press, in press.

Bott, E. *Family and Social Network.* New York: Free Press, 1972.

Bourne, R. "Child abuse and neglect: An overview." In *Critical Perspectives in Child Abuse,* edited by R. Bourne and E.H. Newberge. Lexington, MA: Lexington Books, 1979.

Bradburn, N., and Caplovitz, D. *Reports on Happiness.* Chicago, IL: Aldine, 1965.

Brammar, L.M., and Shostrom, E. L. *Therapeutic Psychology.* 4th ed. Englewood Cliffs, NJ: Prentice-Hall, 1982.

Branch, G. and Paxton, R. "A study of gonococcal infections among infants and children." *Public Health Reports* 80 (1965):347–353.

Brassard, J. "The Nature and Utilization of Social Networks in Families

Confronting Different Life Circumstances." Ph.D. dissertation, Cornell University, 1976.

Brassard, M. R.; Germain, R.; and Hart, S. N. *The Psychological Maltreatment of Children and Youth.* NY: Pergamon, in press.

Bricker, D. "A rationale for the integration of handicapped and non-handicapped preschool children." In *Early Intervention and the Integration of Handicapped and Nonhandicapped Children,* edited by M. Guralnick. Baltimore, MD: University Park Press, 1978.

Briggs, R., ed. *Child Abuse and Developmental Disabilities: Essays.* Washington, D.C.: U.S. Department of Health, Education, and Welfare, DHEW Publication No. (OHDS) 79-30226, 1979.

Brim, J. "Social network correlates of avowed happiness." *Journal of Nervous and Mental Diseases* 158 (1974):432–439.

Brim, O.G. *Education for Child Rearing.* NY: Russell Sage Foundation, 1959.

Brim, O.G. "Macrostructural influences on child development and the need for childhood social indicators." *American Journal of Orthopsychiatry* 45 (1975): 516–24.

Brim, O.G., Jr., and Wheeler, S. *Socialization after Childhood: Two Essays.* NY: Wiley, 1966.

Broadhead, W. E.; Kaplan, B.; James, S. A.; Wagner, E. H.; Schoenbach, V.J.; Grimson, R.; Heyden, S.; Tibblin, G.; and Gehlbach, S.H. "The epidemiologic evidence for a relationship between social support and health." *American Journal of Epidemiology* 117 (1983):521–537.

Broadhurst, D. "Policy making: First step for schools in the fight against child abuse and neglect." *Elementary School Guidance and Counseling* 10 (1975):22–26.

Broadhurst, D. "Project PROTECTION—A school program." *Children Today* (May/June, 1977):22–25.

Bronfenbrenner, U. *Two Worlds of Childhood.* NY: Russell Sage Foundation, 1970.

Bronfenbrenner, U. "The experimental ecology of education." *Teachers College Record* 78 (1976):157–204.

Bronfenbrenner, U. "Towards an Experimental Ecology of Human Development." *American Psychologist* 32 (1977):513–531. (a)

Bronfenbrenner, U. Quoted in M. Senn, *Speaking Out for America's Children.* pp. 105–115. New Haven, CT: Yale University Press, (b)

Bronfenbrenner, U. *The Ecology of Human Development: Experiments by Nature and Design.* Cambridge, MA: Harvard University Press, 1979.

Bronfenbrenner, U., and Cochran, M. "The Comparative Ecology of Human Development: A Research Proposal." Mimeographed. Ithaca, NY: Cornell University, 1976.

Bronfenbrenner, U., and Mahoney, M. "The structure and verification of hypotheses." In *Influences on Human Development*, edited by U. Bronfenbrenner and M. Mahoney. Hinsdale, IL: Dryden Press, 1975.

Brookhouser, P.E., Sullivan, P.; Scanlan, J.M.; and Garbarino, J. "Identification of the sexually abused deaf child: The otolaryngologist's role. *Laryngoscope*, 99 (1986):152–158.

Brown, L.; Branston, M.; Baumgart, D.; Vincent, L.; Falvey, M.; and Schroeder, J. "Utilizing characteristics of a variety of current and subsequent least restrictive environments as factors in the development of curricular content for severely handicapped students." *American Association for the Severely Profoundly Handicapped Review* 4 (1979):407–424.

Bryant, H.D.; Billingsley, A.; Kerry, G.A.; Leafman, M.U.; Merrill, E.J.; Serrecal, C.R.; and Walsh, B. "Physical abuse of children: An agency study." *Child Welfare* 52 (1963):225–230.

Bryce, M., and Lloyd, J. *Treating Families in the Home*. Springfield, IL: Charles C. Thomas, 1981.

Buck v. Bell, 274 U.S. 200 (1927).

Budoff, M., and Gottlieb, J. "Special class students mainstreamed: A study of an aptitude (learning potential) X treatment interaction." *American Journal of Mental Deficiency* 81 (1976):1–11.

Bulkley, J. State Legislative Reform Efforts and Suggested Future Policy Directions to Improve Legal Intervention in Child Sexual Abuse Cases. Washington, D.C.: National Legal Resource Center for Child Advocacy and Protection, American Bar Association, 1985.

Burr, W. *Theory Construction and the Sociology of the Family*. NY: Wiley, 1973.

Burrows, W. E. "Science meets the press: Bad chemistry." *The Sciences* (April 1980):14–15, 18–19.

Bush, M., and Gordon, A. C. "Client choice and bureaucratic accountability: Possibilities for responsiveness in a social welfare bureaucracy." *Journal of Social Issues* 34 (2) (1978):22–43.

Caffey, J. "Multiple fractures in the long bones of infants suffering from chronic subdural hematoma." *American Journal of Roentgenology* Vol 56 (163) (1946):163–173.

Calam, R.M. "The Long-Term Effects of Child Abuse on School Adjustment." Paper presented at the ninety-first annual meeting of the American Psychological Association, Anaheim, CA, 1983.

Camblin, L.D., Jr. "A survey of state efforts in gathering information on child abuse and neglect in handicapped populations." *Child Abuse and Neglect* 6 (1982):465–472.

Cantwell, D.P.; Baker, L.; and Mattison, R.E. "The prevalence of psychiatric disorder in children with speech and language disorder: An epidemiological study. *Journal of Child Psychiary* 18(3) (1979):450–461.

Caplan, G. *Principles of Preventive Psychiatry.* NY: Basic Books, 1964.

Caplan, G. *Support Systems and Community Mental Health.* NY: Behavioral Publications, 1974.

Caplan, G., and Killiea, M. *Support Systems and Mutual Help.* NY: Grune & Stratton, 1976.

Caplan, N.; Morrison, A.; and Stambaugh, R. J. *The Use of Social Science Knowledge in Policy Decisions at the National Level.* Ann Arbor, MI: The University of Michigan, Institute for Social Research, Center for Research on Utilization of Scientific Knowledge, 1975.

Caputo, D., and Mandell, W. "Consequences of low birth weight." *Developmental Psychology* 3 (1970):363–383.

Carlson, A. Testimony to U.S. Justice Department Task Force on Family Violence, Kansas City, MO, 1984.

Carroll, A. The effects of segregated and partially integrated school programs on self-concept and academic achievement of educable mental retardation. *Exceptional Children* 34 (1967):93–99.

Castle v. Castle, 15 Ohio St. 3d 279 (1984).

Catalano, R., and Hawkins, J. *Project Adapt.* Seattle, WA: School of Social Work, University of Washington, 1985.

Causey, J. "Personality characteristics and relationship patterns in parents of physically abused children versus other similar clinical populations." *Dissertations Abstracts International* 44 (6A) (1983):1691.

Center for Applied Urban Research. Housing and Community Development in the Nebraska-Iowa Riverfront Development Project Area. Omaha: Center for Applied Urban Research, 1973.

Chase, J. "Normative criteria for scientific publication." *American Sociologist* 5 (1970): 262–265.

Chennault, G. "Improving the social acceptance of unpopular mentally retarded pupils in special classes. *American Journal of Mental Deficiency* 72 (1967):455–458.

Child Abuse and Neglect in Residential Institutions (1978). NCCAN, DHEW Pub. No. (OHDS) 78-30160, Washington, D.C.: U.S. Government Printing Office.

Child Care Worker Certification Program of Alberta. Edmonton: Child Care Workers Association of Alberta, 1985.

Children's Bureau Act of 1912, 73, 37 Stat. 79 (1912).

Children's Defense Fund. *Children out of School in America.* Washington, D.C.: Washington Research Project, 1974.

Children without Homes. Washington, D.C.: Children's Defense Fund, 1978.

Chotiner, N., and Lehr, W. eds. *Child Abuse and Developmental Disabilities. A Report from the New England Regional Conference.* Sponsored by United Cerebral Palsy of Rhode Island and United Cerebral Palsy Association, 1976.

Christiansen, J. *Educational and Psychological Problems of Abused Children.* Saratoga, CA: Century Twenty One Publishing, 1980.

City of Akron v. Akron Center for Reproductive Health, Inc., 103 S.Ct. 2481 (1983).

Cobb, S. "Social support as a moderator of life stress." *Psychosomatic Medicine* 38 (1976):300–314.

Cochran, M. M., and Brassard, J. A. "Child development and personal social networks." *Child Development,* 50 (1979):601–616.

Cochran, M., and Brassard, J. "Social Networks and Social Development in Childhood." Paper presented in the Biennial Meeting of the Society for Research in Child Development, New Orleans, March 1977.

Cohen, J., and Cohen, P. *Applied Multiple Regression/Correlation Analysis for Behavioral Sciences.* 2d ed. Hillsdale, NJ: Erlbaum, 1983.

Cohen, S., and Syme, L., eds. *Social Support and Health.* NY: Academic Press, 1985. (a)

Cohen, S., and Syme, L. "Issues in the study and application of social support." In *Social Support and Health,* edited by S. Cohen and L. Syme, pp. 3–20. NY: Academic Press, 1985. (b)

Cole, E. "Adoption." In *A Handbook of Child Welfare,* edited by A. Hartman and J. Laird, pp. 638–667. NY: Free Press, 1985.

Colletta, N. The Influence of Support Systems on the Maternal Behavior of Young Mothers. Boston: Biennial Meeting of Society for Research in Child Development, 1981.

Collins, A., and Pancoast, D. *Natural Helping Networks.* Washington, D.C.: National Association of Social Workers, 1976.

Collins, E. "The psychosocial characteristics of child abusers." *Dissertation Abstracts International* 36(6B) (1975):2520.

Commission on Law Enforcement and Administration of Justice. *Report of the Task Force on the Police.* Washington, D.C.: U.S. Government Printing Office, 1967.

Commission on Law Enforcement and Administration of Justice. Reports of the Commission. *The Challenge of Crime in a Free Society.* Washington, D.C.: U.S. Government Printing Office, 1967.

Constantine, L., and Martinson, F. *Children and Sex: New Findings and New Perspectives.* Boston, MA: Little Brown, 1982.

Coolsen, P., Seligson, M., and Garbarino, J. *When School's Out and Nobody Is Home.* Chicago: National Committee for Prevention of Child Abuse, 1985.

Copans, S.; Krell, H.; Gundy, J. H.; Rogan, J.; and Field, F. "The stresses of treating child abuse." *Children Today* 8(1)(Jan.–Feb. 1979):22–78.

Corman, L., and Gottlieb, J. "Mainstreaming mentally retarded children:

A review of research." In *International Review of Research in Mental Retardation*, vol. 9, edited by N.R. Ellis. NY: Academic Press, 1978.

Corrigan, J. "Prevention and appropriate handling of maltreatment of children in residential facilities." In *Multiregional Conference and Institutional Child Abuse and Neglect*, edited by C. Washburne, J. V. Hull, and N. Rindfleisch, pp. 1–14. Columbus, OH: Ohio State University School of Social Work, 1982.

Corrigan, J. P. "National Significance Projects on Developmental Disabilities and Child Abuse and Neglect." Paper read at Region II Conference on Developmental Disabilities in Abused and Neglected Children, May 18, 1983. New York, NY

Cottle, W. C. "Personal characteristics of counselors." *Personnel and Guidance Journal* 31 (1953):445–450.

Cottrell, L. "The adjustment of the individual to his age and sex roles." *American Sociological Review* 7 (7)(1942):617–620.

Council for Exceptional Children. *We Can Help: Specialized Curriculum for Educators on the Prevention and Treatment of Child Abuse and Neglect*. Reston, VA, 1979.

Cowen, E. "Primary prevention in mental health: Past, present, and future." In *Prevention Psychology, Theory, Research and Practice*, edited by R. Felner, L. Jason, J. Nicritsugu, and S. Faber, pp. 11–25. NY: Pergamon Press, 1983.

Craft, A., and Craft, M. *Sex Education and Counseling for Mentally Handicapped People*. Baltimore, MD: University Park Press, 1983.

Crain, R. "Why Academic Research Fails to Be Useful." *School Review* 84 (1976):337–351.

Crewdson, J. "Reports of sexual abuse leap." *Chicago Tribune*, February 17, 1985, p. 1.

Crnic, K.; Friedrich, W.; and Greenberg, M. "Adaptation of families with mentally retarded children: A model of stress, coping and family ecology." *American Journal of Mental Deficiency* 88 (1983):125–138. (a)

Crnic, K.; Greenberg, M.; Ragozin, A.; Robinson, N.; and Basham, R. "Effects of stress and social suport on mothers of premature and full-term infants. *Child Development* 54 (1983):209–217. (b)

Crnic, K.; Greenberg, M.; and Slough, N. "Early stress and social support influences on mothers' and high-risk infants' functioning in late infancy." *Infant Mental Health Journal* 6 (1986): in press.

Crockenberg, S. "Infant irritability, mother responsiveness and social influences on the security of infant–mother attachment." *Child Development* 52 (1981):857–865.

Davis v. Davis, 67 N.W.2d 556 (Iowa 1954).

Day, R.; Powell, T.; and Stowitscheck, J. *Social Competence Intervention Package for Preschool Youngsters (SCIPPY)*. Logan, UT: Exceptional Child Center, Utah State University, 1981.

Dean, A., and Lin, N. "Stress-buffering role of social support." *Journal of Nervous and Mental Diseases* 165 (1977):403–417.

DeFrain, J.; King, K.; *et al.*, eds. *Family Strengths 3: Roots of Well-Being.* Omaha, NE: University of Nebraska Press, 1981.

De Hirsch, K.; Jansky, J.; and Langford, W. "Comparisons between prematurely and maturely born children at three age levels." *American Journal of Orthopsychiatry* 36 (1966):616–628.

DeLa Cruz, F., and LaVeck, G., eds. *Human Sexuality and the Mentally Retarded.* NY: Brunner/Mazel, 1973.

Delaney, J. "New concepts of the family court." In *Child Abuse and Neglect: The Family and the Community,* edited by R. Helfer and C. Kempe. Cambridge, MA: Ballinger, 1976.

Delsordo, J.D. "Protective casework for abused children." *Children* 10 (1963): 213–218.

Department of Health and Human Services, Final Rule, January 26, 1983.

Devoney, C.; Guralnick, M.; and Rubin, H. "Integrating handicapped and nonhandicapped preschool children: Effects on social play." *Childhood Education* 50 (1974):360–364.

Dix, T., and Grusec, J. "Parent attribution processes in the socialization of children." In *Parental Belief Systems,* edited by I. Sigel, pp. 201–233. Hillsdale, NJ: Lawrence Erlbaum, 1985.

Dore, M.M.; Young, T.M.; and Pappenfort, D.M. "Comparison of basic data for national survey of residential group care facilities: 1966–1982." *Child Welfare* 63 (1984):485–495.

Dreikers, R., and Grey, L. *A New Approach to Discipline: Logical Consequences.* NY: Hawthorn Books, 1968.

Dunn, J. "Sibling relationships in early childhood." *Child Development* 54 (1983):787–811.

Dunn, J., and Munn, P. "Becoming a family member: Family conflict and the development of social understanding in the second year." *Child Development* 56 (1985):480–492.

Dunst, C.J. "A Systems-Level, Family-Focused Approach to Assessment and Intervention with Profoundly Handicapped Children." Paper presented at the annual meeting of the Department of Education, Special Education Programs, Handicapped Children's Early Education Program (HCEEP) Conference, Washington, D.C., 1983.

Dunst, C.J. "Parental Styles of Interaction Scale." Unpublished paper, Family, Infant and Preschool Program, Western Carolina Center, Morganton, NC, 1984.

Dunst, C.J. "Rethinking early intervention." *Analysis and Intervention in Developmental Disabilities* 5 (1985):165–201. (a)

Dunst, C.J. "Communicative competence and deficits: Effects on early social interactions." In *Facilitating Social-Emotional Development in the Young Multiply Handicapped Child,* edited by E. McDonald and D. Gallagher, pp. 93–140. Philadelphia, PA: HMS Press, 1985. (b)

Dunst, C.J., and Leet, H. "Family Resource Scale." Unpublished paper, Family Infant and Preschool Program, Western Carolina Center, Morganton, NC, 1985.

Dunst, C.J., and Trivette, C.M. "Differential Influences of Social Support on Mentally Retarded Children and Their Families." Paper presented at the annual meeting of the American Psychological Association, Toronto, Canada, August 1984.

Dunst, C.J., and Trivette, C.M. "Looking beyond the parent–child dyad for the determinants of caregiver styles of Interaction." *Infant Mental Health Journal* 7 (1986):69–80.

Dunst, C.J., and Trivette, C.M. *A Causal Analysis Model for Determining the Effect of Social Support.* In preparation.

Dunst, C.J.; Jenkins, V.; and Trivette, C.M. "Family support scale: Reliability and validity." *Journal of Individual, Family and Community Wellness* 1(4) (1984):45–52.

Dunst, C.J.; Cushing, P.J.; and Vance, S. "Response-contingent learning in profoundly handicapped infants: A social systems perspective." *Analysis and Intervention in Developmental Disabilities* 5 (1985):33–47.

Dunst, C.J.; Trivette, C.; and Cross, A. "Mediating influences of social support: Personal, family, and child outcomes." *American Journal of Mental Deficiency* 90 (1986):403–417. (a)

Dunst, C.J.; Trivette, C.; and Cross, A. "Roles and support networks of mothers of handicapped children." In *Families of Handicapped Children: Needs and Supports Across the Life Span,* edited by R. Fewell and P. Vadasy, pp. 167–192. Austin, TX: PRO-ED, 1986. (b)

Dunst, C.J.; Vance, S.; and Cooper, C.S. "A social systems perspective of adolescent pregnancy: Determinants of parent and parent–child behavior." *Infant Mental Health Journal* 6(1986). (c)

Dunst, C.J.; Trivette, C.; and Cross, A. "Social support networks of Appalachian and non-Appalachian families with handicapped children. In *Mental Health in Appalachia,* edited by S. E. Keefe. Lexington, KY: University of Kentucky Press, in press.

Dunwoody, S. "A question of accuracy." *IEEE Transactions on Professional Communication,* PC-25 (1982):196–199.

Durkin, R. "No one will thank you: First thoughts on reporting institutional abuse." In *Institutional Abuse of Children and Youth,* edited by R. Hanson, pp. 109–114. NY: Haworth Press, 1982.

Education Commission of the States, Child Abuse and Neglect Project. *Education Policies and Practices Regarding Child Abuse and Neglect and Recommendations for Policy Development.* Report No. 8. Denver: Education Commission of the States, April 1976.

Education Commission of the States, Child Abuse and Neglect Project. *Teacher Education: An Active Participant in Solving the Problem of Child Abuse and Neglect.* Denver: Education Commission of the States, April 1977.

Education for All Handicapped Children Act of 1975, 89 Stat. 773.

Egeland, B., and Sroufe, L.A. "Developmental sequelae of maltreatment in infancy. *New Directions for Child Development* 45 (1980):1–64.

Egeland, B., and Brunnquell, D. An at-risk approach to the study of child abuse. *Journal of the American Academy of Child Psychiatry* 17 (1979):219–235.

Egeland, B., and Sroufe, A. "Developmental sequelae of maltreatment in infancy. In *New Directions in Child Development,* edited by R. Rizley and D. Cicchetti. San Francisco, CA: Jossey-Bass, 1981.

Elder, G. *Children of the Great Depression.* Chicago, IL: University of Chicago Press, 1974.

Ellerstein, N.S., and Norris, K.J. "Value of radiologic skeletal survey in assessment of abused children." *Pediatrics* 74 (1984):1075–1078.

Elmer, E. *Children in Jeopardy.* Pittsburgh, PA: University of Pittsburgh Press, 1967.

Embry, L. "Family support for handicapped preschool children at risk for abuse." In *New Directions for Exceptional Children,* vol. 4, edited by J. Gallagher. San Francisco, CA: Jossey-Bass, 1980.

Enelow, A.J. *Elements of Psychotherapy.* NY: Oxford University Press, 1977.

Ettema, J. S.; Brown, J. W.; and Luepker, R. V. "Knowledge gap effects in a health information campaign." *Public Opinion Quarterly* 47 (1983):516–527.

Fanshel, D., and Shinn, E.B. *Children in Foster Care: A Longitudinal Investigation.* NY: Columbia University Press, 1977.

Farber, B. "Effects of a severely retarded child on family integration." *Monographs of the Society for Research in Child Development* 21 (1, Serial No. 75) (1960).

Farber, B., and Jenne, W. "Interaction with retarded siblings and life goals of children." *Marriage and Family Living* 25 (1963):96–98.

Fein, G. G.; Schwartz, P. M.; Jacobson, S. W.; and Jacobson, J. L. "Environmental toxins and behavioral development: A new role for psychological research. *American Psychologist* 38 (1983):1188–11l7.

Felix v. Milliken, 463 F. Supp. 1360 (E.D. Mich. 1978).

Fellin, P., and E. Litwak. "The neighborhood in urban American society." *Social Work* 13 (1968):72–80.

Fewell, R., and Vadasy, P., eds. *Families of Handicapped Children: Needs and Supports across the Life Span.* Austin, TX: PRO-ED, 1986.

Field, T.M. "Interaction patterns of premature and full-term infants." In *Infants Born at Risk: Behavior and Development,* edited by T. M. Field. New York: SP Medical and Scientific Books, 1979.

Figley, C., and McCubbin, H., eds. *Stress and the Family. Volume II: Coping with Catastrophe.* NY: Brunner/Mazel, 1983.

Findall, O., and Hoijer, B. *Fragments of Reality: An Experiment with News and TV Visuals.* Stockholm, Sweden: Svergies Radio, 1976.

Finkelhor, D. *Sexually Victimized Children.* NY: Free Press, 1979.

Finkelhor, D. *Child Sexual Abuse: New Theory and Research.* NY: The Free Press, 1984. (a)

Finkelhor, D. "The prevention of child sexual abuse: An overview of needs and problems." *SIECUS Report* 8(1) (1984):1–5. (b)

Finkelhor, D., and Browne, A. The traumatic impact of child sexual abuse: A conceptualization. *American Journal of Orthopsychiatry* 55 (4) (1985):530–541.

Finkelstein, N. "Family centered group care." In *The Challenge of Partnership: Working with Parents of Children in Foster Care,* edited by A. Maluccio and P. Sinanoglu. NY: Child Welfare League of America, 1981.

Fisch, R.; Graven, H.; and Engel, R. "Neurological status of survivors of neonatal respiratory distress syndrome." *Journal of Pediatrics* 3 (1968):395–403.

Fisher, S. *Stress and the Perception of Control.* Hillsdale, NJ: Lawrence Erlbaum, 1984.

Fitzhardinge, P. "Early growth and development in low birthweight infants following treatment in an intensive care nursery." *Pediatrics* 56 (1975): 162–172.

Fitzharris, T. *The Foster Children of California.* Sacramento: California Association of Services for Children, 1985.

Fixsen, D. L.; Phillips, E.L.; and Wolf, M.M. "The teaching family model: An example of mission-oriented research." In *Handbook of Behavior Analysis,* edited by C.A. Catania and T.A. Brigham. NY: Aalsten Press, 1978.

Flynn, R.J., and Nitsch, K.E. *Normalization, Social Integration and Community Services.* Baltimore, MD: University Park Press, 1980.

Folkman, S.; Schaefer, C.; and Lazarus, R. "Cognitive processes as mediators of stress." In *Human Stress and Cognition,* edited by V. Hamilton and D. Warburton. NY: Wiley, 1979.

Fontana, V. J. "Further reflections on maltreatment of children" *New York State Journal of Medicine* 68 (1968): 2214–15.

Fontana, V. J. "Which parents abuse children?" *Medical Insight* 3 (7) (1971): 195–199.

Fowler, L., and Stenlund, J. "A Multidisciplinary/Multiagency Approach to Families at Risk and Child Abuse/Neglect: The Role of the Schools." Unpublished paper. Milwaukee: Midwest Parent–Child Welfare Resource Center, University of Wisconsin—Milwaukee, 1976.

Freeman, B.J. "Review of child behavior checklist." In *The Ninth Mental Measurements Yearbook,* edited by J. V. Mitchell. Lincoln, NE: Buros Institute of Mental Measurements, 1985.

Friedman, R. "Child Abuse: A Review of the Psychosocial Research." In *Four Perspectives on the Status of Child Abuse and Neglect Research,* edited by Herner & Co. Washington, D.C.: National Center of Child Abuse and Neglect, 1976.

Friedrich, W., and Boriskin, J. A. "The Role of the Child in Abuse: A Review of the Literature." *American Journal of Orthopsychiatry* 46 (1976): 580–90.

Friedrich, W.N., and Boriskin, J.A. "Primary Prevention of Child Abuse: Focus on the Special Child." *Hospital and Community Psychiatry* 29 (4) (1978): 248–251.

Froland, C.; Pancoast, D.L.; Chapman, N.J.; and Kimboko, P.J. *Helping Networks and Human Services.* Beverly Hills: Sage Publications, 1981.

Furman, W., and Buhrmester, D. "Children's perceptions of the qualities of sibling relationships." *Child Development* 56 (1985):448–461.

Furnish, H. "Prenatal exposure to fetally toxic work environments: The dilemma of the 1978 pregnancy amendments to Title VII of the Civil Rights Act of 1964." *Iowa Law Review* 66 (1980):63–129.

Gabel, H.; McDowell, J.; and Cerreto, M. "Family adaptation to the handicapped infant." In *Educating Handicapped Infants,* edited by S. G. Garwood and R. Fewell, pp. 455–493. Rockville, Md: Aspen Corporation, 1983.

Gagnon, J. "Female child victims of sex offenses." *Social Problems* 13 (1965):176–192.

Gallagher, J.J.; Cross, A.H.; and Scharfman, W. "Parent Role Scale." Unpublished instrument, Frank Porter Graham Child Development Center, University of North Carolina, Chapel Hill, NC, 1981.

Gallo, L.B. "Child abuse: Who is involved?" *New York State Dental Journal* (February 1983): 77–78.

Gamble, W., and McHale, S. "Stress and Coping in Siblings of Handicapped Children." Paper presented at the Gatlinburg Conference on Mental Retardation and Developmental Disabilities, Gatlinburg, Tenn., March 1985.

Gampel, D.; Gottlieb, J.; and Harrison, R. "A comparison of the classroom behaviors of special class EMR, integrated EMR, low IQ and nonretarded children." *American Journal of Mental Deficiency* 79 (1974): 16–21.

Gans, H. J. *Deciding What's News.* NY: Vintage Books, 1980.

Garbarino, J. "The family: A school for living." *National Elementary Principal* 55 (May/June 1976): 66–70. (a)

Garbarino, J. "A preliminary study of some ecological correlates of child abuse: The impact of socioeconomic stress on mothers." *Child Development* 47 (1) (March 1976): 178–85. (b)

Garbarino, J. "The human ecology of child maltreatment: A conceptual model for research." *Journal of Marriage and the Family* 39 (1977): 721–27. (a)

Garbarino, J. "The price of privacy: An analysis of the social dynamics of child abuse." *Child Welfare* 56(1977): 565–75. (b)

Garbarino, J. "The role of schools in socialization to adulthood." *Educational Forum* 42 (1978): 169–182.

Garbarino, J. "What kind of society permits child abuse?" *Infant Mental Health Journal* 1 (4) (1980): 270–280.

Garbarino, J. "An ecological approach to child maltreatment." In *The Social Context of Child Abuse and Neglect,* edited by L. H. Pelton, pp. 228–267. NY: Human Sciences Press, 1981.

Garbarino, J. and Associates *Children and Families in the Social Environment.* NY: Aldine, 1982.

Garbarino, J. "What we know about child maltreatment." *Children and Youth Services Review* 5 (1983): 1–6.

Garbarino, J. "What have we learned about child maltreatment." In *Perspectives on Child Maltreatment in the Mid '80s,* pp. 6–7. Washington, D.C.: U.S. Department of Health and Human Services, DHHS Publication NO. (OHDS) 84-30338, 1984.

Garbarino, J. "Prospects for Reducing Child Abuse by 20% in 1990." Paper prepared for The National Committee for Prevention of Child Abuse, Chicago, Illinois, 1985.

Garbarino, J. "The abuse and neglect of special children: An introduction to the issues." In *Special Children/Special Needs* edited by J. Garbarino and Associates. NY: Aldine, 1987.

Garbarino, J., and Bronfenbrenner, U. "The socialization of moral judgment and behavior in cross-cultural perspective." In *Moral Development and Behavior,* edited by T. Lickona. NY: Holt, Rinehart & Winston, 1976.

Garbarino, J., and Bronfenbrenner, U. "Research on Parent–Child Relations and Social Policy: Who Needs Whom?" Paper presented at the Symposium on Parent–Child Relations: Theoretical, Methodological and Practical Implications, Trier, West Germany, May 1977.

Garbarino, J., and Crouter, A. "The problem of construct validity in assessing the usefulness of child maltreatment report data." *American Journal of Public Health* 68 (1978): 598–99. (a)

Garbarino, J., and Crouter, A. "Defining the community context of parent–child relations: The correlates of child maltreatment." *Child Development* 49 (1978): 604–616. (b)

Garbarino, J., and Ebata, A. "The significance of ethnic and cultural differences in child maltreatment." *Journal of Marriage and the Family* 45 (1983): 773–783.

Garbarino, J., and Gilliam, G. *Understanding Abusive Families.* Lexington, MA: Lexington Books, 1980.

Garbarino, J., and Plantz, M. "Child maltreatment and juvenile delinquency: What are the links?" In *Troubled Youth, Troubled Families,* edited by J. Garbarino, C. Schellenbach, J. Sebes, and Associates. NY: Aldine, 1986.

Garbarino, J., and Sherman, D. "High-risk neighborhoods and high-risk families: The human ecology of child maltreatment." *Child Development* 51 (1980): 188–198. (a)

Garbarino, J., and Sherman, D. "Identifying high-risk neighborhoods." In *Protecting Children from Abuse and Neglect*, edited by J. Garbarino and S. Stocking, pp. 94–108. San Francisco, CA: Jossey-Bass, 1980. (b)

Garbarino, J., and Stocking, S. (Eds.) *Protecting Children from Abuse and Neglect*. San Francisco, CA: Jossey-Bass, 1980.

Garbarino, J.; Crouter, A.; and Sherman, D. "Screening neighborhoods for intervention: A research model of child protective services." *Journal of Social Service Research* 1 (1978): 135–45.

Garbarino, J.; Gaboury, M. T.; Long, F.; Grandjean, P.; and Asp, E. "Who owns the children? An ecological perspective on public policy affecting children." In *Legal Reforms Affecting Child and Youth Services*, edited by G. B. Melton, pp. 43–63. New York: Haworth, 1982.

Garbarino, J.; Sebes, J.; and Schellenbach, C. "Families at risk for destructive parent–child relations in adolescence." *Child Development* 55 (1984): 174–183.

Garbarino, J.; Schellenbach, J.; and Sebes, J., Eds. *Troubled Youth, Troubled Families*. NY: Aldine, 1986.

Garbarino, J.; Guttman, E.; and Wilson, J. *The Psychologically Battered Child*. San Francisco, CA: Jossey-Bass, 1986.

Gary, J.; Cutler, C.; Dean, J.; and Kempe, C. H. "Perinatal assessment of mother–baby interaction." In *Child Abuse and Neglect: The Family and the Community*, edited by R. Helfer and C. H. Kempe. Cambridge, MA: Ballinger, 1976.

Gastil, R. "Homicide and a regional culture of violence." *American Sociological Review* 36 (1971): 412–427.

Gath, A. "The impact of the abnormal child on the parents." *British Journal of Psychiatry* 130 (1977): 405–410.

Gaudin, J.M., and Pollane, L. "Social networks, stress and child abuse." *Children and Youth Services Review*, 5 (1983): 91–102.

Gearhart, B.R. *Special Education for the 80's*. St. Louis, MO: C.V. Mosby, 1980.

Geis, C., and Monahan, J. "The social ecology of violence." In *Moral Development and Behavior*, edited by T. Lickona. NY: Holt, Rinehart & Winston, 1976.

Gelles, R. J. "Child abuse as psychopathology: A sociological critique and reformulation." *American Journal of Orthopsychiatry* 43 (1973): 611–21.

Gelles, Richard J. "Child abuse and developmental disabilities." In *Child*

Abuse and Developmental Disabilities: Essays. U.S. Dept. of Health and Human Services, 1980.

Gelles, R. "Problems in defining and labeling child abuse. In *Child Abuse Prediction: Policy Implication,* edited by R. Starr, pp. 1–30. Cambridge, MA: Ballinger, 1982. (a)

Gelles, R. J. "A survey of public perceptions of child abuse." *Prevention Focus,* working paper 003, National Committee for Prevention of Child Abuse and Louis Harris Associates, Chicago, IL, 1982. (b)

Giaretto, H. "The treatment of father–daughter incest: A psychosocial approach." *Children Today* 5 (May 1976): 2–5.

Gil, D.G. "What schools can do about child abuse." *American Education* 5 (1969): 2–4.

Gil, D.G. *Violence Against Children: Physical Child Abuse in the United States.* Cambridge, MA: Harvard University Press, 1970.

Gil, E. *Handbook for Understanding and Preventing Abuse and Neglect of Children in Out-of-Home Care.* San Francisco, CA: Child Abuse Council, 1979.

Gil, E. "Institutional abuse of children in out-of-home care." In *Institutional Abuse of Children and Youth,* edited by R. Hanson, pp. 7–14. NY: Haworth Press, 1982.

Ginsberg v. New York, 390 U.S. 629 (1968).

Giovannoni, J. M., and Becerra, R. M. *Defining Child Abuse.* NY: Free Press, 1979.

Giovannoni, J. M., and Billingsley, A. "Child neglect among the poor: A study of parental adequacy in families of three ethnic groups." *Child Welfare* 49 (1970): 196–204.

Gliedman, J., and Roth, W. *The Unexpected Minority—Handicapped Children in America.* NY: Harcourt Brace Jovanovich, 1980.

Goldman, G.; Drew, J.D.; and Aber, J.L. *Outside In: A Handbook for Citizen Review of Children's Residential Facilities.* Boston, MA: Massachusetts Office for Children, 1980.

Goldstein, J.; Freud, A.; and Solnit, A. J. *Beyond the Best Interests of the Child.* NY: Free Press, 1973.

Goldstein, J.; Freud, A.; and Solnit, A. J. *Before the Best Interests of the Child.* NY: Free Press, 1979.

Gomes-Schwartz, B.; Horowitz, J.M.; and Sauzier, M. "Severity of emotional distress among sexually abused preschool, school-age, and adolescent children." *Hospital and Community Psychiatry* 36(5) (1985):503–508.

Goodman, H.; Gottlieb, J.; and Harrison, R. "Social acceptance of EMRs integrated into a non-graded elementary school." *American Journal of Mental Deficiency* 76 (1972):412–417.

Gordon, B.N. Review of Louisville behavior checklist. In *The Ninth Mental Measurements Yearbook,* edited by Buros. University of Nebraska Press: Lincoln, Nebraska, 1985.

Gore, S. "Social Support and Styles of Coping with Stress." In *Social Support and Health,* edited by S. Cohen and L. Syme, pp. 263–276. NY: Academic Press, 1985.

Gottlieb, B.H. *Social Networks and Social Support.* Beverly Hills, CA: Sage, 1981.

Gottlieb, J. "Mainstreaming: Fulfilling the promise?" *American Journal of Mental Deficiency* 86 (1981): 115–126.

Gottlieb, J.; Cohen, L.; and Goldstein, L. "Social contact personal adjustment as variables relating to attitudes toward EMR Children. *Training School Bulletin* 71 (1974):9–16.

Gottlieb, J.; Gampel, D.; and Budoff, M. "Classroom behavior of retarded children before and after reintegration into regular classes." *Journal of Special Education* 9 (1975):307–315.

Gourash, N. "Help-seeking: A review of the literature." *American Journal of Community Psychology* 6 (1978):413–423.

Gray, J. "Trends in child abuse reporting in New York State, 1966–1972." *Program Analysis Report 51.* Albany: New York State Department of Social Services, 1973.

Gray, J.; Cutler, C.; Dean, J.; and Kempe, C.H. "Prediction and prevention of child abuse and neglect." *Child Abuse and Neglect* 1 (1977): 45–58.

Green, A. "Self-destruction in physically abused schizophrenic children: Report of cases." *Archives of General Psychiatry* 19 (1968): 171–97.

Green, A. "Child abuse by siblings." *Child Abuse and Neglect* 8 (1984): 311–317.

Gregory, T., and Stocking, S. H. "Communicating science to the public through targeted messages." *Children and Youth Services Review* 3 (1981): 277–289.

Gregory, W. L. "Expectancies for controlability, performance attributions, and behavior." In *Research with the Locus of Control Construct,* edited by H. Lefcourt, pp. 67–124. NY: Academic Press, 1981.

Gresham, G. "Misguided mainstreaming: The case for social skills training with handicapped children." *Exceptional Children* 48 (1982): 422–433.

Grodin v. Grodin, 102 Mich APP 396;301NW and 869 (1980).

Grossman, M.L. "Early child development in the context of mothering experiences." *Child Psychiatry and Human Development* 5 (4) (1972): pp. 216–223.

Grunebaum, H.; Weiss, J. L.; Cohler, B. J.; Hartman, C. R.; and Gallant, D. H. *Mentally Ill Mothers and Their Children,* 2d ed. Chicago, IL: University of Chicago Press, 1982.

Guralnick, M. "Integrated preschools as educational and therapeutic environments: Concepts, design, and analyses." In *Early Intervention and the Integration of Handicapped and Nonhandicapped Children,* edited by M. Guralnick. Baltimore, MD, University Park Press, 1978.

Guralnick, M., and Paul-Brown, D. "The nature of verbal interactions among handicapped and nonhandicapped preschool children." *Child Development* 48 (1977): 254–260.

Haddock, M.D., and McQueen, W.M. "Assessing employee potential for abuse." Unpublished paper, W. Carolina University, undated.

Hall, A., and Wellman, B. "Social networks and social support." In *Social Support and Health,* edited by S. Cohen and L. Syme, pp. 23–39. NY: Academic Press, 1985.

Halperin, M. *Helping Maltreated Children: School and Community Involvement.* NY: C.V. Mosby Co., 1979.

Hanson, R. *Institutional Abuse of Children and Youth.* NY: Haworth Press, 1982.

Harrell, S.A., and Orem, R.C. *Preventing Child Abuse and Neglect: A Guide for Staff in Residential Institutions.* Washington, D.C.: U.S. Department of Health and Human Services, DHHS No. (OHDS) 80-30255, 1980.

Harris, O. "Day care: Have we forgotten the school-age child?" *Child Welfare* 55 (1977): 441–448.

Hartman, A., and Laird, J. *Family-Centered Social Work Practice.* NY: Free Press, 1983.

Hartup, W. "Peer Interaction and the Processes of Socialization." In *Early Intervention and the Integration of Handicapped and Nonhandicapped Children,* edited by M. Guralnick. Baltimore, MD: University Park Press, 1978.

Hawkins, R., and Breiling, J. *Issues in Implementing Foster Family Based Treatment.* Rockville, MD: NIMH, in press.

Hawley, A. *Human Ecology: A Theory of Community Structure.* NY: Ronald Press, 1950.

Hayes v. Shelby Memorial Hospital, 726 F.2d 1543, *rehearing denied* 732 F.2d 944 (11th Cir. 1984).

Hearings of Subcommittee on Children and Youth, U.S. Senate, 1974.

Helfer, R. "Basic issues concerning prediction." In *Child Abuse and Neglect: The Family and the Community,* edited by R. Helfer and C. H. Kempe. Cambridge, MA: Ballinger, 1976.

Helfer, R., & Kempe, C.H., eds. *Child Abuse and Neglect: The Family and the Community.* Cambridge, MA: Ballinger, 1976.

Helfer, R.; McKinney, J.; and Kempe, R. "Arresting or freezing the development process." In *Child Abuse and Neglect: The Family and the Community.* Cambridge, MA: Ballinger, 1976.

Helfer, R.E. "Why most physicians don't get involved in child abuse cases and what to do about it." *Children Today* (May–June 1975): 28–32.

Helfer, R.E.; Kempe, C.; Henley, E. eds. *The Battered Child*, 2d ed. Chicago and London: University of Chicago Press, 1974.

Heller, P. "Familism scale: Revalidation and revision." *Journal of Marriage and the Family* 38 (1976): 423–429.

Herrington, Lois H. "Statement before the Senate Subcommittee on Juvenile Justice Concerning *S.1156 Child Witness Protection Act of 1985.*" November 19, 1985.

Hetherington, E., and Martin, B. "Family interaction." In *Psychopathological Disorders of Childhood*, edited by H. Quay and J. Werry. NY: Wiley, 1979.

Hetherington, E.; Cox, M.; and Cox, R. "Divorced fathers." *Family Coordinator* 25 (1976): 427–428.

Hetherington, E.; Cox, M.; and Cox, R. "The aftermath of divorce." In *Mother–Child, Father–Child Relations*, edited by J. Stevens and M. Mathews, pp. 149–176. Washington, D.C.: National Association for the Education on Young Children, 1978.

Hinckley ex rel. Martin v. Secretary of Health and Human Services, 724 F.2d 19 (1st Cir. 1984).

Hingtegen, J.; Saunders, B.; and DeMyer, M.K. "Shaping cooperative responses in early childhood schizophrenics." In *Case Studies in Behavior Modification*, edited by L. Ullman & L. Krasne. NY: Holt, Rinehart, & Winston, 1965.

Hobbes, T. *Leviathan*, edited by Molesworth, vol. 3. London: J. Bohn, 1651/1839–1845.

Hobbs, C.J. "Skull fracture and the diagnosis of abuse." *Archives of Disease in Childhood* 59 (1984): 246–252.

Hobbs, D.F. "Parenthood as crisis: A third study." *Journal of Marriage and the Family* 27 (1965): 367–372.

Hobbs, N. *The Futures of Children: Categories, Labels, and Their Consequences*. San Francisco, CA: Jossey-Bass, 1975.

Hobbs, N. *The Troubled and Troubling Child*. San Francisco, CA: Jossey-Bass, 1982.

Hobbs, N.; Dokecki, P.; Hoover-Dempsey, K.; Moroney, R.; Shayne, M.; and Weeks, L. *Strengthening Families*. San Francisco, CA: Jossey-Bass, 1984.

Hoben, M. "Toward integration in the mainstream." *Exceptional Children* 47 (1980): 100–105.

Hoekstra, K. O.C. "Ecologically defining the mistreatment of adolescents." *Children and Youth Services Review* 6 (1984): 285–298.

Hofstetter, C. R., and Buss, T. F. "Motivation for viewing two types of TV programs." *Journalism Quarterly* 58 (1981): 99–103.

Holahan, C.J.; Wilcox, B.L.; Spearly, J.L.; and Campbell, M.D. "The ecological perspective in community mental health." *Community Mental Health Review* 4(2) (1979): 1–9.

Holmes, T., and Rahe, R. "The social readjustment rating scale." *Journal of Psychosomatic Research* 11 (1967): 212–20.

Holroyd J., and Guthrie, D. "Stress in families of children with neuromuscular disease." *Journal of Clinical Psychology* 35 (1979): 734–739.

Holroyd, J., and McArthur, D. "Mental retardation and stress on the parents: A contrast between Down's Syndrome and childhood autism." *American Journal of Mental Deficiency* 80 (1976): 431–436.

Holroyd, S. "Questionnaire on Resources and Stress Manual." Unpublished paper, Neuropsychiatric Institute, Department of Psychiatry and Biobehavioral Sciences, University of California, Los Angeles, 1985.

Holt, J. *Escape from Childhood: The Needs and Rights of Children.* NY: E. P. Dutton, 1974.

Horner, T.W.; Theut, S.; and Murdoch, W.G. "Discharge planning for the high-risk neonate: A consultation liaison role for the infant mental health specialist." *American Journal of Orthopsychiatry* 54 (4) (1984): 637–647.

Hudzik, John K., *Federal Aid to Criminal Justice.* Washington, D.C., The National Criminal Justice Association, 1984.

Hughes, Ronald C., and Rycus, Judith S. *Child Welfare Services for Children with Developmental Disabilities.* NY: Child Welfare League of America, Inc. 1983.

Hunter, R.S., and Kilstrom, N. "Breaking the cycle in abusive families." *American Journal of Psychiatry* 136 (1979): 1320–1322.

Hyatt, D.; Riley, K.; and Sederstrom, N. "Recall of television weather reports." *Journalism Quarterly* 55 (1978): 306–310.

In re Baby X, 97 Mich. App. 111, 293 N.W.2d 736 (1980).

In re Crystal A., 476 A.2d 1030 (R.I. 1984).

In re Dependency of Joseph Esgate, 990 Wash.2d 210, 660 P.2d 758 (1983) (per curiam).

In re Michael G., 147 Cal.App.3d 56, 194 Cal. Rptr. 743 (3d Dist. 1983).

In re Montgomery, 316 S.E.2d 246 (N.C. 1984).

In re Steven S., 126 Cal.App.3d 23, 178 Cal. Rptr. 525 (2d Dist. 1981).

Inspecting Children's Institutions. Yardley, PA: National Coalition for Children's Justice, 1977.

Institute of Judicial Administration/American Bar Association. *Juvenile Justice Standards Relating to Child Abuse and Neglect.* Cambridge, MA: Ballinger, 1977.

"Institutional Child Abuse" *Human Ecology Forum* 8 (1) (1977): 1–21.

Ipsa, J., and Matz, R. "Integrating handicapped preschool children with a cognitively oriented curriculum." In *Early Intervention and the Integration of Handicapped and Nonhandicapped Children,* edited by M. Guralnick. Baltimore, MD: University Park Press, 1978.

Irving Independent School District v Tatro, 104 S.Ct. 3371(1984).

Jacob, T.; Favorini, A.; Meisel, S. S.; and Anderson, C. M. "The alcoholic's spouse, children and family interaction." *Journal of Studies on Alcohol* 39 (1978): 1231–1251.

Janus, M.D.; Scanlon, B.; and Prince, V. "Youth prostitution." In *Child Pornography and Sex Rings,* edited by A. Burgess. Lexington, MA: Lexington Books, 1984.

Jaudes, Paula Kienberger, and Diamond, Linda J. "The handicapped child and child abuse." *Child Abuse and Neglect* 9 (1985): 341–347.

Jayarantne, S. "Child abusers as parents and children: A review." *Social Work* 22 (1977): 5–9.

Jenkins, L.; MacDicken, R.A.; and Ormsby, N.J. "A Community Approach: The Child Protection Coordinating Committee." U.S. Dept. Health, Education & Welfare, DHEW No. (OHDS) 79-30195, 1979.

Johnson, B., and Morse, H. *The Child and His Development: A Study of Children with Inflicted Injuries.* Denver, CO: Department of Public Welfare, 1968. (a)

Johnson, B., and Morse, H.A. "Injured children and their parents." *Children* 15 (1968): 147–52. (b)

Johnson, R.; Johnson, D.; DeWeerdt, N.; Lyons, V.; and Zaidman, B. "Integrating social adaptively handicapped seventh grade students into constructive relationships with nonhandicapped peers in science class." *American Journal of Mental Deficiency* 6 (1983): 611–618.

Jones, J.G. "Sexual abuse of children." *American Journal of Diseases of Children* 136 (1982): 142–146.

Jones, Nancy Lee. *Major Legal Issues Concerning Discrimination Against Handicapped Persons and Section 504 of the Rehabilitation Act of 1973.* Library of Congress, Congressional Research Service, Report No. 85-192 A, September 16, 1985.

Jones, R.; Gruber, K.; and Timbers, G. "Incidence and situational factors surrounding sexual assault against delinquent youths." *Child Abuse and Neglect* 5 (1981):431–440.

Justice, B., and Duncan, D.F. "Life crisis as a precursor to child abuse." *Public Health Reports* 11 (1976): 110–115.

Justice, B., and Justice, R., eds. *The Abusing Family.* NY: Human Sciences Press, 1976.

Kahneman, D., and Tversky, A. "On the psychology of prediction." *Psychological Review* 81 (1973): 237–251.

Kaplan, P.J., and Hall-McCorquodale, I. "Mother blaming in major clinical journals." *American Journal of Orthopsychiatry* 55(3) (1985): 345–353.

Karchmer, M. "Demographics and deaf adolescents." In *Proceedings of the National Conference on the Habilitation and Rehabilitation of*

Deaf Adolescents, edited by G. B. Anderson & D. Watson, pp. 28–46. Washington, D.C., National Academy of Gallaudet College, 1985.

Katz, E.; Adoni, H.; and Parness, P. "Remembering the news: What the picture adds to recall." *Journalism Quarterly* 54 (1977): 231–239.

Katz, R. "Empowerment and synergy: Expanding the community's healing resources." *Prevention in Human Services* 3 (1984): 201–226.

Katz, S.; Ambrosino, L.; McGrath, M.; and Sawitslsy, K. "The laws of child abuse and neglect: A review of the research." In *Four Perspectives on the Status of Child Abuse and Neglect Research,* edited by Herner & Co. Washington, D.C.: National Center on Child Abuse and Neglect, 1976.

Kauffman, C.; Grunebaum, H.; Cohler, B.; and Gamer, E. "Superkids: Competent children of psychotic parents." *American Journal of Psychiatry* 136 (1979): 1398–1402.

Kaufman, M.; Agard, J.; and Simmel, M. *Mainstreaming: Learners and their Environment.* Baltimore, MD: University Park Press, 1981.

Kelley, M.L. "Review of child behavior checklist." In *The Ninth Mental Measurements Yearbook,* edited by J.V. Mitchell. Lincoln, NE: Buros Institute of Mental Measurements, 1985.

Kelley, S.J. "The use of art therapy with sexually abused children." *Journal of Psychosocial Nursing* 22(12) (1984): 12–18.

Kelly, G.A. *The Psychology of Personal Constructs, Vols. 1 and 2.* NY: Norton, 1955.

Kempe, C. H.; Silverman, F. N.; Steele, B. F.; Droegemueller, W.; and Silver, H. K. "The battered child syndrome." *Journal of the American Medical Association* 181 (1962): 17–24.

Kempe, C.H. "A practical approach to the protection of the abused child and rehabilitation of the abusing parent." *Pediatrics* 51 (1973): 804–12.

Kempe, R.S., and Kempe, C.H. *Child Abuse.* Cambridge, MA: Harvard University Press, 1978.

Kennell, J.; Voos, D.; and Klaus, M. "Parent infant bonding." In *Child Abuse and Neglect: The Family and the Community,* edited by R. Helfer and C.H. Kempe. Cambridge, MA: Ballinger, 1976.

Kent, J. "A follow-up study of abused children." *Journal of Pediatric Psychology* 1(1976): 25–31.

Kett, J. F. *Rites of Passage.* NY: Basic Books, 1977.

Kibby, R. "The abused child: The need for collaboration." *Thrust for Educational Leadership* 4 (1975): 11–13.

Kinard, E.M. "Emotional development in physically abused children." *American Journal of Orthopsychiatry,* 50 (1980):686–696.

King, P. A. "The juridical status of the fetus: A proposal for legal protection of the unborn." *Michigan Law Review* 77 (1979): 1647–1687.

Kirks, D. R. "Radiological evaluation of visceral injuries in the battered child syndrome." *Pediatric Annals* 12 (1983): 880–893.

Kline, Donald F. "The Disabled Child and Child Abuse." Pamphlet. Chicago, IL: National Committee for Prevention of Child Abuse, 1982.

Klopping, H. "The deaf adolescent: Abuse and abusers." In *Proceedings of the National Conference on the Habilitation and Rehabilitation of Deaf Adolescents*, edited by G. B. Anderson and D. Watson, pp. 187–196. Washington, D.C., National Academy of Gallaudet College, 1985.

Kluft, R.P. "Multiple personality in childhood." *Psychiatric Clinics of North America* 7(1) (1984):121–134.

Knitzer, J. *Unclaimed Children: The Failure of Public Responsibilities to Children and Adolescents in Need of Mental Health Services*. Washington, D.C.: Children's Defense Fund, 1982.

Knitzer, J., and Allen, M. "The federal role." *Children Without Homes*. Washington, D.C.: The Children's Defense Fund, 1978.

Knopp, F.H. *Intervention in Adolescent Sex Offenses: Nine Program Descriptions*. Syracuse, NY: Safer Society Press, 1985.

Kogan, L., and Jenkins, S. *Indicators of Child Health and Welfare*. NY: Columbia University Press, 1974.

Korbin, J., ed. *Child Abuse and Neglect: Cross-Cultural Perspectives*. Berkeley, CA: University of California Press, 1981.

Kreighbaum, H. "Public interest in science news." *Science* 129 (1959): 1092–1095.

Kuhn, T. *The Structure of Scientific Revolutions*. Chicago, IL: University of Chicago Press, 1962.

LaFollette, M. C. "Science on television: Influences and strategies." *Daedalus* (Fall 1982): 183–197.

Lamb, M. "Interactions between 18-month-olds and their preschool-aged siblings." *Child Development* 49 (1978): 51–59.

Lamb, M., and Sutton-Smith, B., eds. *Sibling relationships*. Hillsdale, NJ: Lawrence Erlbaum, 1982.

Lambert, N.; Windmiller, M.; Tharinger, D.; and Cole, L. *AAMD Adaptive Behavior Scale*. CA: Publishers Test Service, 1975.

Lamphear, V.S. "The impact of maltreatment on children's psychosocial adjustment: A Review of the research." *Child Abuse and Neglect* 9 (1985):251–263.

Larson, M. *Current Trends in Child Development Research*. Greensboro, NC: University of North Carolina Press, 1975.

Lauer, B.; Ten Brock, E.; and Grossman, M. "Battered child syndrome: Review of 130 patients with controls." *Pediatrics* 54 (1974): 67–70.

Lazar, I., and Darlington, R. "Lasting effects of early education." *Monographs of the Society for Research in Child Development* 47 (2-3, serial no. 195) (1982).

Lefcourt, H., ed. *Research with the Locus of Control Construct,* vol. 1. NY: Academic Press, 1981.

LeMasters, E. "Parenthood as crisis." *Marriage and Family Living* 19 (1957): 352–355.

Lenoski, E. F. "Translating Injury Data into Preventive and Health Care Services—Physical Child Abuse." Unpublished manuscript. Los Angeles: University of Southern California School of Medicine, 1974.

Leonidas, J.C. "Skeletal trauma in the child abuse syndrome." *Pediatric Annals* 12 (1983): 875–881.

Levine, M. "The right of the fetus to be born free of drug addiction." *U.C. Davis Law Review* 7 (1974): 45–55.

Levinson, B.M. "Pets, child development and mental illness." *Journal of the American Veterinary Medical Association* 157 (1979): 1759–1766.

Levy, R. I. "On getting angry in the Society Islands." In Mental Health Research in Asia and the Pacific, edited by W. Candhill and T. Y. Lin. Honolulu: East-West Center Press, 1969.

Lightcap, J.; Kurland, J.; and Burgess, R. "Child abuse: A test of some predictions from evolutionary theory." *Ethology and Sociobiology* 3 (1982): 61–67.

Litwak, E. "The use of extended family groups in the achievement of social goals." *Social Problems* 7 (1960): 177–187.

Lloyd, D.; Melton, G. B.; and Rogers, C. M. *Sexually Abused Children and the Legal System.* NY: Guilford, in preparation.

Lombard, F. K. "1980 Annual survey of Michigan law: Family law." *Wayne Law Review* 27 (1981): 807–826.

Lord, C. "Peer interaction of autistic children." In *Advances in Applied Developmental Psychology,* edited by F. J. Morrison, C. Lord, and D. Keating. NY: Academic Press, 1984.

Luterman, D. *Counseling Parents of Hearing Impaired Children.* Boston, MA: Little Brown & Co., 1979.

Lutzker, J., & Rice, J. "Project '12-ways': Measuring outcomes of a large in-home service for treatment and prevention of child abuse and neglect." *Child Abuse and Neglect* 8 (1984): 519–424.

Lutzker, J.; Wesch, D.; and Rice, J. "A review of Project '12-ways': An ecobehavioral approach to the treatment and prevention of child abuse and neglect. *Advances in Behavior Research and Therapy* 6 (1984): 63–74.

McAlister, A.; Puska, P.; Koskela, K.; Pallonene, U.; and Maccoby, N. "Mass communication and community organization for public health education." *American Psychologist* 35 (1980): 375–379.

McAllister, R.J.; Butler, E.W.; and Lei, T.J. "Patterns of social interaction among families of behaviorally retarded children." *Journal of Marriage and the Family* (February 1973): 93–100.

McCall, R. B. "Family services and the mass media." *Family Relations* 32 (1983): 315–322.

McCall, R. B. "Child development and society: A primer on disseminating information to the public through the mass media." In *Advances in Applied Developmental Psychology,* vol. 1, edited by I. E. Sigel. Norwood, NJ: Ablex, 1985.

McCall, R. B. "The media, society, and child development research." In *Handbook of Infant Development,* edited by J. D. Osofsky. New York: Wiley, 1986.

McCall, R. B.; Lonnborg, B.; Gregory, T. G.; Murray, J. P.; and Leavitt, S. "Communicating development research to the public: The Boys Town experience." *Newsletter of the Society of Research in Child Development* (Fall 1982): 1–3.

McClelland, D. "Testing for competence rather than intelligence." *American Psychologist* 28 (1975): 1–14.

McCombs, M. E., and Shaw, D. L. "The agenda-setting function of mass media." *Public Opinion Quarterly* 36 (1972): 176–187.

McCubbin, H., and Figley, C., eds. *Stress and the Family. Vol. I: Coping with Normative Transitions.* NY: Brunner/Mazel, 1983.

McCubbin, H.; Joy, C.; Cauble, E.; Comeau, J.; Patterson, J.; and Needle, B. "Family stress, and coping: A decade review." *Journal of Marriage and the Family* 42 (1980): 855–871.

McCubbin, H.; Cauble, A.E.; and Patterson, J.M., eds. *Family Stress, Coping, and Social Support.* Springfield, IL: Charles C. Thomas, 1982.

MacEachron, A.E., and Krauss, M.W. "A national survey of handicapped children receiving public social services: Prevalence rates and services patterns in 1977. *Children and Youth Services Review* 5 (1983): 117–134.

McGowan, M. Personal communication, April 1985.

McGuire, I.S., and Wagner, N.N. "Sexual dysfunction in women who were molested as children: On response patterns and suggestions for treatment." *Journal of Sex and Marital Therapy* 4 (1978):11–15.

McHale, S. "Social interactions of autistic and nonhandicapped children during free play." *American Journal of Orthopsychiatry* 53 (1983): 81–91.

McHale, S., and Gamble, W. "Dimensions of Sibling Relationships in Children with Handicapped and Nonhandicapped Siblings." Paper presented at the biennial meeting of the Society for Research in Child Development, Toronto, Canada, April 1985.

McHale, S., and Simeonsson, R. "Effects of interaction on nonhandicapped children's attitudes toward autistic children." *American Journal of Mental Deficiency* 85 (1980): 18–24.

McHale, S.; Olley, J.; Marcus, L.; and Simeonsson, R. "Nonhandicapped peers as tutors for autistic children." *Exceptional Children* 48 (1981): 263–264.

McHale, S.; Simeonsson, R.; and Sloan, J. "Children with handicapped brothers and sisters." In *Current Issues in Autism: The Effects of Autism on the Family,* edited by E. Schopler and G. Mesibov. NY: Plenum, 1984.

McHale, S.; Sloan, J.; and Simeonsson, R. "Sibling relationships with autistic mentally retarded and nonhandicapped brothers and sisters. *Journal of Autism and Developmental Disorders,* in press.

McQuail, D. *Towards a Sociology of Mass Communications.* London: Macmillan, 1969.

Maluccio, A.N., and Sinanoglu, P.A., eds. *The Challenge of Partnership: Working with Parents of Children in Foster Care.* NY: Child Welfare League of America, 1981.

Martin, D. "The growing horror of child abuse and the undesirable role of the schools in putting an end to it." *American School Board Journal* 160 (1973): 51–55.

Martin, H. *The Abused Child.* Cambridge, MA: Ballinger Publ., 1976.

Martin, H. P. "The consequences of being abused and neglected: How the child fares." In *The Battered Child,* edited by C. H. Kempe and R. Helfer. Chicago, IL: University of Chicago Press, 1980.

Martin, H. P. "The neuro-psychodevelopmental aspects of child abuse and neglect." *Child Abuse and Neglect: A Medical Reference,* edited by Norman Ellerstein, pp. 95–119. NY: Wiley, 1981.

Martin, H. P., and Rodeheffer, Martha A. "The psychological impact of abuse on children." *Traumatic Abuse and Neglect of Children at Home,* edited by Gertrude J. Williams and John Money, pp. 254–261.

Martin, H. P.; Beezley, P.; Conway, E. F.; and Kempe, C. H. "The development of abused children." *Advances in Pediatrics* 21 (1974): 25–73.

Martin, H. P., and Beezley, P. "Behavioral observations of abused children." *Developmental Medicine and Child Neurology* 19 (1977): 373–387.

Mash, F. "Families with problem children." *New Directions for Child Development* 24 (1984): 65–79.

Mash, E. J.; Johnston, C.; and Kovitz, K. "A comparison of the mother–child interactions of physically abused and non-abused children during play and task situations. *Journal of Clinical Psychology* 12 (1983): 337–346.

Mead, M. *Sex Temperament in Three Savage Tribes.* NY: William Morrow, 1935.

Meadow, K. "Burnout in professionals working with deaf children." *American Annals of the Deaf* 126 (1981):13–22.

Meadow, K. "Meadow-Kendall Social Emotional Assessment Inventory for Deaf and Hearing Impaired Children." Washington, D.C.: Outreach Pre-College Programs, 1983.

Meddin, B.J., and Hansen, I. "The services provided during a child abuse and/or neglect case investigation and the barriers that exist to service provision." *Child Abuse and Neglect* 9 (1985):175–182.

Meier, J. *Assault against Children*. San Diego, CA: College Hill Press, 1985.

Meier, J. "Current Status and Future Prospects for the Nation's Children and Their Families." Address to the Annual Convention of the National Association for the Education of Young Children, Anaheim, CA, November 13, 1976.

Melton, G. B. "Children's competency to testify." *Law and Human Behavior* 5 (1981): 73–85.

Melton, G. B. "Toward "personhood" for adolescents: Autonomy and privacy as values in public policy." *American Psychologist* 38 (1985): 99–103.

Melton, G. B. "Child witnesses and the first amendment: A psycholegal dilemma. *Journal of Social Issues* 40(2) (1984): 109–123.

Melton, G. B. *Rethinking Child Welfare: International Perspectives*, edited by J. F. Gilgun, Z. Eisikovits, and I. M. Schwartz. Lincoln, NE: University of Nebraska Press, in press.

Melton, G. B., and Scott, E. S. "Evaluation of mentally retarded persons for sterilization: Contributions and limits of psychological consultation." *Professional Psychology: Research and Practice* 15 (1984): 34–48.

Melton, G. B., and Thompson, R. A. "Legislative approaches to psychological maltreatment." In *The Psychological Maltreatment of Children and Youth*, edited by M. R. Brassard, R. Germain, and S. N. Hart. NY: Pergamon, in press.

Melton, G. B., Petrila, J.; Poythress, N. G., Jr.; and Slobogin, C. *Psychological Evaluation for the Courts: A Handbook for Mental Health Professionals and Lawyers*. NY: Guilford, in press.

Menolascino, F. J. *Challenges in Retardation: Progressive Ideology and Services*. NY: Human Services Press, 1977.

Menolascino, F. J. "Overview: Bridging the gap between mental retardation and mental illness." In *Mental Health and Mental Retardation: Bridging the Gap*, edited by F. J. Menolascino and B. M. McCann. Baltimore, MD: University Park Press, 1983.

Menolascino, F. J., and McCann, B. M., eds. *Mental Health and Mental Retardation: Bridging the Gap*. Baltimore, MD: University Park Press, 1983.

Mercer, J. R. *Labeling the Mentally Retarded: Clinical and Legal Perspectives on Mental Retardation*. Berkeley, CA: University of California Press, 1973.

Merril, E. J. *Protecting the Battered Child*. Denver, CO: Children's Division, American Human Association, 1962.

Meyer, A. J.; Nash, J. D.; McAlister, A. L.; Maccoby, N.; and Farquhar,

J. W. "Skills training in a cardiovascular health education campaign." *Journal of Consulting and Clinical Psychology* 48 (1980): 129–142.

Meyer v. Nebraska, 262 U.S. 390 (1923).

Meyers, D.; MacMillan, E.; and Yoshida, R. "Regular class education of EMR students from efficacy to mainstreaming: A review of issues and research." In *Educating Mentally Retarded Persons in the Mainstream,* edited by J. Gottlieb. Baltimore, MD: University Park Press, 1980.

Milgram, S. *Obedience to Authority.* NY: Harper & Row, 1974.

Miller, A. *For Your Own Good: Hidden Cruelty in Child Rearing and the Roots of Violence.* NY: Farrar, Straus, Giroux, 1983.

Miller, B., and Myers-Walls, J. "Parenthood: Stresses and coping strategies." In *Stress and the Family. Vol. I: Coping with Normative Transitions,* edited by H. McCubbin and C. Figley, pp. 54–73. NY: Brunner/Mazel, 1983.

Miller, J. D., and Barrington, T. M. "The acquisition and retention of scientific information." *Journal of Communication* 31 (1981): 178–189.

Miller, L. C. *Louisville Behavior Checklist.* Los Angeles, CA: Western Psychological Services, 1981.

Miller, N., and Cantwell, D. "Siblings as therapists: A behavioral approach." *American Journal of Psychiatry* 133 (1976): 447–450.

Miller, N., and Miller, W. "Siblings as behavior change agents." In *Counseling Methods,* edited by J. Kromboltz and C. Thoresen. NY: Holt, Rinehart & Winston, 1976.

Miller, S. "An exploratory study of sibling relationships in families with retarded children." Unpublished Ph.D. dissertation, Columbia University. *Dissertation Abstracts International* 35 (2) (1974): 994B - 2, 995B.

Mills, C. W., *The Sociological Imagination.* NY: Oxford University Press, 1975.

Milner, J. S. *The Child Abuse Potential Inventory.* Webster, NC: Psychtech Corp., 1980.

Milner, J. S., and Ayoub, C. "Evaluation of at-risk parents using the child abuse potential inventory." *Journal of Clinical Psychology* 36 (1980): 945–948.

Milner, J.S., and Wimberley, R. C. "Prediction and explanation of child abuse. *Journal of Clinical Psychology* 36 (1980): 875–884.

Mink, I.T.; Nihira, K.; and Meyers, C.E. "Taxonomy of family life styles: I. Homes with TMR children." *American Journal of Mental Deficiency* 87 (1983): 484–497.

Missing Children's Assistance Act of 1984, 98 Stat. 2125

Mitchell, J. *Social Networks in Urban Situations.* Atlantic Highlands, NJ: Humanities Press, 1969.

Mitchell, R.E., and Trickett, E.J. "Task force report: Social networks as mediators of social support." *Community Mental Health Journal* 16 (1980): 27–43.

Mnookin, R. H. "Foster care: In whose best interest?" *Harvard Educational Review* 43 (1973): 599–638.

Mnookin, R. H. "Child custody adjudication: Judicial functions in the face of indeterminancy." *Law and Contemporary Problems* 39 (1975): 226–293.

Monahan, J. *The Clinical Prediction of Violent Behavior.* Beverly Hills, CA: Sage, 1981.

Monahan, J., and Walker, L. *Social Science in Law: Cases and Materials.* Mineola, NY: Foundation Press, 1985.

Moos, R. *Family Environment Scale.* Palo Alto, CA: Consulting Psychologists Press, 1974.

Morris, J. L.; Johnson, C. F.; and Clasen, M. "To report or not to report: Physician's attitudes toward discipline and child abuse." *American Journal of Diseases of Children* 139 (1985): 194–197.

Morris, M. G., and R. W. Gould. "Role reversal: A necessary concept in dealing with the 'battered child syndrome'." In *The Neglected/Battered Child Syndrome.* NY: Child Welfare League of America, 1963.

Morris, R. A., and Sonderegger, T. B. "Legal applications and implications for neurotoxin research of the developing organism." *Neurobehavioral Toxicology and Teratology* 6 (1984): 303–306.

Morse, C. W.; Sahler, O. J.; and Friedman, S. B. "A three-year follow-up study of abused and neglected children." *American Journal of Diseases of Children* 120 (1970): 439–46.

Mussen, P.; Conger, J.; and Kagan, J. *Child Development and Personality.* NY: Harper & Row, 1974.

Nage, S. "Child abuse and neglect problems: A national overview." *Children Today* 7 (May–June 1975): 13–17.

Nagi, Saad. *Child Maltreatment in the United States.* NY: Columbia University Press, 1977.

Naisbitt, J. *Megatrends.* NY: Warner Books, 1984.

Nakashima, I. "Runaway girls." *Medical Aspects of Human Sexuality,* 16(8) (1982):49–50.

National Academy of Sciences. *Toward a National Policy for Children and Families.* Washington, D.C.: U.S. Government Printing Office, 1976.

National Center for Child Abuse and Neglect. *Child Abuse and Neglect: The Problem and Its Management.* Washington, D.C.: U.S. Government Printing Office, 1975.

National Commission on Children in Need of Parents: Final Report. NY: NCCINP, 1979.

Navarre, E.L. *Sexually Abused Children—Prevention, Protection and*

Care: A Handbook for Residential Child Care Facilities. Indianapolis, IN: Indiana University School of Social Work, 1980.

Nelson, B.J. "The politics of child abuse and neglect: New governmental recognition for an old problem." *Child Abuse and Neglect* 3 (1979): 102.

Nelson, Barbara J. *Making an Issue of Child Abuse.* Chicago, IL: University of Chicago Press, 1984.

Neuman, W. R. "Patterns of recall among television news viewers." *Public Opinion Quarterly* 40 (1976): 115–123.

New American Humane Association. "Guidelines for Schools to Help Protect Neglected and Abused Children." Pamphlet, 1971.

Nihira, K.; Meyers, C.E.; and Mink, I. "Home environment, family adjustment, and the development of mentally retarded children." *Applied Research in Mental Retardation* 1 (1980): 5–24.

Nordstrom, J. "Child Abuse: A School District's Response to Its Responsibility." *Child Welfare* 53 (1974): 257–60.

Oates, R.K.; Forrest, D.; and Peacock, A. "Self-esteem of abused children." *Child Abuse and Neglect* 9 (1985): 159–163.

O'Brien, Shirley. *Child Abuse: A Crying Shame.* Provo, Utah: Brigham University Press, 1980.

O'Day, B. *Preventing Sexual Abuse of Persons with Disabilities.* St. Paul, MN: Minnesota Program for Victims of Sexual Abuse, 1983.

Ogle, P. *The sibling relationship: Maternal preceptions of the nonhandicapped on handicapped/nonhandicapped sibling dyads.* Unpublished Ph.D. dissertation, University of North Carolina, Chapel Hill, 1982.

Oil, Chemical and Atomic Workers International Union v. American Cyanamid Co., 741 F.2d 444 (D.C. Cir. 1984).

Olmstead v. United States, 277 U.S. 438 (1928).

Olweus, D. "Stability of aggressive reaction patterns in males: A review." *Psychological Bulletin* 86 (1979):852–875.

Oregon Association of Treatment Centers: Handbook. Redmond: Oregon, 1985.

Pahl, J. M., and Pahl, R. E. *Managers and Their Wives: A Study of Career and Family Relationships in the Middle Class.* London: Allen Lane, 1971.

Pancoast, D.L. "Finding and enlisting neighbors to support families." In *Protecting Children from Abuse and Neglect,* edited by J. Garbarino & S. Stocking, pp. 109–132. San Francisco, CA: Jossey-Bass, 1980.

Pappenfort, D.M.; Kilpatrick, D.M.; and Roberts, R.W., eds. *Child Care: Social Policy and the Institution.* Chicago: Aldine, 1973.

Pappenfort, D.M.; Young, T.M.; and Marlow, C.R. *Residential Group Care: 1981: 1966 and Preliminary Report of Selected Findings from the National Survey of Residential Group Care Facilities.* University of Chicago, School of Social Service Administration, 1983.

Parke, R. "Theoretical models of child abuse: Their implications for prediction, prevention, and modification." In *Theoretical Models of Child Abuse,* edited by R. Starr, pp. 31–66. Cambridge, MA: Ballinger, 1982.

Parke, R., and Slaby, D. "The development of Aggression in Children." In *Social Development: Carmichael's Manual of Child Psychology,* edited by M. Hetherington. NY: Wiley, 1983.

Parke, R., and Collmer, C. W. "Child abuse: An interdisciplinary analysis." In *Review of Child Development Research,* vol. 5, edited by E. M. Hetherington. Chicago, IL: University of Chicago Press, 1975.

Parloff, M.B.; Waskow, I.E.; and Wolfe, B.E. "Research on therapist variables in relation to process and outcome." In *Handbook of Psychotherapy and Behavior Change,* 2d ed., edited by S. L. and H.E. Bergin, pp. 233–282. NY: Wiley, 1978.

Pascoe, J.M.; Hildebrandt, H.M.; Tarrie, A.; and Murphy, M. "Patterns of skin injury in non-accidental and accidental injury." *Pediatrics* 64 (1979): 245–247.

Pascoe, J.; Loda, F.; Jeffries, V.; and Earp, J. "The association between mothers' social support and provision of stimulation to their children." *Developmental and Behavioral Pediatrics* 2 (1981): 15–19.

Pastor, D., and Swap, S. "An ecological study of emotional disturbed preschoolers in special and regular classes. *Exceptional Children* 45 (1978): 213–215.

Patterson, G. "Mothers: The unacknowledged victims." *Monographs of the Society for Research in Child Development* 45 (5) (1980).

Patterson, J., and McCubbin, H. "Chronic illness: Family stress and coping." In *Stress and the Family. Vol. I: Coping with Catastrophe,* edited by H. McCubbin & C. Figley, pp. 21–36. NY: Brunner/Mazel, 1983.

Pattison, E.; DeFrancisco, D.; Wood, P.; Frazier, H.; and Crowder, J. "A psychosocial kinship model for family therapy. *American Journal of Psychiatry* 132 (1975);1246–1251.

Paulson, M. "Multiple intervention program for the abused and neglected child." *Journal of Pediatric Psychology* 1 (1976): 83–87.

Paulson, M., and P. Blake. "The physically abused child: A focus on prevention." *Child Welfare* 48 (1969): 86–95.

Paykel, E. S. "Life stress, depression and attempted suicide." *Journal of Human Stress* (September 1976): 3–12.

Pearlin, L. "Social structure and processes of social support." In *Social Support and Health,* edited by S. Cohen and L. Syme, pp. 43–59. NY: Academic Press, 1985.

Pearlin, L., and Schooler, C. "The structure of coping." In *Family Stress, Coping, and Social Support,* edited by H. McCubbin, A. Cauble, and J. Patterson, pp. 109–135. Springfield, IL: Charles C. Thomas, 1982.

Pelton, L. H., ed. *The Social Context of Child Abuse and Neglect.* NY: Human Sciences Press, 1981.

People v. Pointer, 151 Cal. App.3d 1128, 199 Cal.Rptr. 357 (1st Dist. 1984).

Perlman, D., and Peplau, L.A. "Loneliness research: A survey of empirical findings." *Preventing the Harmful Consequences of Severe and Persistent Loneliness.* Rockville, MD: U.S. Department of Health and Human Services, DHHS Publication No. (ADM) 84-1312, 1984.

Perry, M.A.; Doran, L.D.; and Wells, E.A. "Developmental and behavioral characteristics of the physically abused child. *Journal of Clinical Child Psychology* 12 (1983):320–324. (a)

Perry, M.A.; Wells, E.A.; and Doran, L.D. "Parent characteristics in abusing and nonabusing families." *Journal of Clinical Child Psychology* 12 (3) (1983): 329–336. (b)

Pettis, K.W., and Hughes, R.D. "Sexual victimization of children: A current perspective." *Behavioral Disorders* (February 1985): 136–144.

Philliber, S., and Graham, E. "The impact of age of mother and mother–child interaction patterns." *Journal of Marriage and Family* 43 (1981): 109–115.

Phillips, E.L.; Phillips, E.A.; Fixsen, D.L.; and Wolf, M.M. *The Teaching Family Handbook.* Lawrence, KS: Bureau of Child Research, University of Kansas, 1974.

Piaget, J. *The Moral Judgment of the Child.* Glencoe, IL: Free Press, 1932.

Pierce v. Society of Sisters, 268 U.S. 510 (1925).

Platt, A. M. *The Child Savers: The Invention of Delinquency,* 2d ed. Chicago, IL: University of Chicago Press, 1977.

Polansky, N. "Analysis of research on child neglect: The social work viewpoint." In *Four Perspectives on the Status of Child Abuse and Neglect Research,* edited by Herner & Co. Washington, D.C.: National Center on Child Abuse and Neglect, 1976.

Polsky, H. *Cottage Six.* NY: Russell Sage, 1962.

Pomeroy, W. *Your Child and Sex.* NY: Delacorte, 1974.

Poorman, C. "Mainstreaming in reverse with a special friend." *Teaching Exceptional Children* 12 (1980): 136–142.

Powell ex rel. Powell v. Schweiker, 514 F. Supp. 439, aff'd, 688 F.2d 1357, rehearing denied, 694 F.2d 727 (11th Cir. 1981).

Powell, D. R. "Personal social networks as a focus for primary prevention of child mistreatment." *Infant Mental Health Journal* 1 (4) (1980): 232–239.

Powell, T. *Parents, Siblings, and Handicapped Children: A Social Interaction Program.* Storrs, CT: The University of Connecticut, 1982.

Powell, T., and Ogle, P. A. *Brothers and Sisters: A Special Part of Exceptional Families.* Baltimore, MD: Paul H. Brookes, 1985.

Powell, T.; Salzberg, C.; Rule, S.; Levy, S.; and Itzkowitz, J. "Teaching mentally retarded children to play with their siblings using parents as trainers." *Education and Treatment of Children* 6 (1983): 343–362.

Price-Bonham, S., and Addison, S. "Families and mentally retarded children: Emphasis on the father." *The Family Coordinator* 3 (1978): 221–230.

Prince v. Massachusetts, 321 U.S. 158 (1944).

Programs to Strengthen Families. Yale Bush Center in Child Development and Social Policy and the Family Resource Coalition. Chicago, IL: Family Resource Coalition, 1984.

Project FEED, Fact Sheet and Curriculum Guide, Indiana University Institute for Child Study, Bloomington, Indiana. N.D.

Radbill, S. "A history of child abuse and infanticide." In *The Battered Child,* edited by R. Helfer and C. H. Kempe. Chicago, IL: University of Chicago Press, 1974.

Raleigh Fitkin–Paul Morgan Memorial Hospital v. Anderson, 42 N.J. 421, 201 A.2d 537, *cert. denied,* 377 U.S. 985 (1964).

Rappaport, J. "In praise of paradox: A social policy empowerment over prevention." *American Journal of Community Psychology* 9 (1981): 1–25.

Reece, R. M., and Grodin, M. A. "Recognition of nonaccidental injury." *Pediatric Clinics of North America* 32 (1985): 41–60.

Reed, E. W., and Reed, S. C. *Mental Retardation: A Family Study.* Philadelphia, PA: Saunders, 1965.

Rehabilitation Act of 1973, 87 Stat. 504.

Reidy, T. J. "The aggressive characteristics of abused and neglected children." *Journal of Clinical Psychology* 33 (1977): 1140–1145.

Rementeria, J. L., ed. *Drug Abuse in Pregnancy and Neonatal Effects.* Saint Louis, MO: C. V. Mosby, 1977.

Report of the Attorney General's Task Force on Family Violence. William L. Hart, Chairman. Washington, D.C.: U.S. Government Printing Office, 1984.

Report of the President's Task Force on Victims of Crime. Lois H. Herrington, Chair. Washington, D.C.: U.S. Govt. Printing Office, 1982.

Residential Child Care Guidebook. Trenton, NJ: Interstate Consortium on Residential Child Care, 1980.

Reskow, J. "Child abuse: What the educator should know." *New Jersey Education Association Review* 47 (1973): 14–15.

Reyes v. Superior Court, 75 Cal.App.3d, 141 Cal. Rptr. 912 (4th Dist. 1977).

Richards, L. "Can the schools help prevent child abuse?" *Illinois Teacher* 17 (1973): 43–52.

Rindfleisch, N. *Identification, Management and Prevention of Child Abuse and Neglect in Residential Facilities.* Columbus, OH: Ohio State University Research Foundation, 1984.

Robertson, J.A. "Procreative liberty and the control of conception, pregnancy, and childbirth." *Virginia Law Review* 69 (1983): 405–464.

Rodee, M. "A Study to Evaluate the Resource Teacher Concept When Used with High Level Educable Retardation at a Primary Level." Unpublished Ph.D. dissertation, University of Iowa, 1971.

Roe v. Wade, 410 U.S. 113 (1973).

Roos, R. "The handling and mishandling of parents of mentally retarded persons." In *Mental Health and Mental Retardation: Bridging the Gap*, edited by F.J. Menolascino and B.M. McCann. Baltimore, MD: University Park Press, 1983.

Rosenberg, M. S. Memorandum to M. Brewster Smith on behalf of the Division of Child, Youth, and Family Services, American Psychological Association, September 15, 1984.

Rosenberg, M. S., and Hunt, R. D. "Child maltreatment: Legal and mental health issues." In *Children, Mental Health, and the Law*, edited by N. D. Reppucci, L. A. Weithorn, E. P. Mulvey, and J. Monahan, pp. 79–101. Beverly Hills, CA: Sage, 1984.

Rosenberg, M. S., and Reppucci, N. D. "Child abuse: A review with special focus on an ecological approach in rural communities." In *Rural Psychology*, edited by A. W. Childs and G. B. Melton, pp. 305–336. NY: Plenum, 1983.

Ross, G.S. "Home intervention for premature infants of low-income families." *American Journal of Orthopsychiary* 54 (2) (1984): 263–270.

Routh, D. K. Memorandum to M. Brewster Smith on behalf of the Division of Clinical Psychology, American Psychological Association, July 18, 1984.

Rubin, R.L. "Bridging the gap through individual counseling and psychotherapy with mentally retarded people." In *Mental Health and Mental Retardation: Bridging the Gap*, edited by F.J. Menolascino and B.M. McCann. Baltimore, MD: University Park Press, 1983.

Rucker, C., and Vincenzo, F. "Mainstreaming social acceptance gains made by mentally retarded children." *Exceptional Children* 36 (1970): 679–680.

Russell, Alene Bycer, and Trainor, Cynthia Mohr. *Trends in Child Abuse and Neglect: A National Perspective*. Denver, CO: The American Humane Association, Children's Division. 1984.

Russo, D., and Koegel, R. "A method for integrating an autistic child into a normal public school classroom." *Journal of Applied Behavior Analysis* 10 (1977): 579–590.

Russo, E.M., and Shyne, A.W. *Coping with Disruptive Behavior in Group Care*. NY: Child Welfare League of America, 1980.

Ruth, R.A.; Snell, T.B.; Tajalli, I.Q.; and Navarre, E.L. *The Care of Minority Children in Residential Facilities*. Indianapolis, IN: Indiana University, School of Social Work, 1982.

Ryan, W. *Blaming the Victim*. NY: Vintage, 1971.

Sameroff, A., and Chandler, M. "Reproductive risk and the continum of caretaking causality." In *Review of Child Development Research*, edited by F. D. Horowitz. Chicago, IL: University of Chicago Press, 1975.

Samuels, H. "The effect of an older sibling on infant locomotor exploration in a new environment." *Child Development* 51 (1980): 607–609.

Sanders, L. "Child abuse: Detection and prevention." *Young Children* 30 (1975): 332–38.

Sandgrund, A.; Gaines, R.; and Green, A. "Child abuse and mental retardation: A problem of cause and affect." *Journal of Mental Deficiency* 19 (1975): 327–330.

Sarason, I.; Johnson, J.; and Siegel, J. "Assessing the impact of life changes." *Journal of Consulting and Clinical Psychology* 45 (1978): 932–946.

Schilling, R.F., and Schinke, S.P. "Personal coping and social support for parents of handicapped children." Children and Youth Services Review 6 (1984): 195–206.

Schilling, R.F.; Schinke, S.P.; Blythe, B.J.; and Barth, R.P. "Child maltreatment and mentally retarded parents: Is there a relationship?" *Mental Retardation* 20 (1982): 201–209.

Schlosser, P. "The abused child." *Bulletin of the Menninger Clinic* 28 (1964): 260.

Schmitt, B.D. "What teachers need to know about child abuse and neglect." *Childhood Education* 52 (1975): 58–62.

Schmitt, B.D., ed. *The Child Protection Team Handbook: A Multidisciplinary Approach to Managing Child Abuse and Neglect*. NY: Garhand ST PM Press, 1978.

Schneider, C.; Hoffmeister, J.; and Helfer, R. "A predictive screening questionnaire for potential problems in mother–child interaction." In *Child Abuse and Neglect: The Family and the Community*, edited by R. Helfer and C. H. Kempe. Cambridge: Ballinger, 1976.

Schopler, E. "Parents of psychotic children as scapegoats." *Journal of Contemporary Psychology* 4 (1) (1971): 17–22.

Schopler, E., and Reichler, R. *Psychopathology and Child Development*. NY: Plenum, 1976.

Schramm, W., and Wade, S. *Knowledge and the Public Mind*. Stanford: Stanford University Press, 1967.

Schreibman, L.; O'Neill, R.; and Koegel, R. "Behavioral training for siblings of autistic children." *Journal of Applied Behavior Analysis* 16 (1983): 129–138.

Schroeder, C. "The Psychologist's Role in PL 94-142: Consultation Strategies with Peer Groups of Handicapped Children." Paper presented at the annual meeting of the American Psychological Association, Toronto, Canada, August 1978.

Schuchter, Arnold. *Child Abuse Intervention*. Prescriptive Package. Washington, D.C.: U.S. Government Printing Office, 1976.

Seattle Rape Relief. *Special Education Curriculum on Sexual Exploitation*. Seattle, WA: Developmental Disabilities Project, 1979.

Select Committee on Children, Youth and Families. *Federal Programs Affecting Children*. Washington, D.C.: U.S. Government Printing Office, 1984.

Selected Readings and Adolescent Maltreatment. U.S. Department of Health and Human Services, Washington, D.C.: DHHS # (OHDS) 81-30301, 1981.

Selman, R. "Social cognitive understanding: A guide to educational and clinical practice." In *Moral Development and Behavior*, edited by T. Lickona. NY: Holt, Rinehart, and Winston, 1976.

Senn, M. *Speaking Out for America's Children*. New Haven, CT: Yale University Press, 1977.

Sgroi, S. *Handbook of Clinical Intervention in Child Sexual Abuse*. Lexington, MA: D.C. Heath and Company, 1982.

Shanas, B. "Child abuse: A killer teachers can help control." *Phi Delta Kappan* 56 (1975): 479–82.

Shapiro, A. "The evaluation of clinical prediction: A method and application." *New England Journal of Medicine* 296 (1977): 1509–1514.

Shatz, M., and Gelman, R. "The development of communication skills: Modifications in the speech of young children as a function of listener. *Monographs of the Society for Research in Child Development* 38 (1973): (5).

Shores, R. E. *Social Competence Intervention Project: Final Report*. Nashville, TN: Vanderbilt University (U.S. Office of Education Grant No G007802088), 1973.

Sidel, R. *Women and Child Care in China*. NY: Hill & Wang, 1974.

Siker, E. "First year's experience in Connecticut with a child abuse law." *Connecticut Health Bulletin* 81 (1967): 53–59.

Silverberg, N.E., and Silverberg, M.C. "Abusing poor children by trying to protect them." In *Institutional Abuse of Children and Youth*, edited by R. Hanson, pp. 133–138. NY: Haworth Press, 1982.

Simeonsson, R., and Bailey, D. "Siblings of Handicapped Children." Paper presented at NICHD Conference on Research on Families with Retarded Children, September 1983.

Simeonsson, R., and McHale, S. "Review: Research on handicapped children's sibling relations." *Child: Care, Health, and Development* 7 (1981): 153–171.

Simpson, R. "Mainstreaming behavior disordered students: A perspective." *Journal of Research and Development in Education* 13 (1980): 58–73.

Singer, Michael, ed. *Developmental Disabilities*. Washington, D.C.: National Association of Counties Research, Inc., 1982.

Sininger v. Sininger, 300 Md.604, 479 A.2d 1354 (1984).

Skoler, G. "New hearsay exceptions for a child's statements of sexual abuse." *John Marshall Law Review* 18 (1984): 1–48.

Small, R.W., and Whittaker, J.K. "Residential group care and home-based care: Toward a continuity of family service. In *Home-based Services for Children and Their Families,* edited by S. Maybanks and M. Bryce, pp. 77–91. Springfield, IL: Thomas, 1979.

Smith, S. M.; Hanson, R.; and Noble, S. "Social aspects of the battered baby syndrome." *British Journal of Psychiatry* 125 (1974): 458–82.

Social Security Amendments of 1972, 86 Stat. 1329.

Soeffing, M. "Abused children are exceptional children." *Exceptional Children* 42 (1975): 126–33.

Solomons, Gerald. "Child abuse and developmental disabilities." *Developmental Medicine and Child Neurology* 21 (1979): 101–106.

Solomons, Gerald. "Child abuse and developmental disabilities." *Looking Back, Looking Ahead: Selections From the Fifth National Conference on Child Abuse and Neglect,* pp. 251–256, 1981.

Souther, M.D. "Developmentally disabled, abused, and neglected children: In *Perspectives on Child Maltreatment in the Mid '80s.* Washington, D.C.: U.S. Department of Health and Human Services, DHHS Publication No. (OHDS) 84-30338, 1983.

Spinetta, J.J., and Rigler, D. "The child-abusing parent: A psychological review." *Psychological Bulletin* 77 (1972): 296–304.

Stack, Carol. *All Our Kin.* NY: Harper & Row, 1974.

Stainbeck, W.; Stainbeck, T.; and Jaben, T. "Providing opportunities for interaction between severely handicapped and nonhandicapped students. *Teaching Exceptional Children* 13 (1981): 72–75.

Standards for Residential Child Care. NY: Child Welfare League of America, 1985.

Stark, R., and J. McEvoy. "Middle class violence." *Psychology Today* 4 (1970): 52–65.

Starr, R. H.; Dietrich, K. N.; Fischhoff, J.; Ceresnie, S.; and Zweier, D. "The contribution of handicapping conditions to child abuse. *Topics in Early Childhood Special Education* 4(1) (1984): 55–69.

State of Illinois, Department of Children and Family Services: A Survey of the First year. Springfield: State of Illinois, 1966.

State of Maryland. Department of Public Welfare: Incidence of Suspected Child Abuse. January–June 1967. Research Report no. 4. Baltimore: State of Maryland, 1968.

State v. Pendleton, 10 Kan.App.2d 26, 691 P.2d 959 (1984).

Steele, B. F., and Pollock, C. B. "A psychiatric study of parents who abuse infants and small children." In *The Battered Child,* 2d ed., edited by R. E. Helfer and C. H. Kempe, pp. 89–134. Chicago, IL: University of Chicago Press, 1974.

Steele, B.F., and Pollock, D. "A psychiatric study of parents who abuse infants and small children." In *The Battered Child*, 2d ed., edited by C. H. Kempe and R. E. Helfer, pp. 89–134. Chicago, IL: University of Chicago Press, 1968.

Steinmetz, S. "Disciplinary techniques and their relationship to aggressiveness, dependency, and conscience." In *Contemporary Issues about the Family*, vol. 1, edited by W. Burr, R. Hill, F. Nye, and I. Reiss, pp. 405–438. NY: Free Press, 1979.

Stern v. Stern, 58 Md. App. 280, 473 A.2d 56 (1984).

Stevenson, H.W. "Developmental Psychology." In *International Encyclopedia of the Social Sciences*, edited by D. Sills. NY: Macmillan, 1968.

Stocking, S. H., and Dunwoody, S. L. "Social science in the news media: Images and evidence." In *The Ethics of Social Research: Fieldwork, Regulation, and Publication*, edited by J. Sieber. NY: Springer-Verlag, 1982.

Storr, A. *Sexual Deviation*. London: Heineman, 1965.

Strain, P., Kerr, M., and Ragland, E. "Effects of peer-mediated social initiations and prompting/reinforcement on the social behavior of autistic children." *Journal of Autism and Developmental Disorders* 9 (1979): 41–54.

Straus, M. "Stress and child abuse." In *The Battered Child*, edited by C. H. Kempe and R. E. Helfer, pp. 86–103. Chicago, IL: University of Chicago Press, 1980.

Straus, M.; Gelles, R.; and Steinmetz, S. *Behind Closed Doors*. Garden City, NY: Doubleday, 1980.

Subcommittee on Juvenile Justice, United States Senate. *Child Sexual Abuse Victims in the Courts*. Proceedings of Senate hearing 98-1207, May 1984.

Sullivan, P. "Adaptations for special populations." In *Trainee's Manual: Kidability*, edited by M. Mitchel. Omaha, NB: Girls Club of Omaha, 1985.

Sullivan, P.; Scanlan, J.; Brookhouser, P.; and Andrew, J. The impact of sexual abused on handicapped children: A follow-up study. In preparation.

Summit, R. "What Makes Children Worth Stealing?" Presentation at Interdisciplinary Conference on the Sexual Victimization of Children, Virginia Beach, Virginia, September 25, 1985.

Summit, R., and Kryso, J. "Sexual abuse of children: A clinical spectrum." *American Journal of Orthopsychiatry* 48(2) (1978): 237–251.

Supplemental Security Income for the Aged, Blind, and Disabled, 20 C.F.R. 416.906 (1985).

Tankard, J., and Rayn, M. "News source perceptions of accuracy of science coverage. *Journalism Quarterly* 51 (1974): 219–225, 334.

Tarkington, C. "Mental health services for the Deaf. *APA Monitor,* June 1982.

Taylor, D.A., and Alpert, S.W. *Continuity and Support Following Residential Treatment.* NY: Child Welfare League of America, 1975.

Taylor, R.B. *The Kid Business.* Boston, MA: Houghton Mifflin, 1981.

The Parents Anonymous Chairperson—Sponsor Manual. Parents Anonymous, 1982.

Thomas, B.R. "Protecting abused children: Helping until it hurts." In *Institutional Abuse of Children and Youth,* edited by R. Hanson, pp. 139–154. NY: Haworth Press, 1982.

Thomas, G. "The responsibility of residential placements for children's rights to development." *Child and Youth Services* 4 (1982): 23–47.

Thomas, M. "Child abuse and neglect, Part I: Historical overview, legal matrix, and social perspectives." *North Carolina Law Review,* 50 (1972).

Thompson v. Arkansas Social Services, 282 Ark. 369, 669 S.W.2d 878 (1984).

Thurman, S. K., ed. *Children of Handicapped Parents: Research and Clinical Perspectives.* Orlando, FL: Academic Press, 1985.

Tichenor, P.; Olien, C.; Harrison, H.; and Donohue, G. A. "Mass communication systems and communication accuracy in science news reporting." *Journalism Quarterly* 47 (1970): 673–683.

Tietjen, A.M. "Formal and Informal Support Systems: Services and Social Networks in Swedish Planned Communities." Ph.D. thesis, Cornell University, 1977.

Trieschman, A.E.; Whittaker, J.K.; and Brendtro, L.K. *The Other 23 Hours: Child Care Work in a Therapeutic Milieu.* NY: Aldine, 1969.

Trigger stories: Preventing Institutional Child Abuse through the Development of Positive Norms for Staff. Trenton, NJ: Interstate Consortium on Residential Child Care, undated.

Trivette, C.M. "The Study of Role Division and Stress in Families of Handicapped Children." Unpublished Masters Thesis, Appalachian State University, Boone, NC, 1982.

Trivette, C.M., and Dunst, C.J. "Proactive influences of social support in families of handicapped children." In *Family Stengths,* Vol. 8, edited by N. Stinnet *et al.* Lincoln, NE: University of Nebraska Press, 1986.

Trivette, C.M., and Dunst, C.J. "Characteristics and influences of role division and social support among mothers of handicapped preschoolers." *Parenting Studies,* in press.

Tsai, M.; Feldman-Summers, S.; and Edgar, M. "Childhood molestation: Variables related to differential impacts on psychosexual functioning in adult women." *Journal of Abnormal Psychology* 88 (1979):407–417.

Tulkin, S. R. "An analysis of the concept of cultural deprivation." *Development Psychology* 6 (1972): 326–39.

Turnbull, H.R., and Turnbull, A.P. *Parents Speak Out.* Columbus, OH: Merrill, 1984.

Twardosz, S.; Cataldo, J.; and Risley, T. "An open environment design for infant and toddler day care." *Journal of Applied Behavior Analysis* 7 (1974): 529–546.

The Urban Institute, Report of the Comprehensive Service Needs Study. Washington, D.C.: Urban Institute, 1975.

U.S. Children's Bureau *Child Welfare Research Note No. 1.* Washington, D.C.: Department of Health and Human Services, 1983.

U.S. Department of Education. *Summary of Existing Legislation Relating to the Handicapped.* Washington, D.C.: Publication No. e-80-22014, August 1980.

U.S. Department of Education. *To Assure the Free Appropriate Public Education of All Handicapped Children."* Sixth Annual Report to Congress on the Implementation of Public Law 94-142: The Education for All Handicapped Children Act. Washington, D.C., 1984.

U.S. Department of Health and Human Services. "Overview." In *Child Abuse and Developmental Disabilities: Essays.* pp. 1–9. Washington, D.C.: DHEW Publication No. (OHDS) 79-30226, 1980.

U.S. Department of Health and Human Services. "Overview." In *Perspectives on Child Maltreatment in the Mid '80s.* Washington, D.C.: DHHS Publication No. (OHDS) 84-30338, 1984. (a)

U.S. Department of Health and Human Services. *The Status of Handicapped Children in Head Start Programs.* Tenth Annual Report of the U.S. Department of Health and Human Services to the Congress of the United States on Services Provided to Handicapped Children in Project Head Start. Washington, D.C., 1984. (b)

U.S. Department of Justice, Office of Justice Programs, *Categorical Awards Relating to Child Abuse.* Washington, D.C., November 1985.

United Nations. *Declaration of the Rights of the Child.* Resolution adopted by the General Assembly, 1959.

United States Senate, Committee on Labor and Public Welfare, Child Abuse Prevention and Treatment Act of 1974; Questions and Answers, Analysis and Text of the Act. Washington, D.C.: U.S. Government Printing Office, 1974.

Vaillant, G. E. *The Natural History of Alcoholism.* Cambridge, MA: Harvard University Press, 1983.

Vietze, P.; Falsey, S.; Sandler, H.; O'Connor, S.; and Altemeier, W. "Transactional approach to prediction of child maltreatment. *Infant Mental Health Journal* 1 (1980): 248–261.

Wadlington, W. J.; Whitebread, C. H.; and Davis, S. M. *Children in the Legal System: Cases and Materials.* Mineola, NY: Foundation Press, 1983.

Wakefield, W. E. "Annotation: Validity of state statute providing for termination of parental rights." *ALR 4th, 22* (1983): 774–825.

Wald, M. "Legal policies affecting children: A lawyer's request for aid." *Child Development* 47 (1976): 1–5.

Wald, M. S. "State intervention on behalf of 'neglected' children: A search for realistic standards." *Stanford Law Review* 27 (1975): 985–1040.

Wald, M. S. "State intervention on behalf of 'neglected' children: Standards for removal of children from their homes, monitoring the status of children in foster care, and termination of parental rights." *Stanford Law Review* 28 (1976): 625–706.

Wald, M. S. "State intervention on behalf of endangered children: A proposed legal response." *Child Abuse and Neglect* 6 (1982): 3–45.

Walker, K.; Macbride, A.; and Vachon, M. "Social support networks and the crisis of bereavement. *Social Science and Medicine* 11 (1977): 35–42.

Wandersman, L.; Wandersman, A.; and Kahn, S. "Social support in the transition to parenthood." *Journal of Community Psychology* 8 (1980): 332–342.

Washburne, C.; Van Hull, J.; and Rindfleisch, N., eds. *Multi Regional Conference on Institutional Child Abuse and Neglect*. Columbus, OH: Ohio State University, College of Social Work, 1983.

Weber, G., and Parker, T. A study of family and professional views of the factors affecting family adaptation to a disabled child. In *Family Strengths 3: Roots of Well-Being*, edited by N. Stinnett, J. DeFrain, K. King, *et al*. Omaha, NE: University of Nebraska Press, 1981.

Weinraub, M., and Wolf, B. "Effects of stress and support on mother–child interactions in single- and two-parent families." *Child Development* 54 (1983): 1297–1311.

Weinrott, M. "A training program in behavior modification for siblings of the retarded." *American Journal of Orthopsychiatry* 44 (1974): 362–375.

Weisberg, D. K. "The 'discovery' of sexual abuse: Experts' role in legal policy formulation." *U.C. Davis Law Review* 18 (1984): 1–57.

Weiss, C. H. "What America's leaders read. *The Public Opinion Quarterly* 38 (1974): 1–21.

Weiss, C. H. "Translation of Social Science Research into Public Knowledge." Paper presented at the meeting of the Association for Public Policy Analysis and Management, New Orleans, La., October 19, 1984.

Weiss, R. "The provisions of social relationships." In *Doing unto Others*, edited by Z. Rubin, pp. 17–26. Englewood Cliffs, NJ: Prentice-Hall, 1974.

Weissman, M., and Paykel, E. "Moving and Depression in Women." Chicago, IL: University of Chicago Press, 1974.

Weithorn, L. A. Memorandum to M. Brewster Smith on behalf of the Division of Psychology and Law, American Psychological Association, May 11, 1984.

Westervelt, V., and McKinney, J. "Effects of a film on nonhandicapped children's attitudes toward handicapped children." *Exceptional Children* 46 (1980): 294–296.

Wetzel, R.J., and Hoschouer, R.L. *Residential Teaching Communities.* Glenview, IL: Scott, Foresman and Company, 1984.

Whalen v. Roe, 429 U.S. 589 (1977).

Whitcomb, Debra; Shapiro, Elizabeth; and Stellwagen, Lindsey D., Esq. *When the Victim is a Child: Issues for Judges and Prosecutors.* Washington, D.C.: U.S. Government Printing Office, 1985.

White, S. T.; Loda, F. A.; Ingram, D. L.; and Pearson, A. Sexually transmitted diseases in sexually abused children. *Pediatrics* 72 (1983): 16–21.

Whittaker, J.K. *Caring for Troubled Children: Residential Treatment in a Community Context.* San Francisco, CA: Jossey-Bass, 1979.

Whittaker, J.K. "Family involvement in residential child care: A support system for biological parents." In *The Challenge of Partnership: Working with Parents in Foster Care,* edited by A. N. Maluccio and P. Sinanoglu, pp. 67–89. NY: Child Welfare League of America, 1981.

Whittaker, J.K., and Maluccio, A.N. "Changing paradigms in substitute care services for children and youth: Retrospect and prospect." In *Foster Family Based Treatment and Special Foster Care,* edited by R. Hawkins and J. Breiling. Washington, D.C.: NIMH, in press.

Whittaker, J.K., and Pecora, P. "A research agenda for residential care." In *Group Care Practice: The Challenge of the Next Decade,* pp. 71–87. Surrey, UK: Community Care-Business Press International, 1984.

Whittaker, J.K., and Trieschman, A.E., eds. *Children Away from Home: A Sourcebook of Residential Treatment.* New York: Aldine, 1972.

Whittaker, J.K.; Garbarino, J.; and Associates. *Social Support Networks: Informal Helping in the Human Services.* New York: Aldine, 1983.

Whittaker, J.K.; Gilchrist, L.D.; and Schinke, S.P. "The ecological paradigm in child, youth and family services: Implications for policy and practice. *Social Service Review,* in press.

Wikler, L.; Wasow, M.; and Hatfield, E. "Chronic sorrow revisited: Parent vs. professional depiction of the adjustment of parents of mentally retarded children." *American Journal of Orthopsychiatry* 51 (1981): 63–70.

Wilbur, C.B. "Multiple personality and child abuse: An overview." *Psychiatric Clinics of North America* 7(1) (1984): 3–7.

Wilkinson, T. "Covering abuse: Content and policy." In *Child Abuse: An Agenda for Action,* edited by G. Gerbner, C. J. Ross, and E. Zigler. NY: Oxford University Press, 1980.

Willems, E. "Relations of Models to Methods in Behavioral Ecology." Paper presented at the Biennial Conference, International Society for the Study of Behavioral Development, Guildford, July 13–19, 1975.

Williams, W. "Firing the woman to protect the fetus: The reconciliation of legal protection with employment opportunity goals under Title VII." *Georgetown Law Journal* 69 (1981): 641–704.

Willner, S. K., and Crane, R. "A parental dilemma: The child with a marginal handicap." *Social Casework* 60 (1979): 30–35.

Wilson, C. E. "The effect of medium on loss of information." *Journalism Quarterly* 51 (1974): 111–115.

Winett, R. A.; Leckliter, I. N.; Chinn, D. E.; and Stahl, B. "Reducing energy consumption: The long-term effects of a single TV program." *Journal of Communication* 34 (1984): 37–51.

Wisconsin v. Yoder, 406 U.S. 205 (1972).

Wolfe, D., and Manion, E. "Impediments to child abuse prevention: Issues and directions." *Advances in Behavior Research and Therapy* 6 (1984): 47–62.

Wolfe, D.A., and Mosk, M.D. "Behavioral comparisons of children from abusive and distressed families." *Journal of Consulting and Clinical Psychology* 51 (1983): 702–708.

Wolfensberger, W. *Normalization*. NY: National Institute on Mental Retardation, 1972.

Wolman, B. "The patient–doctor relationship. In *The Therapist's Handbook: Treatment of Mental Disorders*, edited by B. Wolman, pp. 3–21. NY: van Nostrand Reinhold, 1983.

Woodall, W. G.; Davis, D. K.; and Sahin, H. "From the boob tube to the black box: Television news comprehension from an information processing perspective." *Journal of Broadcasting* 27 (1983): 1–23.

Wynn V. Carey, 599 F.2d 193 (7th Cir. 1979).

Yates, A. *Sex without Shame: Encouraging the Child's Healthy Sexual Development*. NY: Morrow, 1978.

Young, C. "Children as instructional agents for peers: A review and analysis." In *The Utilization of Classroom Peers as Behavior Change Agents*, edited by P. Strain. NY: Plenum, 1981.

Young, L. *Wednesday's Children*. NY: McGraw-Hill, 1964.

Zalba, S.R. "The abused child, II: A typology for classification and treatment." *Social Work* 12 (1967): 70–79.

Zigler, E. "Controlling Child Abuse in America: An Effort Doomed to Failure." Mary Elaine Meyer O'Neal Award Lectureship. Meyer Children's Rehabilitation Institute, University of Nebraska Medical Center, Omaha, Nebraska, May 25, 1976.

Zimbardo, P., and F. Ruch. *Psychology and Life*. Glenview, IL: Scott, Foresman, 1975.

APPENDIX: MATERIALS FOR CHILDREN, THEIR PARENTS, AND THEIR TEACHERS

BOOKS FOR PARENTS AND TEACHERS

Braun, S., and Lasher, M. *Are You Ready to Mainstream? Helping Preschoolers with Learning and Behavior Problems.* Columbus, OH: Charles E. Merrill, 1978.

This book presents practical information for those who work with children in preschool and day-care. Included is information on organizing the classroom environment and using community resources. A list of children's books about handicapped individuals also is provided.

Fetherstone, H. *A Difference in the Family: Life with a Disabled Child.* New York: Basic Books, 1980.

The author is a parent of a handicapped child as well as a special educator. This book deals with a variety of aspects of family life with a handicapped child, including sibling relationships.

Gearhart, B., and Weishahn, M. *The Handicapped Child in the Regular Classroom.* St. Louis, MO: C. V. Mosby, Co., 1984.

This book deals with mainstreaming in the school environment. Included in the appendixes are lists of organizations serving disabled youngsters and an annotated bibliography of children's books about handicapped individuals.

Powell, T., and Ogle, P. *Brothers and sisters: A Special Part of Exceptional Families.* Baltimore, MD: Paul H. Brookes, 1985.

The authors describe what life is like for nonhandicapped children growing up in families with a handicapped child. Several chapters are devoted to ways of helping children adjust to their handicapped siblings' directed to providing information and services to families with a disaled member. A bibliography of books for children also is included; some of these are listed below.

BOOKS FOR CHILDREN

Adams, B. *Like It Is: Facts and Feelings about Handicaps from Kids Who Know.* NY: Walker & Company, 1979.

Edrington, M. J.; Moss, S. A.; and Young, J. *Friends.* Monmouth, OR: Instructional Development Corporation, 1978.

Meyer, D. K.; Vadasy, P. F.; and Fewell, R. *Living with a Brother or Sister with Special Needs.* Seattle, WA: University of Washington Press, 1985 (P.O. Box C-50096, Seattle, WA 98145-0096).

Sullivan, M. B.; Brightman, A. J.; and Blatt, J. *Feeling Free.* Reading, MA: Addison-Wesley, 1979.

The Sun is a newspaper published by Siblings Understanding Needs (SUN) (Department of Pediatrics C-19, University of Texas Medical Branch, Galveston, TX 77550).

ORGANIZATIONS

In addition to these organizations for siblings, local and national organizations such as the Association for Retarded Citizens, Easter Seals, and March of Dimes Foundation may have materials that can be used to educate siblings and peers about handicapped children.

Sibling Information Network
The University of Connecticut
Department of Educational Psychology
Box U-64
Storrs, CT 06268

This organization publishes a quarterly newsletter that includes discussion of programs directed toward siblings and relevant publications.

Siblings for Significant Change
Room 808
823 United Nations Plaza
New York, NY 10017

Siblings Helping Persons with Autism through Resources and Energy (SHARE)
c/o National Society for Children and Adults with Autism (NSAC)
Suite 1017
1234 Massachusetts Avenue, NW
Washington, D.C. 20005-4599

SIBS
123 Golden Lane
London, EC1Y ORT
ENGLAND

PROGRAMS

Kids on the Block, Inc.
822 N. Fairfax Street
Alexandria, VA 22314
(800) 368-KIDS

This organization has produced programs for educating children at school about youngsters with special needs. Puppets displaying a variety of special needs are a central part of these programs.

Sibshops
Produced by D. Meyer, P. Vadasy, and R. Fewell
P.O. Box 855 569
Seattle, WA 98145
(202) 543-4050

A handbook for implementing workshops for siblings of children with special needs.

FILMS

One of our Own Produced by Canadian Broadcasting Corporation
16 mm., color, 55 minutes
Filmmakers Library, Inc.
133 East 58th Street
New York, NY 10022
(212) 355-6545

One of the Gang Filmstrip and tape, color, 20 minutes
Cuyahoga Association for Retarded Citizens
1001 Huron Road
Cleveland, OH 44115
(216) 621-4505

AUTHOR INDEX

A

Abel, E. L., 185, *245*
Aber, J. L., 85, 98, *261*
Achenbach, T. M., 88, 132, *245*
Adams, B., *290*
Adams, C., 151, *245*
Addison, S., 48, *278*
Adler, A., 51, 52, *245*
Adoni, H., 214, *267*
Agard, J., 58, *267*
Alexander, J., *245*
Allen, K., 65, *246*
Allen, M., *268*
Aloia, G., 65, *246*
Alpert, S. W., 89, *284*
Altemeier, W., 18, *285*
Ambrosino, L., 72, *267*
Anastasiow, N. J., 235, *246*
Anderson, C. M., 192, *266*
Andrade, B., 186, *246*
Andrew, J., 133, 134, *283*
Apollini, T., 55, 59, *246*
Aragona, J. A., 129, *246*
Asp, E., 182, *260*
Atkin, C. K., 215, 216, 217, *246*
Attneave, C., 45, *246*
Ayoub, C., 24, 25, *246*, 273

B

Bailey, D., 61, *281*
Bakan, D., 179, *246*, 247
Baker, L., 142, *250–251*

Ballew, J., 41, *247*
Ball-Rokeach, S. J., 216, *247*
Banagale, R., *247*
Bandura, A., 137, *247*
Bank, S., 56, *247*
Barber, T. S., *247*
Bardon, J. I., 149, *247*
Barrington, T. M., 214, 217, *273*
Barry, R. J., 167, 173, *247*
Barsh, E. T., 95, *247*
Barth, R. P., 80, *280*
Basham, R., 22, 32, *253*
Baumgart, D., 65, *250*
Beaver, R., 65, *246*
Becerra, R. M., 183, *261*
Beckman, P., 29, 39, *247*
Beckman-Bell, P., 60, *247*
Beezley, P., 129, *271*
Beitchman, J. H., 142, *247*
Bell, R. Q., 189, *247*
Belsky, J., 19, 20, 21, 24, 34, 36, 40, *247*
Bennett, C. W., *247*
Bennett, V. C., 149, *247*
Benning, P., 65, *246*
Benward, J., 131, *248*
Bernstein, B., 94, *248*
Berry, C., 214, *248*
Berry, F. C., Jr., 224, *248*
Besharov, D., *248*
Bettelheim, B., *248*
Bijou, S. W., 70, *248*
Billingsley, A., 22, *250*, 261
Blacher, J., 27, 28, 29, 235, *248*
Blake, P., *276*

*Numbers in italics indicate the page where the complete reference is given.

293

SUBJECT INDEX